The Birth of
THE ASHES

In Affectionate Remembrance

OF

ENGLISH CRICKET,

WHICH DIED AT THE OVAL

ON

29th AUGUST, 1882,

Deeply lamented by a large circle of sorrowing
friends and acquaintances.

R. I. P.

*N.B.—The body will be cremated and the
ashes taken to Australia.*

The Amazing Story of the First Ashes Test

The Birth of
THE ASHES

CHRISTOPHER HILTON

First published in Great Britain in 2006 by
The Breedon Books Publishing Company Limited
Breedon House, 3 The Parker Centre, Derby, DE21 4SZ.

This edition published in Great Britain in 2012 by The

Derby Books Publishing Company Limited, 3 The

Parker Centre, Derby, DE21 4SZ.

Distributed in Australia by
Renniks Publications Pty Limited,
3/37-39 Green Street,
Banksmeadow NSW 2019

ISBN 978-1-78091-180-9

Contents

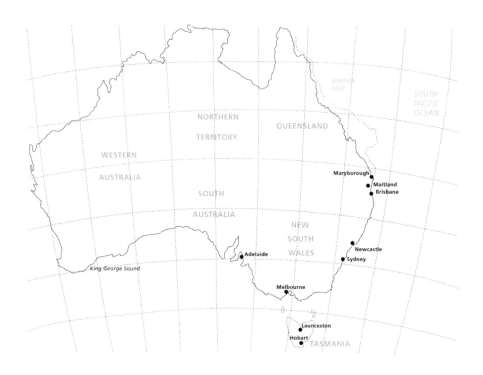

Ivo Bligh set out to win The Ashes in 1882–83. This is where his tour went beyond the State of Victoria.

The hub of the tour in and near Melbourne, with
Rupertswood at Sunbury.

Acknowledgements

This book is about two days in 1882 which changed the course of cricket, gave to it one of sport's most famous trophies and enriched the lives of two nations forever afterwards. The two days, when England and Australia moved to a truly desperate finish at the Oval in South London, are set into their historical context with descriptions of what went before and what has come after, all the way to today – to Vaughan, Flintoff, Pietersen, to Ponting, McGrath, Warne and co. What they all did at the Oval in September 2005 was not only the direct descendant of 1882, it was the same thing in spirit, intensity and execution.

I owe thanks to many people, particularly John Kobylecky who has recreated many of the early matches ball by ball and particularly, in the case of this book, the Oval. He did this by a meticulous study of the Australian scorebook. (The whereabouts of the English scorebook appears to be unknown.) Mr Kobylecky, a charming and generous man, emailed me his work and said 'Help yourself!' He has also kindly allowed me to reproduce, as an appendix, his actual handiwork. He describes his fascination with recreating the matches as a cross between being a detective and an engineer who takes a machine apart to see how it works.

Glenys Williams, the MCC Archivist at Lord's, has allowed me to quote from a talk she gave on the origins of The Ashes and gave permission to reproduce an MCC letter to Ivo Bligh's widow.

Dominic and Marie Romeo are managers of the Rupertswood Mansion near Melbourne, site of the birth of The Ashes. (They restored the mansion and it is used as a function venue and accommodation.) Dominic sent photographs and background information, and Marie kindly gave permission to quote insights from her research into several aspects of what happened.

My old sports editor at the *Daily Express*, Ken Lawrence – a Surrey stalwart, incidentally – pointed me in several directions, including the Oval librarian Trevor Jones. He laid their resources before me, handled the photocopying I needed and emailed invaluable pictures. Iain Taylor, who happened to be in the library that day, kindly delved into his own library to help me with the background.

Medway Council in Kent were, by my good fortune, having an exhibition of direct relevance to The Ashes as well as holding correspondence by the Hon. Ivo Bligh, the man responsible – one way or another – for The Ashes coming into existence and remaining in existence. Derek Moore and Stephen M. Dixon, Borough Archivist at the Medway Archives and Local Studies Centre, were enormously helpful. The correspondence is reproduced by kind permission of the Earl of Darnley and the Director of Community Services, Medway Council.

The British Newspaper Library at Colindale, North London, is a bottomless mine of information, the staff always helpful, and you can't really begin a book like this without going there. To them, my gratitude.

The website cricinfo.com, part of the Wisden Group, is an astonishing and invaluable resource and I offer humble thanks to everyone there.

Matters arising. In 1882 overs were of four balls and wicketkeepers habitually stood up to the bowling. Whether all batsmen wore gloves is doubtful, although clearly some did because reports mention them being 'caught off the glove' – and some didn't, including one of the Australians, Tom Horan.

The standard of play is difficult to judge but that in no way detracts from the drama of the games themselves. To risk a generalisation, however, the first 20 years of Test cricket (which began in 1877) were dominated by bowlers, and if a team did make a large total it was invariably because one batsman scored heavily rather than several batsmen making substantial contributions. Runs were a more precious commodity then, and rarely more so than at the Oval in August 1882.

Because the two days are where the great, dynastic saga of The Ashes began, the 22 players who contested them are by definition central, too. I signal the first appearance of each of them in the text by setting their names in bold type. All else aside, it helps to get to know them.

W.G. Grace, the colossus who almost won The Ashes match – there would have been no Ashes if he had.

Michael Vaughan, who won them back 123 years later.

Billy Murdoch, the Australian skipper who did win.

Ricky Ponting, whose 2005 side drew at the Oval – and a draw wasn't enough.

One Cold Afternoon

IT MUST have seemed a long journey as the Yorkshireman with the strong, solid face, swept back hair and drooping moustache came down the pavilion steps. **Edmund Peate** moved between the ranks of men severely dressed in the Victorian way – long coats, top hats, bowler hats – and stepped out onto the pitch.

He was very alone.

If he looked at the scoreboard he saw:

ENGLAND
Runs   75
Wickets   9

For long hours the match had been building – run by run, wicket by wicket, maiden over by maiden over – so remorselessly that one spectator died of a heart attack, another gnawed the handle off his umbrella and an England player wrapped himself in a blanket and ran round, unwilling or unable to watch. As Peate began the walk towards the distant wicket, with the 11 predatory Australians waiting there for him, the tension struck the England scorer who tried to write *Peate* in the scorebook but his hand scribbled something resembling *Geese*.

The 20,000 packed deep all round the ground knew that England still needed 10 runs to win and each stride brought Peate, in all his loneliness, closer to confronting that. He had been given instructions: stay there, survive, let the chap at the other end get them. He's a batsman.

If Peate looked about him he saw low stands full of people, and, between them, the crowd standing eight and 10 deep on banking. They, too, were mostly dressed severely. If he looked beyond he saw a dense press of square, brick residential buildings, the line of them broken by tall trees here and there. South London hadn't been rural for generations, but the trees seemed to carry a lingering memory of that.

What did Peate think on that journey? Was his mind in turmoil? Was he phlegmatic or fatalistic as each stride brought him closer and closer? Had the tension struck him?

At 26 he was a brilliant left-arm spinner but was only in his fourth season. He'd toured Australia the previous winter and batted at his natural position, this same number 11, in all four Test Matches, so he understood – or ought to have understood – tension. He'd been not out 4; run out 2; not out 1 twice; not out 11 and 8; caught and bowled 13, giving him an average of 20. Now, as he neared the Australians, all he and that batsman at the other end, C.T. Studd, needed was 9 between them to tie the match, 10 to win it.

Henry Boyle, a wiry-looking man with a flowing beard who bowled just under medium pace with a round arm action, had just taken the ninth wicket with the opening ball of his 20th over. The delivery leapt, rasped a glove and the fielder at point caught it.

Boyle had long mastered the subtleties of flight and to exploit that he could pitch the ball on a precise length and whip in leg-breaks. Scoring off him was always difficult, and so far he'd bowled 11 maidens and conceded only 17 runs. It made even singles a precious commodity to draw out of him.

As Peate came, what did Boyle think? There are clues. In his career he'd invented a fielding position, silly mid-on. Although many leading English players said he'd be killed standing that close, he never flinched and reaped a harvest of catches from prods and pushes and fumbles. He didn't flinch, either, if his bowling came under attack. He weathered it, then counter-attacked. At 35 he was the oldest of the Australians, on his third tour and worldly enough to become a tour manager himself one day. He wasn't the sort to flinch now, as Peate reached the middle and took guard.

Australia had never beaten England – the Mother Country – in England, and if they did it would be a moment of genuine nation building far beyond cricket. Edmund Peate, now preparing to take strike, stood quite literally between them and that.

Studd had been held back as insurance while the wickets fell, this Studd who'd scored 100 against the Australians for Cambridge University and could surely win it, this Studd who within months would find God – but he watched helpless and impotent from the non-striker's end.

The whole ground fell silent.

Boyle ran in, and Peate hit the ball towards square-leg. They ran 2. The thousands must have thought, in something approaching collective horror, that it was not the shot of a man determined on survival in order to bring Studd's skills into play, however nourishing the runs were: 8 for the win now, 7 for a tie.

Boyle ran in and Peate mishit the ball so badly someone called it a fluke he connected with it at all: no wicket, no run.

Boyle ran in and Peate slogged, wielding his bat like a flail. He missed. The ball struck the stumps and the crowd, suddenly released from their agony, gave a sort of animal roar so tremendous that W.G. Grace in the pavilion said he never forgot it.

The Kennington Oval at 5.45 on the cold afternoon of Tuesday 29 August 1882.

The crowd were already swarming the pitch.

As Peate turned away and set off on the long journey back to the pavilion, all unknowing, he was no longer alone. He had set in motion a path that generations of others would tread: Victor Trumper carrying with him the soul of the game, God-fearing Jack Hobbs and, the greatest of all, Don Bradman, quiet Len Hutton and noisy Denis Compton, bustling, boisterous Ian Botham, the extraordinary Chappell and Waugh brothers, the even more extraordinary Shane Warne, yeoman Freddie Flintoff, the very modern Michael Vaughan and Ricky Ponting...

On that cold afternoon nobody among the 20,000 at the Oval knew The Ashes had been born – but they had.

The 1882 match opened the way to an amazing and enduring future. Don Bradman would make 232 and 244 at the Oval in the 1930s and Len Hutton would make the then highest Test score there, 364 in 1938.

The Kindling

AUSTRALIA had never beaten a full England team before – as we have just seen – and that stands in direct contrast to the Australian teams of the 1990s and early 2000s which, until 2005, nobody could beat. Some said that the sides of the 1990s–2000s were the greatest there had ever been, all the way back to the August afternoon and beyond, into the very mists of the game.

By then Australia itself had evolved quite naturally into a self-confident nation in its own right with a distinct multi-racial character, a salty phraseology, plenty of provocative personalities, robust politics and cuisine to make the world envious. In February 2006 the Australian Prime Minister, John Howard, speaking at a memorial service to Kerry Packer – the tycoon who changed cricket by buying the leading players and creating his own series in the 1970s – said: 'He was a larrikin [rascal], but he was also a gentleman and that's a dual description that any Australian would be proud to have.'

If Britain had a great past, an Australian – seafood platter before him or her, glass of wine in hand – had a great future.

To what extent sport helped in shaping it is material for a scholarly treatise rather than a book like this, although learned works have already appeared about how Bradman gave the country hope and a sense of purpose in the impoverished Depression years of the 1920s and 1930s.

It makes the victory in the Test Match of 1882 more intriguing still and explains in the immediate aftermath the subsequent strong reaction of condemnation for the England players by domestic press and public alike. This was rendered more than an affront by colonists: the English batsmen were widely held to have 'funked' the second innings – an old word much used then which my dictionary defines as 'flinch, shirk, show cowardice'. This was not what the breed of Empire builders was supposed to do.

The two countries which met at the Oval in 1882 could not, in the essences of their being, have been more similar. Today they are not remotely recognisable except in measuring how much about each has changed.

In 1882 Britain bestrode the world as its only superpower. Her writ, enforced by military and economic muscle, ran across an enormous empire and anywhere else it chose to flex it. Effortlessly, and as a by-product, the British invented or shaped virtually all modern sport: tennis at Wimbledon, golf at St Andrews, Rugby at Rugby School. Soccer goes a long way back but in 1815 Eton College drew up rules which passed into common usage. The English Football League came into existence six years after the Oval match.

Cricket goes a long way back, too, but by 1744 there were laws.

The Olympic Games had lay dormant since ancient Greek times, although a sports festival was held at Much Wenlock, Shropshire, with Dr William Penney Brookes a moving force. In 1850 he set up an Olympic society to revive the Games, and they were revived when Baron Pierre de Coubertin came to see him.

The Australia of 1882 was not only a British sibling spiced by a lot of Irish but also a young country feeling its way, if it thought of itself as a country at all rather than an extension of the Mother Country. The Australia of today was surely as unimagined, and unimaginable, as what Peate inadvertently created by slogging at a cricket ball – once – and missing it.

Leading on from this, and of direct relevance to our story, there are two contexts at work here, ancient and modern (if I can put it like that).

We know a great deal, maybe too much, about the modern players, foibles and failings as well as feats. Their faces are comfortingly familiar, sometimes inescapable, and so are their mannerisms. Think Flintoff; think Warne.

The players on that cold afternoon are visibly remote as well as remote in time. They look forbiddingly serious in photographic portraits, their personalities hidden somewhere behind severe, almost dehumanised, faces as they hold rigid poses even when they pretend to bat or bowl. The team photographs are just as severe, just as formalised. Scarcely one of them is without either moustache or beard, sometimes beards of biblical proportions. Of action photographs there is no more than a precious little hoard, much of it taken from a distance and conveying little sense of letting you see it as a spectator on the ground would have done. Artists, acting as surrogates for the photographs which didn't exist, did drawings of the action, trying to distil the drama and personalities into them. The fact that this was the only way to do it heightens the sense of remoteness.

To appreciate them as real people at all – with foibles and failings – is extremely difficult. I have scoured the contemporary literature for those precious details which humanise them. Much is lost beyond retrieval. How fast were the fast bowlers, really? How much did the spinners spin, and how accurate were they? How good was the fielding? How intelligent was the field placing? How technically competent were the batsmen? Would W.G. Grace have feasted on Warne or been endlessly his victim? There's a surviving film clip of Grace practising, and for a big man he stepped sprightly – but against Warne? What would Flintoff the batsman have done to Boyle with the flowing beard?

In a sense, the answers only matter in helping to cross the arch of time and finally see the remote people as they really were.

The journey to the Oval had been a long one, beginning on 20 April 1770 when Captain James Cook reached the coast of New South Wales in his ship *Endeavour*. Others visited before, perhaps from as early as 1606, but Cook held royal instructions. Within a week he moved up to Botany Bay and landed there. He spent that summer mapping the coastline as far as the northernmost part of Queensland, and on the evening of 22 August, at Possession Island, made a declaration. He remembered that although 'I had in the Name of His Majesty taken possession of several places upon this coast, I now once more hoisted English Colours and in the Name of His Majesty King George the Third took possession of the whole Eastern Coast... by the name New South Wales, together with all the Bays, Harbours, Rivers and Islands situate upon the said coast, after which we fired three Volleys of small Arms...'

Australia would be born British. Cook returned to England in May 1771 and his maps must have been of particular value because, seven years later, the government decided to establish a colony at Botany Bay. The outward influence was very strong. The British Empire had been acquiring territories since the early 1600s, for political as well as commercial reasons.

The British had used their colonies for 100 years and more as a place where they could send criminals. By the 1780s the North American colonies were gone after the War of Independence and 'somewhere new had to be found to prevent British prisons – not to mention the new prison hulks along the south-east coast – from overflowing with untransportable inmates.'[1]

And here was Australia.

Botany Bay proved to be swampy and unsuitable for a naval base or anything else, so on 26 January 1788, 11 ships with some 1,350 people on them – half convicts – swung into what was called Port Jackson and is now called Sydney.

The journey would be extraordinary now. The earth has been exhaustively mapped to the point where finding unknown jungle tribes, however small, creates great excitement. The early colonists to the United States, Canada and Australia found that, factoring in the indigenous populations, they were

It all started here. This is believed to be the only photograph of the match in progress. The pavilion and long grandstand are on the right.

standing on virgin continents. It would be brutally hard, and deadly, from the beginning but the potential was inherent, and inevitably they had brought English society with them, because that was all they knew.

One human being casting a ball to another human being for it to be hit or missed seems to be a very basic English impulse, and 'we may assume that some of those' on the original 11 ships 'would have either brought, or manufactured, bats to play the game'.[2] More than that, it seems peculiarly English because the only two sports where it happens – cricket and rounders, becoming baseball – were both English. Perhaps it accorded with the adversarial nature of law and politics, something else the Australians would inherit in full measure. All the other sports are adversarial in a different way: golfers all play with similar clubs, footballers all kick the same ball except the two goalkeepers, who can both handle it. Rugby players can all handle the ball, swimmers all swim up and down, and so it goes.

The bowler and the batsman are demonstrating precisely opposed skills, to the point where the batsman is not allowed to touch the ball.

The impulse was not so much recreated in Australia as continued. Certainly cricket has been recorded at Sydney by 1803 and may well have been played before, no doubt informally in clearings with rudimentary implements, to satisfy the impulse. The 'pioneers were not greatly worried about' the 'niceties… they hewed, or fashioned, their bats out of ironbark [a king of eucalyptus tree], cedar, or other substantial timber which would stand the strain of heavy hitting.'[3]

It remains little short of astonishing that within just over 70 years Australia would be fielding teams capable of competing against England and, in less than 80, find themselves at the Oval with imperious, imperial England at their mercy.

Brutally hard from the first moments after landing? A report[4] from the early days describes 'the colony barely emerging from infantile imbecility, and suffering from various privations and disabilities; the country impenetrable beyond forty miles from Sydney; agriculture in a yet languishing state; commerce in its early dawn; revenue unknown; threatened with famine; distracted by factions; the public buildings in a state of dilapidation and mouldering to decay.'

Yet, by 1810, cricket had 'become a popular recreation'.[5] It seems to have grown quite naturally after that. By 1826 clubs were being formed and cricket played in Tasmania by that same year at least. The first mention of a game in Western Australia is 1835.

The Melbourne Cricket Club was founded in 1838, a match played at Adelaide in 1839. Queensland's history of cricket is slightly mysterious with no reference until 1857.

Like the United States and Canada, however unremittingly harsh the beginnings had to be, inhabiting a virgin continent allowed the possibilities of fantastic wealth for the successful, and William Clarke, known as 'Big Clarke', was one such person. Born in 1805 in Somerset, his parents – already wealthy – died when he was young and he became a stockman. Married, he and his wife emigrated to Van Diemen's Land [later Tasmania] in 1929. Throughout the voyage Clarke travelled in the hold of the ship to look after the stock he'd brought. It suggests a very determined man, the kind who fully intended to exploit the opportunities the continent offered. He set up as a butcher but found money lending more lucrative and in time owned or controlled *all* the land between the two main towns, Hobart and Launceston – 120 miles apart.

The Clarke family moved to the mainland, eventually to Sunbury near Melbourne because the land was not freehold. Sunbury had been founded in 1836 and from about 1850 Clarke became a major landowner there. It was the shrewd thing to do. Up to 1850 the Australian economy relied on producing wool but by a most natural process of land settlement that emphasis shifted to what has been quaintly termed 'pastoral businesses', and they drove the economy.

Brothers called Jackson occupied the land Clarke wanted but 'unfortunately, they neglected to register their claim. After having the land surveyed, Clarke approached the Government with gold and purchased 31,000 acres. He bought another 36,000 acres throwing 9 squatters off their holdings. ... When "Big Clarke" had purchased his land in Sunbury, he lived in the Jackson's 2-roomed cottage... Later the cottage was increased to a 12-room homestead. "Big Clarke" was responsible for the introduction of Border Leicester sheep and trout into the Port Phillip District. He also started the Colonial Bank. Said to be an absolute miser...'[6]

Fifty-three years after 'Big Clarke' landed, his heir and successor would invite the touring England cricket team to spend Christmas at the Clarkes' Sunbury mansion and, there, the ball that Peate had missed set in train a set of circumstances which reached out to the cricket ground 200 yards from the mansion, to a match against the staff and a little urn which likely stood in all its ordinary anonymity on a ladies' dressing table.

While Australia was taking the first faltering steps towards becoming a nation, England 'became the workshop of the world'. In the 1850s Britain produced more than half of all the coal, iron, steel, cotton cloth and hardware. It manufactured all the machine tools. The world was able to industrialise because Britain could, and did, provide the expertise and had the money to finance it. 'By 1840 Britain had £160 million invested abroad; by 1873 nearly £1,000 million.'[7]

The contrast with Australia could hardly be more stark, and what they would do on the cricket field in a comparatively short space of time is even more astonishing as well as significant. When Australians spoke of the 'Mother Country', they were speaking of the place whose 'ideas, institutions, attitudes, tastes, pastimes, morals, clothes, laws, customs, their language and literature, units of measurement, systems of accountancy, company law, banking, insurance, credit and exchange, even [...] their patterns of education and religion became identified with progress across the planet.'[8]

The political story of Australia sets the context for the cricket because it is one of gradual, sometimes painful, coming together and discovering – or creating – a national identity. Clearly by that cold afternoon, whatever the politics of suspicion and self-interest, the major aspects of this had already happened, because the Australians refer to themselves just as Australians and *The Age* writes of all Australia waiting breathless on their doings. They would continue to refer to Britain as the Mother Country quite naturally for a long time afterwards but that wasn't quite the same thing. The difference may have begun as a nuance, especially with so many Australians born in the Mother Country, but each successive generation born in Australia added physical substance to the political fact that they were becoming a nation in their own right.

In the international sphere, *nothing* defines nationhood so passionately and comprehensively as its own sporting teams. If you disagree with this statement, ask yourself how many current cricketers you can name and then how many politicians at the United Nations...

Profound undercurrents travelled all down Australia's journey to the Oval on the cold afternoon. Initially there was the problem of *being* a continent and the wide geographical separation of colonists into separate colonies in an era when travel was slow, arduous and full of perils.

Within 50 years of the landing at Port Jackson some wanted self-government and by 1850 the British government looked favourably on this. (It's an interesting sub-current that Britain expected the colonies it seeded with its own blood-lines to become mature and independent, and welcomed this.) From 1855 to 1859, five groups of colonists – New South Wales, Victoria, Tasmania, South Australia and Queensland – were granted what has been described as 'responsible government', meaning they elected their own governing bodies. They went their own way (New South Wales, for example, built a railway using a different gauge to the others). A national government would be long in coming – not, in fact, until after the cold afternoon. What the colonies did want was proper defence, and for that they looked to Britain.

In terms of cricket a firm of Melbourne caterers called Spiers and Pond were poised to change everything. They were among the 700,000 migrants who arrived in the 1850s when gold had been discovered and although neither Spiers nor Pond made fortunes from that (which was why they were now in catering) they saw there was money to be made and publicity to be had by bringing a team from England to make a tour.

The discovery of gold altered the whole direction of the economy and surpassed the staple, wool. News of gold brought a rush of migrants – one source estimates the population of 400,000 hit a million by 1860. By a paradox, this increase 'put a burden on the gold supply' and a return of the importance of wool.

By now cricket was popular in Australia and 'there were more than 70 clubs in Victoria and many Victorian and New South Wales pastoral properties maintained their own teams.'⁹ It was time to look outwards, and that could only mean the Mother Country.

Cricket inspires romantic souls and it's temptingly easy to portray the early touring parties as missionaries and pioneers, proud in their breasts to be spreading the gospel of the game. The truth is much more prosaic. Money runs through the early tours like an imperative and many players, offered less than what they imagined to be the going rate, simply stayed at home. These early tours give authentic glimpses of life in Australia and, because they deepen the understanding of the events of the cold afternoon, I propose to give you the full flavour in several extracts. You'll note that many of the matches were against teams of more than XI to give the locals a chance against the mighty masters from England.

Spiers and Pond sent a man to England and, after negotiations, secured a team of mostly Surrey players under H.H. (Heathfield Harman) Stephenson. The team sailed in October 1861. William Caffyn, an all-rounder, described the trip evocatively. The night before they left London for Liverpool and the ship, they stayed at an hotel in the Haymarket and had their photograph taken in the stable yard next morning. At Liverpool 'the team sang "The Anchor's weighed", and I gave them "Cheer, Boys, Cheer", on the cornet as the vessel moved off... The only unpleasant part of the voyage was the trouble caused by the mosquitoes. These tiresome insects seem to have singled me out as their special prey, and tormented the life out of me. I was quite ill for a time and had to consult the doctor. I used to get a large piece of muslin and wrap round my head before going to bed, and also put a pair of stockings on my arms. I shall never forget the laugh that was raised when my fellow-cricketers first saw me in this disguise.'[10]

Caffyn records that 'several of the passengers' were 'sorely puzzled to know who and what we were, and when they were informed that we were English cricketers they did not appear to be much wiser than before.'

The ship reached Melbourne on Christmas Eve.

'There were great demonstrations on our arriving [...] flags being hoisted on most of the ships in the harbour, and a crowd of over 10,000 people gathered to welcome us as we came ashore. [...] Messrs Spiers and Pond came aboard and presented us with an address of welcome. As soon as we got on *terra firma* we were driven off in a coach-and-four to the café of Messrs Spiers & Pond in Burke [Bourke] Street, a great crowd of people following us. We were photographed on the coach before alighting. We all wore white pot-hats [hats with a stiff crown] with a blue ribbon. The following day we were driven seven miles into the bush to practise on a piece of ground which had been previously selected by Spiers & Pond. The locality had been kept a secret, as had it been known we should have been followed by a mob of people.'[11]

As the All England XI, they played Eighteen of Victoria at Melbourne, starting on New Year's Day.

'There was a great stir in the city at an early hour of the morning. People flocked in from the surrounding country in all directions, in coaches, waggons, cars, and conveyances of every description. The trains, too, were filled to overflowing. More than 15,000 people were on the ground when the English Eleven arrived. We lost the toss, and H.H. Stephenson [...] led us into the field. We had all been supplied with very light white hats of the helmet shape. Each of us had a coloured sash and a ribbon round his hat – one man's colour being blue, another green, another crimson, and so on. These colours were printed against each of our names on the score-card, so that any one provided with one of these could at once identify every member of our team. My own colour was dark blue. The National Anthem was played as we entered the field, amidst the silence of the vast concourse of spectators. When the band stopped playing a tremendous burst of cheering rent the air.'[12]

Caffyn bowled the very first ball to James Bryant, himself a Surrey man who had emigrated. He played the first ball defensively,[13] and although this was in no sense a Test Match it *was* the first ball which led to the cold afternoon, and from there, to the dynasty to Vaughan and Ponting. The All England team won by an innings and 96 runs on the fourth day of the match, 4 January.

They went on to play at Beechworth, a town made by the gold rush in 1852 some 200 miles north-east of Melbourne, returned to Melbourne for another match, went to Geelong, Sydney, Bathurst, Sydney again and Hobart before they returned to Melbourne. They went to Ballarat, Bendigo and Castlemaine with a final match in Melbourne finishing on 22 March. They'd played 14 matches and the tour proved such a financial success that a second followed, in 1863–64 under George Parr of Nottinghamshire. It, too, was a financial success.

From 1863 conferences were held bringing the various colonies together to discuss what might be called national matters, like defence – again – and external trade.

The contrast – again – with wealthy, imperial London could hardly be more marked, even under the ground. In 1863, for example, the first section of underground railway in the world opened between Paddington and Farringdon Street with stations along it at Edgware Road, Baker Street, Great Portland Street, Euston Square and King's Cross. During the 1860s the city's modern sewerage network was built to combat disease and very unpleasant smells. The man who built it also built the Embankment. Gas light had been in use all over the city for 20 years and so had horse-drawn buses. Electric street lighting was not far away.

By a great curiosity the first Australian tour to Britain, where they'd witness these miracles of modernity, was by a team of Aborigines in 1868. However vivid they were – what else could they be with names like Dick-a-Dick, Red Cap and Bullocky? – their tour remains slightly quixotic and, in a sense, a diversion.

In retrospect the past seems a logical place, one step leading to the next as if it was all meant to be. That is not at all true of cricket because it was not a regulated, regimented thing with tours allocated years in advance on a rotational basis. Teams went because promoters and players saw the money: hence the profusion of tours. For ease of comprehension from where we've reached, 1868, to the creation of The Ashes this is what happened:

1873–74	W.G. Grace's team to Australia
1876–77	James Lillywhite's team to Australia
1878	Dave Gregory's Australians to England
1878–79	Lord Harris's team to Australia
1880	W.L. Murdoch's Australians to England
1881–82	Lillywhite's team to Australia
1882	Murdoch's Australians to England
1882–83	Ivo Bligh's team to Australia

Grace went at the invitation of the Melbourne Cricket Club and captured how rugged an experience it was. They played Eighteen of Victoria at Melbourne, starting on 26 December, travelled to Ballarat for a draw and continued. 'Our troubles began in earnest when we turned our backs upon Ballarat, and our faces towards Stawell [another gold rush town], where we were to play our next match. The journey of 74 miles had to be made in an old-fashioned Cobb's coach over a rough bush track, quite undeserving of the name of road. At the outset there were difficulties to overcome. When they saw the vehicle in which they had to make the journey several members of the team flatly refused to take their seats, and were only after much coaxing prevailed upon to do so. We left Ballarat at 8.30 a.m. The first fifteen miles were through cultivated country, and the roads were tolerably decent, but for the remaining sixty miles we endured agonies. The horses laboured along up to their hocks in white dust, with which we were literally cloaked, so that we looked for all the world like so many millers as we sat on the ailing and rickety vehicle.'[14]

In order to 'break the monotony', two team members, who had guns with them, took pot shots at magpies and parrots. Grace excused this by explaining that they were as plentiful as sparrows in London.

'The secretary of the Stawell Cricket Club, and a few other cricket enthusiasts in the neighbourhood, came 20 miles from home to meet us at Ararat. Four miles off Stawell itself it seemed as if the whole town had turned out en masse to greet us. As we approached, the crowd cheered wildly, and two brass bands struck up a welcoming strain. The horses in one of the waggonettes at once took fright, and overturned the vehicle. Luckily, though the trap was smashed to atoms, no one was injured. Stawell was reached at 8.30. We had been twelve hours on the road, travelling under the most uncomfortable conditions, but our reception made us forget the trials and troubles of the long drive.'[15]

Stawell had a population of some 8,000 with a mine reputed to be the most profitable in Victoria. The professionals in the party went to have a look at it the following day but Grace and his cousin W.R. Gilbert 'hired a buggy and drove about 10 or 12 miles to a lagoon in the bush, where we had a fine day's sport with our guns. On the way we came across an Irish settler, a wonderfully hospitable old man, who, when we made ourselves known to him, could scarcely do enough for us. He showed us where to find the best sport, and then left us for about a couple of hours, returning with a big basket of luscious peaches, which he had ridden over to a neighbouring squatter's to procure for us.'[16]

The day after that they prepared to play Twenty-Two of Stawell but found the ground in a 'deplorable condition. Here and there were small patches of grass' – with none on the rest of it. The ground had been ploughed only three months before and grass sown because the tourists were coming. Grace judged the wicket 'execrable' and added that during the match one delivery stuck in the dust and 'never reached the batsman'. England, hampered by a plague of flies, were all out for 43 and lost by 10 wickets.

They left for Warrnambool on the coast, going via Ararat. The 'rain, which was very much wanted, fell in torrents, and when we started at 4.30 a.m. on Monday for our ninety-one miles drive we found the tracks in an appalling state. They were bad enough in all conscience when we traversed them en route to Stawell, but the rain had converted the dust into thick mud, in which the wheels sank almost to the axles.

'Of all my travelling experiences that coach drive to Warrnambool was the most unpleasant. Rain fell pitilessly all the time, and we were soon drenched to the skin. The first thirty-one miles took five hours and a quarter, and though we changed horses now and again our progress was exasperatingly slow. On leaving Hexham, where we halted for dinner, we came to a slight incline. Here two of our horses jibbed, and refused to budge.'[17]

Several players stayed at Hexham, an 'entertainment centre' during the gold rush, to 'lighten the load' and in the circumstances perhaps entertain themselves while 'we managed to make the horses convey the rest of us to Warrnambool, which we reached at half-past eleven at night, after a ride of nineteen hours. We were wet through, and our cricket bags and portmanteaus were soaking. Notwithstanding the rain a large number of the people at Warrnambool, who expected us to arrive in the afternoon, had gone out to meet us, but as we made no appearance they assumed that our coaches had broken down.'[18]

England won the match, returned to Melbourne and caught a boat up to Sydney to play Eighteen of New South Wales. There, for the first time, Grace played against a tall, lean 19-year-old from Balmain called **Frederick Robert Spofforth**, 'quite a youngster' but 'a very fair bowler, and he took two of our wickets for 16 runs in the second innings'.

Grace and Spofforth would meet again many times, and Spofforth became known as 'The Demon'. Apart from Grace himself, he is the first of the Oval people to make their entrance into our story.

The tourists played another 10 matches and when they got back to England 'we found that our doings in Australia had been followed by cricketers at home with the keenest possible interest and that for the first time people in England had received the results of matches in Australia by means of the telegraph.'[19]

By definition this was a long way from modern communications, and not as quick as perhaps you'd imagine – as we shall see when news of the Oval Test was being relayed round the world to Australia – but it must have been a revolution compared to sending letters by boat.

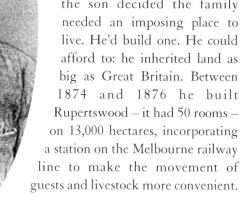

At Sunbury, William Clarke – son of 'Big Clarke' – took on a woman called Janet to be companion and helper to his wife. His wife died and Clarke married Janet. 'Big Clarke' died the following year – 1874 – and the son decided the family needed an imposing place to live. He'd build one. He could afford to: he inherited land as big as Great Britain. Between 1874 and 1876 he built Rupertswood – it had 50 rooms – on 13,000 hectares, incorporating a station on the Melbourne railway line to make the movement of guests and livestock more convenient.

Fred Spofforth, who meant terror to a generation of batsmen.

In 1876–77 James Lillywhite of Sussex took a team to Australia, the fourth to tour and still the only tourists to England were the Aborigines. Evidently there had been some friction between the amateurs and professionals on the Grace tour and, to circumvent that, Lillywhite took only professionals.

One of them, a dangerous practical joker called **George Ulyett**, would play at the Oval. Known as Happy Jack, the 25-year-old from Sheffield was a leading all-rounder – he'd have earned his place for his bowling alone never mind an extraordinary ability in the field or his fine batting. Typically, he ignored all this and said Yorkshire picked him for his 'whistling and good behaviour'[20] – and added irreverently that whenever he went out to open an innings with Grace it was to give the Old Man confidence. Ulyett must have smiled a wicked smile every time he said that.

Of him, Grace wrote that he was a clean hitter, confident, easy and a great punisher of bowling whatever its quality. He 'threw all his gigantic strength into his strokes. The secret of his bowling success was a combination of pace and off break, coupled with the fact that he made the ball rise very rapidly. On bumping wickets it was no pleasure to play Ulyett's bowling. In the field he was almost infallible, and any one who saw the superb catch with which he dismissed Mr Shuter at Lord's[21] ... will never forget the roar of applause which went up when Ulyett, fielding at extra long-on, leaped up and caught the ball just as it was dropping on the awning over the spectators' seats.'[22]

Ulyett could take the passion for practical joking too far, a failing of so many of that devious art. Grace again:

'On the occasion of the picnic down Sydney Harbour, given to the team then in Australia, Ulyett, who went out in a small boat towed by a steamer, conceived the idea of frightening one of the gentlemen in the boat. He pretended to scuffle with the gentleman, and while doing so purposely fell overboard—a foolhardy trick, as sharks are not uncommon in those waters. George, who was a splendid swimmer, struck out for the shore, but was fished up. Then he proceeded to frighten the gentleman by accusing him of pushing him overboard and demanding compensation.'[23]

Grace emphasised the point by recounting a further example, although this happened in England.

'Ulyett, who was also a good boxer, was invited... to the house of a gentleman, who, after being introduced to some of the Yorkshire cricketers, asked if anyone would like a little "mill" [old usage for boxing match] with the gloves. Someone suggested that Ulyett should have a round or two, but he pretended that he knew nothing about boxing. However, after some persuasion he did put the gloves on, and in a few minutes convinced his host that he had him at his mercy.'[24]

Lillywhite's 1876–77 team holds its place in history because it played what is now recognised as the first Test Match against Australia, at Melbourne. Ulyett played in that and so did a great slow bowler, Alfred Shaw of Nottinghamshire. He remembered 'it was on the night of Monday, November 6th, 1876, at eleven o'clock, that the *Tanjore* reached Adelaide. The following day we made our entry into the city in state – that is, in a coach, drawn by six greys, and preceded by a band of music. It was all wonderful to me then. The experience of after years enabled me to regard these pleasant receptions more as matters of course.

'If it had been difficult for some of us to keep our sea legs on board ship for a few days before landing, it was even more so for one or two of the party to regain their land legs. It surely must have been this difficulty that caused [Harry] Jupp, on spending his first night in an hotel in Adelaide, to so far forget his location as to crawl carefully under the bed in the belief that he was getting into his bunk on board ship.'[25]

Nor would Shaw forget the Adelaide wicket for their first match.

'The Adelaide Cricket Association had been afraid to use the roller for fear it would bruise and kill the grass! They were dumfounded when they saw Southerton's preparations.[26] He got them to borrow the Corporation roller, and then he took one of the four horses by the head and led the team right across the centre of the ground. Perhaps it was not singular that on a wicket that had received so little preparation I should have been able to claim an analysis of 226 balls, 46 maidens, 12 runs, 14 wickets, at my first turn with the ball.'

He wouldn't forget his first ball, either. The 'wicket was sandy, and broke up quickly'. Another era of course: a public holiday was declared for the match, as it would be at Melbourne – and, Shaw pointed out, the team was given free railway passes for the tour which 'meant a considerable saving to those who financed the trips'. This 'privilege' lasted until 1881.

Tours were hard. At one point, leaving Melbourne, Shaw felt 'we must have been a miserable party [...] Jupp was suffering martyrdom from rheumatism, sciatica, or something of the kind, and became so helpless from pains in the hips and loins that he could not walk, or even get out of his berth without assistance. Selby and myself were as miserable from cold as two men could well be, Hill appeared to be sickening for the measles or something of that kind, Ulyett said he wished himself at Sheffield, never to be tempted to go to sea again; and all the party had an acute attack of the doldrums. But it is wonderful what a change comes over a man when he sets foot on *terra firma*.'[27]

They played nine matches, including Adelaide, Sydney and Melbourne before travelling to New Zealand, where the wicketkeeper Ted Pooley of

Surrey, who liked a bet, tricked one of the locals, a surveyor. The tourists were due to play Eighteen of Canterbury, and it went like this: Pooley wagered that he'd predict the Canterbury batsmen's scores but demanded odds of 20–1 for each one he got right. The surveyor thought that reasonable – but Pooley wrote down 0 against each batsman, knowing that in such matches ducks abounded. There were 11. The surveyor claimed trickery and a brawl developed resulting in Pooley's arrest.

As a consequence he was not with the team when it sailed back to Australia for the first Test, starting on 15 March. Before they sailed for New Zealand the tourists lost to Fifteen of New South Wales and Fifteen of Victoria. It seems to have made the Australians think they should meet, and perhaps could beat, them in an 11-a-side match. No such match was on the schedule but the Victorian Cricket Association, the tour promoters, saw the potential benefit, especially financial. The match, billed as All England v All Australia, wasn't that at all: the leading English amateurs were all at home and the Australian side selected only from Victoria and New South Wales.

Australia took the field without three of their leading bowlers, including Spofforth – who refused to play because **Billy Murdoch** hadn't been selected: throughout Spofforth's career Murdoch had kept to him and Spofforth believed nobody else could.

The Oval people were making their entrances now.

Murdoch, born in Sandhurst, Victoria in 1855, combined 'a perfect style with splendid defence'[28] and on this he constructed a career as the first Australian batsman who could be compared to the best of the English. In 1882 he was one of only two men who had ever made 300 in a First Class innings (Grace inevitably the other).

Thomas Garrett, born at Wollongong, was an all-rounder who never quite found his true form in England. A solicitor by profession, he worked for the civil service in New South Wales and bowled a mean off-break.

Thomas Horan was the leading Victorian batsman whose patience could make spectators despair. He worked in a Melbourne audit office and soon would have connections with the *Australiasian,*

All-rounder Thomas Garrett.

writing for it and, long into the future, giving an evocative account of the cold August afternoon.

One beginning had been at 12.20 on Wednesday 1 January 1862 when William Caffyn bowled to James Bryant. Here was another when, at 1.05 on Thursday 15 March 1877, Shaw ran up and bowled to **Charles Bannerman** of Sydney. At that instant Test cricket began (although the term Test Match would come later), and, just like Caffyn and Bryant, the first ball produced no run.

Bannerman, who worked in the government printing office in Sydney, had an organised technique and a solid defence. He was 'short, dour... could defend for long periods and like it.'[29] He scored 165, retired hurt and Australia won by 45 runs. England extracted some sort of revenge two weeks later in a second match, again at Melbourne. This time Spofforth played, and so did Murdoch, although he wasn't keeping wicket.

John McCarthy Blackham did that, as he had done in the first match, and soon enough people would be speaking of his astonishing speed of reaction and judging a genuinely great wicketkeeper. There is some argument about whether he was the first to do without a long stop to back him up. Standing up to all the bowling, his body and head received plenty of blows, but he was never seen to flinch.

On the cold August afternoon he never made a mistake and would be crouched behind the stumps when Peate had made his long journey...

Now, in Melbourne, he stumped Shaw off Spofforth, who took 3 – 67, although England won by four wickets.

Shaw remembered the 'success of the Australians created immense jubilation in Melbourne and other Colonial centres. It would have been strange, indeed, had the effect been otherwise. For the time being the defeated English-men and their associates in the Colonies had to be content to eat humble pie – sweetened, it is true, with the thought that it was members of their own race who had offered it – but humble pie all the same.'[30]

The next logical step was a tour of England, which happened in 1878, although many in Australia thought they weren't strong enough yet. The team which arrived at Liverpool on 13 May lost little time in demonstrating that they were. Across a long, arduous, nomadic summer from May to mid-September they played 37 matches and lost only seven, four against leading teams: Nottinghamshire, the Gentlemen of England, Yorkshire and Cambridge University.

Captained by 32-year-old Dave Gregory – a New South Wales all-rounder known as 'Handsome Dave' who did have a biblical beard – the side formed the matrix which would eventually take Australia to parity with England.

Among them was Boyle, the oldest member of the 1882 party at 35. He was useful in the sense that he batted and bowled effectively, at medium pace and breaking the ball both ways.

A glimpse of the times: Spofforth wrote that 'no one but the very best cricketers owned pads or even bats... the team had an immense canvas bag with "Australian Eleven" in bold letters across it. We used to draw lots to decide who would look after it from match to match. [...] The "Caravan", we called it. [...] We carried it to England, and landed it safely at Nottingham, but in London it was lost, and no man knows its burying-place.'[31]

They did have a growing awareness of being Australian, although the population had not yet reached two million, breaking down to approximately 60 percent born in Australia and 30 percent British migrants.

London alone had about three million inhabitants and was poised to become the world city, spreading outwards because the construction of railways, beginning in the 1830s, allowed people to live in the suburbs and

This was the Oval in the early days but the picture is alas undated. (Courtesy of Surrey County Cricket Club)

commute to work. By 1900 the population had doubled and the city occupied an area of more than a hundred square miles. The railways brought mobility, and that brought all manner of people to London – many poor and looking for a chance. Steamships brought mobility, and that brought all manner of other people – the poor of Europe, political refugees, people from the empire (notably Indians and Chinese).

There was an underside. One medical student, wandering the Haymarket, remembers 'at least a thousand ladies of easy virtue... of all nationalities, some of whom were anxious to do business with me, which honour, however, I naturally declined.'

And 'the East End had become as potent a symbol of urban poverty... as Manchester had been of industrial conditions in the 1840s.' Many in the West End viewed the East as a place where the 'vilest practices are looked upon with the most matter-of-fact indifference... [and where] the filthy and abominable from all parts of the country seem to flow. Entire courts are filled with thieves, prostitutes, and liberated convicts.' Whitechapel had almost 40 percent of its 76,000 inhabitants on or below the poverty line. Work was hard to find, whether regular or intermittent. Sweat shops – primitive working conditions where long hours of toil yielded meagre reward – were widespread. Working days of as long as 18 hours were not unknown in the East End among those who tried to wring a living out of employment in places like furniture makers and tailoring.

This is the city the Australians would soon be confronting. Their presence would be lost on many of the inhabitants.

'Many of the lower classes were so ignorant of Australia itself, to say nothing of the cricket capabilities of its inhabitants, that they fully expected to find the members of Gregory's team black as the Aborigines. We remember the late Rev. Arthur Ward "putting his foot into it" on this subject before some of the Australians. One day in the pavilion at Lord's, the writer, who had been chosen to represent the Gentlemen of England against the visitors in a forthcoming match, was sitting beside Spofforth watching a game, in which neither was taking part. Mr Ward coming up, accosted the writer, "Well, Mr Steel, so I hear you are going to play against the niggers on Monday?" His face was a picture when Spofforth was introduced to him as the "demon nigger bowler".'[32]

Of Allan Steel, more in a moment. The tourists lost the first game, at Nottingham, by an innings and 14 runs, in filthy weather – it prevented them practising before the match – then journeyed to London to meet the MCC.

What impact did the city have on them? It is lost.

Because they had yet to prove themselves, the attendance at Lord's was small and the MCC picked a strong side with W.G. and Hornby to open.

Albert Neilson 'Monkey' Hornby, medium height (5ft 9in) and medium weight (11st 7lb), was full of restless energy. Hence his nickname. He was the sixth son of William Henry Hornby, MP for Blackburn from 1857 to 1869. One author describes him as an 'inspired amateur, excitable, dashing, immensely combative and slightly outrageous. He was an England rugger three-quarter (nine caps) and he tackled cricket *like* a rugger player. He … was on the small side and made up for his lack of inches by a determination to fight any enemy in sight. […] he was capable of chasing a barracker twice his size out of Old Trafford. If he did not like what a sports writer had said of him, he did not pen him a pained note. He did not write to *The Times,* pleading for higher standards of objectivity in sporting journalism. He simply darted up the steps of the old Press Box at Old Trafford, seized the feller by the collar – anybody who offended Hornby was always "the feller" – and ran him downstairs, out of the ground, and probably out of Manchester altogether.'[33]

Grace, who opened the England second innings with Hornby at the Oval in 1882, wrote of him as one of

'our brilliant amateurs. I have been associated very closely with him […] and we have fought side by side or against each other at home every year in the last twenty. Very few cricketers have so attractive a style, and it has always been a treat to watch his dashing play. Perhaps he is a little too anxious to score at times; but when he makes up his mind to defend his wicket, the bowling has a heavy problem to solve. […] He had a wonderful eye, and at his best was very quick on his legs for a short run, at times accomplishing extraordinary things which electrified his opponents and the spectators. I know he used to be the terror of

Ex-rugby international Albert Hornby.

some batsmen who were in with him, and one or two have said they never knew whether they were on their heads or their legs while the partnership continued.'[34]

Spofforth recorded how, when the tourists reached Lord's, they 'were not very confident'. The MCC batted first – again in filthy weather – and Grace was caught off the second ball. Spofforth announced himself as a destroyer with six wickets for 4 off 5.3 overs. Boyle took six wickets for 3 in the second innings (Spofforth four for 16) and the tourists won by nine wickets. The result 'created a sensation in London and throughout England, and our hotel was almost besieged'.[35]

Spofforth remains in historical terms touched by greatness, similar – in forbidding reputation – to the destroyers who came long after him: Harold Larwood, Ray Lindwall, Keith Miller, Frank Tyson, Fred Trueman, Dennis Lille and Jeff Thomson. Perhaps a better analogy would be Glenn McGrath, in pace and execution.

Dick Lilley, a shrewd observer from the vantage point of keeping wicket for Warwickshire, explained: 'One of the reasons that may account for Spofforth's phenomenal success was the exhaustive study he made of the art. He varied his bowling to a wonderful extent from slow to very fast, and by studying his opponents' weaknesses added considerably to the strength of his attack.'[36]

In retrospect, the victory at Lord's, as well as Spofforth's bowling, became even more significant.

'Not until Monday, May 27, 1878, did the English public take any real interest in Australian cricket, though in 1877 in their own country the Australians had defeated Lillywhite's eleven on even terms. Prior to this date four English teams had visited Australia, but their doings, though recorded in the press, did not interest the cricket community at home. The Australian players met with in the Colonies were no doubt learning from the English teams they had seen and played against, but the idea that they were up to the standard of English first-class cricket seemed absurd; and to a certain extent this estimate was justified by the records of the English visitors.

'Now, though English cricketers had been beaten on even terms as recently as 1877, the fact seemed to have been lost sight of at home in 1878, and when the first Australian eleven that ever visited [...] it never occurred to anyone that it could have any chance of actually storming the citadel of English cricket with success. On May 27 English cricket and its lovers received a serious shock, as on that day, in the extraordinarily short space of four and a half hours, a very fair team of the MCC were beaten by nine wickets. The famous English club was certainly well represented.'[37]

They beat Yorkshire at Huddersfield and on 3 June came to the Oval to play Surrey, a match which generated so much enthusiasm it drew 30,000 spectators who 'broke down fences in the crush and spilled onto the field'.[38] Technically the Aborigines had been the first Australian team to play at the Oval, because they'd begun their 1868 tour there, but in a very real sense this 1878 match was the beginning of a tradition which has continued in unbroken sequence ever since.

South London in the 1880s had been steadily developed for a couple of hundred years and offered entertainment – music hall and theatre – as well as housing. The Vauxhall Pleasure Gardens opened in 1661 and became extremely popular while the construction of Vauxhall Bridge, in 1816, enabled the area around Brixton to be developed. This was now in full flow, fed by railway and tram lines from the middle of London.

The Oval, set amid all this, had originally been a big cabbage patch, the ground made fertile perhaps by the River Effra which rose near Crystal Palace and flowed through Norwood, Dulwich, Herne Hill, Brixton and Kennington before entering the Thames beside Vauxhall Bridge. Originally small boats could navigate it (Queen Elizabeth I may have gone by barge to visit Sir Walter Raleigh at his home), and, as late as 1860, Dulwich was drawing fresh water from it. 'When the Albert embankment was built, however, much of the water from the River Effra was diverted into a sewer whilst the remaining flow was enclosed in a covered culvert.'[39]

The Oval took its shape from the road around the patch and in 1846 became a cricket pitch because various proposals for buildings did not materialise. (It was turfed by sod from Tooting Common.)

The Australians won by five wickets and went on a mini tour – Elland, Batley, Longsight – against minor teams before playing the Gentlemen of England at Prince's, a ground in Chelsea. Here they'd meet **Allan Gibson Steel**, gentleman, barrister and evidently a shooter of grouse who was an outstanding all-rounder – he bowled round arm and made the ball break both ways. One judge placed him 'second only' to Grace and 'emphatically the greatest after him [...] he never seemed to want practice, and he always played the first ball as if he had been at the wicket a week.'[40]

Of him, Grace said:

'It is very difficult to arrive at a proper estimate of his abilities as a cricketer. Before he had completed his sixteenth year he had played well enough to warrant the prediction that he would do as well as any one since the game began. Unfortunately, professional and other duties interfered very much with his cricketing career [...] For weeks and months he would be unable to play in first-class cricket and then suddenly appear in some great

Allan Steel in classical pose.

match and astonish everyone by his brilliant form.'[41]

The Australians lost to the Gentlemen by an innings and 1 run (Steel 4 for 37 and 7 for 35), which suggested they weren't as good as the MCC result might imply. Two days later they were due to meet Middlesex at Lord's and there the Australians and Grace fell into a bitter dispute. It concerned William Midwinter, born in Gloucestershire but an immigrant to Australia at the age of nine. He had represented Australia in the First Test but also played for Gloucestershire.

The tourists selected him in advance, and when they reached England he joined them, playing in every match. However, at Lord's, before he went out against Middlesex, Grace appeared in the pavilion and told Midwinter that under his contract he had to go to the Oval and play for Gloucester against Surrey. The Australians voiced their objections very strongly – there was, as someone has noted, an exchange of bad language – but Midwinter went. Eventually Grace apologised.

John Conway, the tour manager, had already lodged an objection to Grace being paid £60 for an appearance with the Gentlemen's team at Prince's because, logically, if Grace received payment he could no longer be an amateur. Grace had not forgotten this, and when he apologised he did so to Boyle and Gregory but not Conway until well afterwards.

Perhaps England v Australia has always been a hard place, even in the supposedly refined and, forgive me, gentlemanly era of 'gentlemen'.

Astonishingly, the Australians played 28 matches after Lord's against a wide variety of opponents in a wide variety of places but no Test Match. They weren't ready yet, and Steel passed this judgement. The team 'contained four really good bowlers: Spofforth, Boyle, Allan, and Garrett, and two fair changes in Midwinter and Horan, but as batsmen they were poor when compared with England's best. Charles Bannerman was a most dashing player, his off-driving being magnificent, and Horan and Murdoch were fairish batsmen. Murdoch then was very different […] but the rest were rough and untutored, more like country cricketers than correct players. Had this team come to England in a dry instead of a wet season, it would probably have had a very different record at the end of its visit. Spofforth, Boyle and Garrett were most deadly to the best batsmen on the soft, caked wickets they so often had to assist them; and the Australian batsmen, with the rough crossbat style which distinguished the majority, were just as likely to knock up fifteen to twenty runs on a bad wicket as on a good one. Nothing brings good and bad batsmen so close together as bad wet seasons. When Cambridge University met them the match was played on a hard true wicket, the Australian bowling was thoroughly collared, and none of the eleven, except Murdoch, C. Bannerman, and perhaps Horan, showed any signs of being able to play correct cricket on a hard ground.

'Gregory's team, however, had a wonderfully stimulating effect on English cricket. Their record taught us that the Australians could produce men to beat most of the counties, and who *might,* after a year or two of experience, play a very good game with a picked team of England.'[42]

The hardness lingered into the following winter when Lord Harris took a side to Australia. The original idea had been to take amateurs only, but Ulyett and another Yorkshire professional, Tom Emmett, were added for strength. Hornby went as one of the amateurs, and so did **Alfred Perry 'Bunny' Lucas**, a Londoner whose batting was 'free and correct, and he had great patience. He made the most of his height, and came down on the ball with great force; and he was particularly strong in driving.'[43] He watched the ball closely and cut well; as a round-arm bowler at slightly above medium pace he brought the ball in from the off, exploiting a high action, and could be virtually unplayable.

Richard Gorton Barlow from Bolton, who'd open for England as he did for Lancashire, was 'the straight man' to Hornby, 'the sturdy professional, sober, slow, resourceful and stead'.[44] He batted with an infinity of patience and once took five and a half hours over 5. Grace was almost acerbic.

'His play was monotony incarnate, and could be relied on to send spectators to sleep on a sultry day. I have seen Mr A.N. Hornby, who always opened the Lancashire innings with Barlow, score a century while his partner made a tedious dozen – principally in singles. Stonewallers have their uses, but it is a blessing that Nature is sparing with the supply of the requisite patience necessary for making a stonewaller. One in a team is sometimes very useful, but a second is more than spectators can stand.'[45]

They played a single Test, at Melbourne, which Australia won by 10 wickets (Spofforth 13 wickets in the match) but encountered serious trouble against New South Wales when Murdoch was given run out by the Australian umpire travelling with the English team. The crowd, incensed, rushed the pitch and one spectator struck Harris – perhaps with a stick, perhaps with a whip – before Hornby got hold of him and hauled him to the pavilion. As Hornby did this, he was struck by another spectator and 'had his shirt nearly torn off his back', as Harris subsequently described. For a while it looked very ugly.

Grace gave a subsequent description, too: 'It was George Ulyett who distributed the wickets – as weapons of offence and defence [...] Luckily there was no need for the wickets to be brought into active service. George Ulyett armed with a wicket would have been a desperate antagonist even for an Australian larrikin.'[46]

The New South Wales captain, Sid Gregory, objected to the umpire and asked for him to be changed. Harris refused. The match was eventually completed and Harris bore no grudges because when the Australians toured England in 1880 and found difficulty in attracting matches against the leading teams Harris helped organise a Test at the Oval, the first to be played in England.

The 1880 Australian party included **George John Bonnor**, of whom little was known. It soon would be. Bonnor stood 6ft 6in and came originally of solid Yorkshire stock: his parents emigrated to Gisburn, and although their herd of pedigree cattle was rustled by bushrangers they prospered. Bonnor's style was to use his strength to hit cricket balls immense distances as often as he could and, despite his height, his body was perfectly proportioned so that his movements looked elegant. The hitting excited crowds everywhere, in anticipation and – when the hitting came off – in execution as well. If he looked big he made grounds look small.

'Bonnor was by nature a friendly soul, with malice towards none. With his happy nature, he bore no ill-will towards any person or object, except a small red ball. Like many another giant, he was shy in the presence of women, but warmly approved of by dogs and children. He would take his turn at ship's concerts or pavilion sing-songs and when he "rendered" in his pleasant tenor voice "The Tear in Every Eye" he quivered with honest emotion, all six foot six of him. He had another trait in common with many a famous man: he longed to be famous for something else.'[47]

Even his feet were remarkable. He 'wore the largest size of cricket boots I have ever seen. For many years a pair of his boots were exhibited by way of an advertisement in a boot shop in the Strand.'[48]

Bonnor's contemporary, George Giffen, said of him:

'One of the most interesting figures that have strutted on the cricket stage, and one of the finest specimens of manhood I have ever met. When, exerting all the strength of that herculean frame he smote the bowling, it was a sight for the gods. […] He was born to be a hitter; he had a distinct mission as a demoraliser of bowlers and fieldsmen, and if he had always adhered to the strict terms of his unwritten commission he would have made a great many more runs. […] His great reach |enabled him| to kill good length balls which would have given other batsmen no end of worry.'[49]

The 1880 tour was a nomadic marathon, as 1978 had been, and took the tourists all over the land, meeting another wide variety of opponents. Steel paid tribute to the progress they were making. 'The close of the season showed that in the 11-a-side matches, Derbyshire, Yorkshire, Gloucestershire, and a good 11 of the Players of England had been beaten, while only two matches had been lost: Nottingham succeeded in winning by one wicket, and England by five wickets.'

This was the first Test Match played in England. The **Hon. Alfred Lyttelton** kept wicket for England and **William Barnes** batted at number 4.

Lyttelton, according to Grace, as a batsman had 'a most commanding and beautiful style, and scored at a very fast pace against all kinds of bowling. I remember hearing someone remark that his style was the champagne of cricket.'[50]

England's first innings at the Oval in 1880.

The England bowling when Australia batted. From the original scorebook. (Courtesy of John Kobylecky)

'I would,' Lord Hawke wrote, 'sum him up as a typical Sahib [gentleman], endowed with tremendous enthusiasm. In no one did I ever find the spirit of the game more absolutely true than in Alfred. It did not matter what he played, you never saw him play the fool in any game [he] was a magnificent wicket-keeper, and, rightly, the first ever selected to wear the gloves for England at home. He was particularly strong on the leg-side.'

England batted first, Grace and his brother E.M. putting on 91 for the first wicket. W.G. went on to 152 and in the context of the era a total of 420 put the match beyond Australia. They made 149, followed on, and although Murdoch made 153 not out England won by five wickets. The match provoked intense excitement and, of real significance for the future, Australia had not been disgraced.

In retrospect, it opened the way to 1882 and the tours were coming hard and fast by now. England toured in 1881–82 and played 30 matches between October and March. Edmund Peate played in all three Tests. The first, at Melbourne, was drawn (Horan 124) and Australia won the second, at Sydney, by five wickets.

Thereby hangs a tale, recounted by Shaw who played in it.

'It was a very hot day and we were wearing thin silk shirts. Tom, as it happened, was fielding at short slip and long field alternately, and having had a lot of running about to do he had become very warm, and his shirt worked up and floated freely in the light breeze. Tom was all unconscious of the amusing figure he was cutting with his silk shirt blowing out from the rearward like a miniature balloon. Ladies tittered, the roisterers of the crowd guffawed, and Sammy Jones lay down on the wicket and roared. "What's t' matter?" innocently asked Emmett, but with a suspicion of rising anger in his tone. We all laughed then in chorus, and the more we laughed the redder and more angry did genial Tom become. At last he found out that the breeze had taken unwarrantable liberties with his silk shirt, and at the same time a voice floated over the breeze, "Tom, your swag's out." For the rest of that tour "Tom, have you got your swag out?" was a very popular inquiry.'[51]

What Peate made of this is lost, and so is what he made of the Third Test which Australia won by six wickets. The tourists left Melbourne on 22 March and reached Naples on 2 May when some went overland and others steamed to Plymouth.

Whichever route Peate followed, overland or staying on the ship, he had four months of just being another cricketer before he confronted the cold afternoon and the long journey.

As a bowler there would be no problems. 'Peate was blessed with the most perfect action of any man I have seen deliver the ball [...] he began as a very fast bowler, though throughout his career in big cricket his pace was slow. He had no theories. Nobody ever bowled more with his head, but his only principle, with all his variations, was always to bowl with a length – a golden rule he acquired from watching Alfred Shaw. He was a really charming fellow. When Bates was married in the middle of the cricket season, Peate said "Bates is a fool! 'E's gone and got married in middle o' soomer. 'E should have got married in middle o' winter so that 'e could pay 'is oondivided attention to it."'[52]

Whether Edmund Peate paid his undivided attention to the final ball of Harry Boyle's 19th over on the cold afternoon is something we are still wondering about.

Notes

1. *Empire*, Niall Ferguson.
2. *Australian Cricket, A History*, Johnny Moyes.
3. Ibid.
4. NSW Governor Lachlan Macquarie, quoted in *The Story of Cricket In Australia*, Jack Egan.
5. Egan op.cit.
6. home.vicnet.net.au/~pioneers/pppg5v.htm
7. *The Offshore Islanders*, Paul Johnson.
8. Ibid.
9. *Cricket Walkabout*, John Mulvaney and Rex Harcourt.
10. *71 Not Out*, William Caffyn.
11. Ibid.
12. Ibid.
13. *The Trailblazers*, David Frith.
14. *Cricket Reminiscences & Personal Recollections*, W.G. Grace.
15. Ibid.
16. Ibid.
17. Ibid.
18. Ibid.
19. Ibid.
20. *Odd Men In*, A.A. Thomson.
21. In the Gentlemen v Players match at Lord's – Grace says 1891 but it was 1890. Wisden: 'Shuter was splendidly caught at extra long-on by Ulyett, the fieldsman taking the ball with his right hand close to the boundary.'
22. *Cricket Reminiscences*, Grace.
23. Ibid.
24. Ibid.
25. *Alfred Shaw Cricketer*, A.W. Pullin.
26. James Southerton was vice-captain of the touring side and, according to Wynne-Thomas in *The Complete History of Cricket Tours at Home & Abroad*, 'spent a week before the game preparing the wicket and in consequence run-getting was much easier than on the previous tour.'
27. Shaw op. cit.
28. *Australians in England 1881 and 1884*, Charles F. Pardon in *Bell's Life*.
29. Moyes op. cit.
30. Shaw op. cit.
31. Quoted in Egan.
32. Ibid.

33. *Odd Men In*, A.A. Thomson.

34. *Cricket*, Grace.

35. Quoted in Egan.

36. *Twenty Four Years Of Cricket,* A.A. Lilley.

37. *The Badminton Library: Cricket,* A.G. Steel and R.H. Lyttelton.

38. Egan op. cit.

39. www.vauxhallsociety.org.uk/Effra.html

40. *Recollections And Reminisces,* Lord Hawke.

41. Grace op. cit.

42. Steel op. cit.

43. Grace op. cit.

44. Thomson op. cit.

45. *Cricket Reminiscences*, Grace.

46. Ibid.

47. Thomson op. cit.

48. Lilley op. cit.

49. *With Bat And Ball,* George Giffen.

50. *Cricket*, Grace.

51. Shaw op. cit.

52. Hawke op. cit.

Hotting Up

O N WEDNESDAY 3 May 1882 the *Assam* sailed into Plymouth and four members of the party, manager C.W. Beal, Murdoch, Bonnor and Garrett, got off. They would take the night train to London, arriving the following morning, while the rest of the party stayed on board until it docked in London.

Perhaps these four had had enough of *Assam* and the sea – they'd sailed on 16 March – but Bonnor had his own reason. During the voyage a passenger had bet him that as soon as he stood on dry land he could not send a cricket ball 110 yards with his first throw. No other attempt would be allowed. If Bonnor succeeded, he won £100. If he failed, he paid the passenger £100.

They drove to a local businessman and amateur cricketer called William Hearder and asked him to act as referee. How they knew of Hearder is unclear because neither the 1878 nor 1880 sides had played at Plymouth. In the era there were at least two prominent William Hearders, one a printer and another involved in the fledgling telephone service. It may be, however, that Hearder ran some kind of sports shop because Bonnor bought a ball off him. This would explain how Bonnor found him: when the ship docked he asked 'Where can I buy a ball?'

Hearder took them to the cricket ground, but Bonnor 'objected to the grass and said he would prefer a hard road or parade-ground. We then drove to the Raglan Barracks, where there is plenty of space.' There certainly was. Finished 24 years earlier, it embraced squares and streets over 11 acres. The parade ground measured 4.5 acres, enough even for Bonnor.

'He said that would suit very well. The distance was marked off by newspapers, and he took his stand, toeing a line. The ball [...] was an ordinary match ball. This I handed to him, and I had placed in my hand the two cheques for £100 a piece.

'He threw the ball from where he stood at the line and did not run. It was a grand throw. It seemed as if the ball would never stop rising; and it pitched on a spot which was measured after to be 119 yards 5 inches from where he stood. As there was no objection made I handed over the two cheques to Mr Bonnor, who then said, "I will back myself for £200 to throw the ball 120 yards the next throw." Of course 120 yards is a fair throw, but the conditions were that it was to be his first throw on landing and after he had been cooped up on board ship for six weeks you can imagine he would be out of training. Mr Bonnor kindly presented me with the ball after the event and we adjourned to their hotel to wash off the dust.'[1]

The Australia which the tourists left was changing because, by the 1880s, decisions needed to be made about the extent of Chinese immigration and the kidnapping of islanders from the South Seas as workers for the Queensland sugar and cotton farms. Of more importance, there was a chance other European powers might cast covetous eyes on Australia's potential and the colonies took a view that perhaps a national government could best deal with that. (The Irish liked that because it separated the country from the British.) If Britain didn't produce one for them they must consider doing it themselves. Equally, the ordinary citizen began to feel Australian rather than from the individual colonies.

By this decade some 75 percent of Australians had been born in Australia, a powerful current because inevitably they felt Australian rather than the cargo from somewhere else. Australian art would soon be reflecting this, painting Australia and spawning the legend of the man of the Australian Bush, rugged, self-sufficient, trusting only his mates. That moved in the background.

The tourists, so firmly in the foreground, faced another nomadic marathon: 38 matches, the Oval Test the 30th of them. They certainly had the players to cope.

'Everyone in that Australian side was a master of some department of cricket. Massie, Bonnor and Percy McDonnell were superb hitters. The stylist was Billy Murdoch, the captain, one of the most elegant and admirable bats I ever fielded out to. The amazing thing was that he came originally from the Antipodes as their leading wicket-keeper with the incomparable Blackham as second string. Australian common sense soon reversed this departmental error [...] In 1882 he was *hors concours* among the Australian giants.

'Horan never came subsequently to this country, and always wore brown pads when batting. He had great command over all sorts of bowling [...] Bannerman was a caution as a stone-wailer. George Giffen, the greatest Australian all-rounder, except perhaps M.A. Noble, with S.P. Jones, were novices. What a quartet Spofforth, Boyle, Palmer and Garrett were, especially on the queer wickets they often bowled on.

'It was "Spof" who was the star turn. He has often said of himself that he was the fastest bowler that ever was. Of course, this is a harmless delusion [...] whilst he had the good fortune never to be overworked, because he was blessed with plenty of support.

'As for Blackham at the wicket, well, he conjured. His hands were all gnarled and his fingers misshapen from blows, but he never winced. Quick as the proverbial lightning, he could take any bowling apparently as if it were aimed to come straight to his hands, and he was the W.G. of his own department.'[2]

The tour began against Oxford University on 15 May. Jones would say: 'Twice daily we practised, with no restrictions as to "a modest quencher". I shall always remember breakfasting at Magdalen College. Champagne cup was sent round with monotonous regularity, with old Oxford Ale as a sort of topper to the function.'[3] At 9.00 that morning the selectors 'were hesitating whether to play him. [...] He was regarded as a batsman who could hit hard and might at any time make a good score, but was a very uncertain quantity.'[4] They played him.

Murdoch won the toss, and Massie made 104 before lunch, pressing on afterwards to 206. He had only been in England for 10 days, never seen an English wicket before – and he made his second hundred in 59 minutes. People were already asking what Massie might do to England.

They beat the University by nine wickets.

'A saloon carriage attached to the 9.30 train from London Bridge [station] down to Brighton on Thursday morning'[5] took them to the second match, against Sussex, who medium-pace bowler George Palmer (8 for 48) cut to pieces. Murdoch compiled a mighty 286 not out after Massie and Bannerman put on 96 in 35 minutes for the first wicket. The Australian total, 643, was the highest ever made in England in a first-class match. The tourists won by an innings and 355 runs.

They played the Orleans Club at Twickenham, Palmer bowling Grace for 34 and Murdoch making 107 not out, the match drawn. It allowed them to get to Epsom on the Wednesday for The Derby. There were no reports of any Australian winning much, and some reports of one or two losing a little.

Surrey, with Lucas and **Maurice Read**, ought to have provided the first real threat of the tour, but Boyle (7 for 52 and 4 for 16) bowled the Australians to a six-wicket win. Read was 'a magnificent batsman who never had pretensions to be even a moderate change bowler'[6] and 'one of the most genuine cricketers I met'.[7]

Cambridge University were strong, fielding three Studd brothers, J.E.K.,

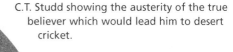

C.T. Studd showing the austerity of the true believer which would lead him to desert cricket.

C.T. and G.B. – Charles Thomas – was a right-hand bat and right-arm medium pacer. The Australians batted and Studd took 5 for 64 then made a masterfully confident 118 as the University won by six wickets.

They recovered against Lancashire – with Hornby, Barlow and Steel – and won by four wickets before they drew with Yorkshire at Bradford (Peate 3 for 40 and 5 for 75, Ulyett bowled Spofforth 0) and Nottinghamshire. **William Barnes** was a stalwart all-rounder who would play for the county for 20 years, a reliable batsman who hit the ball cleanly and, when set, scored quickly. The Australians made 140 and in reply Notts were all out for 110. Garrett bowled the last man, Fred Morley, for a duck, and Morley said memorably: 'It beat me in the pace, it beat me in the pitch, and it beat me in the flight.'

They beat Derbyshire comprehensively, beat Yorkshire – at Sheffield this time – by six wickets and the Gentlemen of England by an innings at the Oval. Australia made 334 and Grace opened for the Gentlemen. Giffen remembered 'W.G. was scoring freely when I went on, and as this was the first time I had bowled at the champion batsman of the world, I tried for his wicket as though my life depended on the result. Success rewarded my efforts because I bowled out his middle stump.'[8]

The tourists beat a team called the United Eleven at Chichester by an innings and 263. All the Australians made runs and Horan 112.

To emphasise the strength of the side, they played a further 17 matches up to the Test Match and lost only twice – one of them against the Players of England, ironically at the Oval and also in August.

Along the way they drew with the MCC at Lord's, a significant match in that the MCC made 302 (Grace 46, Hornby 45, Lucas 45, Studd 114, while Barnes and Steel also played). When the Australians batted, Studd took 4 for 26 and Steel 2 for 39.

Amazingly, they played Yorkshire in three consecutive matches, Dewsbury on 13, 14 and 15 July, Bradford on 17, 18 and 19 July, and Middlesbrough on 20, 21 and 22 July. Lord Hawke, opening for Yorkshire, remembered 'I had a chance of pulling off the second game. I managed to get a good sight of the ball when Boyle and Spofforth were at their deadliest, but I was badly run out – one of the few occasions when I yielded to the too-excited call of a more experienced comrade. In the last match I enjoyed the earliest of my many partnerships with a tail batsman. Ted Peate stuck in with me, to the delight of the crowd at Middlesbrough.' Hawke made 30 and Peate 20.

For the Players of England, Barnes made 87 and Read 130, while Peate, Barnes and Ulyett took wickets. The Players won by an innings and 34 runs. During the match Palmer was injured, a strain.

They played Cambridge University Past and Present at Portsmouth. Lyttelton opened and kept wicket. Studd and Steel made runs, and Steel settled the match with 5 for 24 – Cambridge won it by 20.

They battered Somerset at Taunton by an innings and went to Clifton to play Gloucestershire. Palmer was still unwell and so, now, was Murdoch. Rain affected the match, although Massie showed his form with 39 and 55 not out while Spofforth took 5 for 60. After the match – drawn – the Australians caught the 6.40 train which pulled into Paddington at 10.40. They took carriages to the Tavistock Hotel in Covent Garden and spent a quiet Sunday there. Covent Garden was then a poor, noisy area that smelt, but the Tavistock was a familiar haunt for the Australians: a 200-room establishment which long before had been a bordello with a woman in every room.

The President of the Melbourne Cricket Club, William Clarke – son of 'Big Clarke' – was in London with his wife Janet and attendants, including a close friend of Mrs Clarke, Florence Rose Morphy. Daughter of a magistrate from the gold-rush town of Beechworth in north-east Victoria, she was the music teacher at Rupertswood and very beautiful.

'Florence is no mere servant. She is very much loved by the Clarke family and had gone to live with them a few years earlier out of a necessity of earning her own living.'9

The Clarkes were enjoying their second grand tour of Europe. Whether he went to the Tavistock to meet the team is unknown. Clarke, enormously wealthy of course, was making both a favourable impression and influential friends. He would certainly be at the Oval on the morrow for the Test.

The Age newspaper in Melbourne previewed the match. 'With such a large number of first-class players to select from, and the fact that no stone will be left unturned to win, the 11 representing England will be wonderfully strong in all departments of the game, and their opponents will have the toughest job set them they have yet attempted.

'Every one of them with the exception of Peate (the best bowler of the lot) is a first-class batsman. The others comprise the cream of English batting and A. Lyttelton, who will keep wicket, while perhaps a little inferior to Pilling, is a most punishing and dashing batsman, and has shown himself to be in great form this season. The aggregation of talent in these names is something exceptional [...] it is not necessary to refer particularly to the Australian players, but if Murdoch and Palmer are well enough to play it will probably be found that Jones and Boyle will stand out [down]. [News of] the first day's play can scarcely be expected before a late hour this evening, and will be awaited with considerable interest in all parts of Australia.'

It would.

The obituary which appeared in the *Sporting Times* three days after the Oval Test – rarely reproduced in the context of the page on which it appeared.

Notes

1. *Cricket Reminiscences,* Grace.
2. *Recollections And Reminiscences,* Hawke.
3. Jones's Obituary in *Wisden,* 1952 edition.
4. *With Bat And Ball,* Giffen.
5. Pardon in *Bell's Life.*
6. Hawke op. cit.
7. Giffen op. cit.
8. Ibid.
9. *'The Lion and the Kangaroo': The Ashes Story,* an essay by Marie Romeo of Rupertswood Mansion.

28 August 1882

AT BREAKFAST at the Tavistock the 'anxieties' in the Australians' minds 'must sure have concerned the weather and the toss'.[1] Heavy rain drowned Saturday in London and more rain fell during Sunday night. The wicket wouldn't be easy and could only deteriorate.

Anticipation ran strong and hard all down an overcast morning, spiced because of all the matches this long summer here was the only one pitting the full might of England against the tourists.

The Australians arrived at 10.30 and wrestled with their team selection. They made an immediate decision to leave out McDonnell and, assuming Palmer – still suffering from his strain – would be fit enough to play, left Jones out. But was Palmer fit? Was Murdoch himself? The Australians decided to find out. Palmer, ball in hand, and Murdoch, bat in hand, emerged from the pavilion and walked over to the nets in front of the score box. Palmer bowled to Murdoch who 'appeared far from well but hit in his usual vigorous style'. Palmer 'looked really ill'. Back in the pavilion a doctor examined Palmer and told him that if he did play he risked severe damage. Jones came in. Giffen judged that the team 'suffered irreparable' from Palmer's absence – Jones, 'the one unsuccessful player on the tour, being but an inefficient substitute'.[2]

The mood was one of delicious and rising anticipation towards the start at midday.

'After the close finish and the creditable display made in 1880 against England by worse players, the match created the most intense excitement.'[3]

Some 20,000 people were making their way to the Oval to witness it: 420 must have been members because 19,580 paid. No crowd as big as this had, some reporters insisted, ever been seen at a cricket match in England before, and 'the public swarmed the gates, which were totally inadequate to the calls made upon them.'[4]

The picture is undated but the presumption is that this was what the entrance looked like in 1882 and the Australians arrived here. It seems to have acquired windowboxes since the photograph earlier in this book! (Courtesy of Surrey County Cricket Club)

No doubt, in the best stoical British tradition, those trying to get in formed queues and waited with murmurings of discontent. It may be that – because things which didn't work properly offended Victorians, and Victorian gentlemen disliked waiting in herds – the murmurings grew louder and louder. The sounds of it are in the great silence now, but we might hear rasping noises of complaint.

Soon the ground 'presented indeed a striking scene. None of its green surface was visible except the enclosure. All else was a dense border of eager, interested, and generally silent onlookers. They reclined on the turf, filled the seats, stood behind in ranks six or seven deep and crowded the mound which runs round the boundary.'[5] The mound had been made of earth from the excavations taking the River Effra underground. The pavilion, main grandstand (a seat costing five shillings = 25p, but a lot then) and the rest of the ground were full by mid-morning.

The clock moved to 11.45 and a bell rang: 'anyone still on the pitch please vacate it now'.

In the pavilion just before 12.00 Hornby spun the coin and Murdoch called correctly. He decided to bat, the only prudent decision when he weighed up the uncertain weather, the wicket – it had a reputation for being notoriously unreliable and would almost certainly break up on the second day – and the season: almost September and at this time of year the light became murky in early evening when, Murdoch could anticipate, England would be batting to win or save the match on the second day, and his Australians bowling to win it.

As someone noted, England took the field with no out-and-out pace bowler, although Ulyett could be brisk enough.

The six gentlemen in the England team came down the pavilion steps and out onto the pitch at 12.03, followed a moment later by the five professionals. The team was greeted by a reverberating cheer and that established a mood which lasted throughout the match. The 20,000, whether they sensed it at this moment or not, would exhibit very unVictorian public displays of emotion.

Massie and Bannerman followed the Englishmen.

Peate prepared to open the bowling from the Gasometer end to Bannerman, and arranging the field took a few minutes. Lyttelton, gloves on, stood behind the wicket, Steel positioned as the only slip beside him, Lucas at short-leg the other side of the wicket. Grace loomed, a great threatening presence, at point. Hornby loomed at silly mid-on, making himself another threatening presence. Barnes stood at mid-off, and Studd patrolled the broad acres beyond him. Ulyett must have been given the covers for reasons other than geographical. It was handy because he'd be bowling the second over. Read went over to long-off, Barlow down to third man.

The field was set for a left-arm bowler who knew what he was about. Peate would be attacking from outside the off stump and, if he could hold a length, hitting him anywhere else but the off-side on this wicket had to be extremely difficult: hence only two men to leg, Lucas and Hornby, and Hornby, as one account relates, was unusually close for mid-on – his positioning suggested aggression rather than run saving.

Bannerman faced a web of fielders on the off-side, artfully placed so that tame shots for singles would be ensnared and more robust strokes cut off in penetrating the defensive arc of three – Ulyett, Studd and Barnes – beyond them. Bannerman was known for his defence, and Peate must have been concentrating on keeping him defensive.

On a wicket which one account says, with unexpected frankness, was 'bumpy' – and partially sodden, anyway, so the ball wouldn't be coming onto the bat – runs were looking precious even before Peate bowled the first ball to Bannerman.

At 12.10 the 20,000 created an 'anxious excitement'[6] as Peate ran up.

The view from the pavilion to the Gasworks in 1887 but the view can't have changed much since 1882. This is what the players saw. (Courtesy of Surrey County Cricket Club)

Over 1: Peate to Bannerman

Where the ball pitched, whether Bannerman left it or it struck the bat, that also is lost in the great silence. Bannerman certainly did not score off it. The great match – arguably the greatest match in terms of the longevity of its impact – had begun in the most modest, mundane way possible. The scorers recorded such balls with a dot in the scorebook. They inscribed a dot. It would be the first of many.

Bannerman habitually employed a tactic at the beginning of an innings, taking easy runs on the leg-side before the bowler found line and length. He must have been trying to do that now, canny Peate denying him.

Nothing happened to the second ball.

Nothing happened to the third.

Bannerman moved into position for an off drive to the fourth, and they ran three, although he was so slow getting to the bowler's end on the last of them that sharper fielding might have run him out. The great match – the greatest match – had really begun. Bannerman, of course, kept strike, Massie watching from the other end.

Over 2: Ulyett to Bannerman

Aggression: Ulyett bowled like that from a high delivery, cutting the ball back or making it leap – he was agile enough to keep goal for Sheffield Wednesday

in the winters. He prepared to bowl from the pavilion end, and to a field more evenly balanced: Lyttelton keeping wicket, of course, Steel at slip and Peate at 'cover slip', Barnes at third man, Grace at point, Studd in the covers, Barlow at mid-off, Read at long-leg, Lucas at short-leg, Hornby at mid-on. That still left a yawning gap on the leg-side between Hornby and Lucas, but, to exploit it, Bannerman – a right-handed batsmen – would have to hit across the line of the ball. The famed, infuriating stonewaller was unlikely to do that unless one of those loose ones he liked so much came along. Massie, the 'most brilliant and dashing batsmen in the Colonies',[7] and also right-handed, might, but Massie might do anything.

Bannerman, entirely in keeping with the whole of his career up to this moment, played out a maiden to Ulyett.

It may be that Bannerman set the tone for the whole match in these two overs, from which the three runs had come from one stroke: trench warfare with psychological overtones, each run a cautious and precious gain. It may be that the state of the wicket decreed caution. It may be that Bannerman would have batted the way he did regardless of all that.

Over 3: Peate to Massie

Massie seemed to be in the mood to set his own tone because he struck the third ball for a single.

Over 4: Ulyett to Massie

They ran a bye to the first ball, Bannerman snicked the second for a single, and that brought Massie back on strike. Ulyett's third ball, a yorker, struck his leg-stump. The crowd erupted – they knew all about how dangerous Massie could be. The innings had lasted seven minutes, and Massie faced four balls including this one. Aggressive: like so many openers down the ages who preferred attack, it worked or it didn't.

Australia 6 – 1.

The considerable figure, in body and stature, of Murdoch safely negotiated the final ball.

Over 5: Peate to Bannerman

A maiden. They settled to the trench warfare, the wicket made visibly slow by the rain and Bannerman in no hurry.

Over 6: Ulyett to Murdoch

Ulyett containing Murdoch – he batted 'carefully' – for the first three balls, but the fourth pitched short and outside the off stump. Murdoch cut it 'prettily' all along the ground to the boundary between Grace at point and Studd in the covers. Studd turned, gave chase and almost overhauled the ball before it reached the boundary and the crowd there. This, too, set a tone. The match would be held between batsmen surviving and sudden flurries of movement.

Over 7: Peate to Bannerman

A maiden.

Over 8: Ulyett to Murdoch

A maiden.

Over 9: Peate to Bannerman

From the third ball Peate beat Bannerman, who was playing a leaden stroke on the leg-side, but the ball nicked the bat and ran away for 2. That was a minute or two before 12.30, and Bannerman now sank himself so deeply into the trench warfare that he would not score again until a quarter past one.

Over 10: Ulyett to Murdoch

A maiden.

Over 11: Peate to Bannerman

A maiden.

Over 12: Ulyett to Murdoch

Murdoch played Ulyett to the leg-side for two consecutive 2s from the first two balls, and Read was loudly cheered for the way he fielded and returned the ball to one of them. Murdoch didn't score off the last two.

Over 13: Peate to Bannerman

A maiden. Aggression: the crowd openly enjoyed how close Grace came to Bannerman, trying to intimidate him, and cheered Grace when he stopped a tremendous cut stroke. Nimble, he'd be cheered again and again for excellent fielding.

Over 14: Ulyett to Murdoch

Murdoch took 2 from the third ball with a drive but nothing from the last ball.

Over 15: Peate to Bannerman

A maiden.

Over 16: Barlow to Murdoch

Barlow came on for Ulyett at the pavilion end, this Barlow who Grace described as bowling 'above medium pace, keeps a good length and is very seldom off the wicket'.[8] His second ball came as near as possible to bowling Murdoch off his pad, and Grace was applauded for a stop at point. A maiden.

Over 17: Peate to Bannerman

A maiden.

Over 18: Barlow to Murdoch

Murdoch hit the first ball into the leg-side for a single. The three maidens between this and Murdoch's drive for 2 have, for the modern reader, a deceptive quality implying an extended period of stalemate. Murdoch's 2 came at about 12.36 and the single in this over at 12.41 – five minutes. The four-ball maidens were taking only a minute to bowl. In other words, the overall rhythm of the game was brisk. Put another way, Australia were 19 for one scored in half an hour, a reasonable strike rate at the beginning of any Test. That, however, was about to change. Bannerman didn't score off the last three balls.

Over 19: Peate to Murdoch

Murdoch took a single off the final ball to bring up the 20 after 76 deliveries – at just before 12.44 – but now a combination of factors did bring stalemate: the wicket, the relentlessly accurate English bowling and eager fielding. One report says it did not permit anything approaching a run as if, in context, even a single would have been an enormity. It would.

Barlow bowled seven maidens to Murdoch, and Peate bowled seven to Bannerman who, watchful and infinitely patient, was beaten only twice. The bowlers were containing the batsmen so completely that sustained cheering greeted the end of each over. It

All-rounder Richard Barlow.

developed into a profound examination of technique, nerve and willpower on both sides.

Giffen, watching intently from the pavilion – he was due to bat at number six – wrote: 'Who could wish for finer all-round play... not a loose one from either of them, while the way the ball came back on the treacherous wicket put the batsmen through a severe ordeal.'[9] A light shower brought a flurry of movement in the pavilion and grandstands, and a forest of umbrellas went up, but the shower wasn't heavy enough to stop play and it soon passed.

Over 34: Barlow to Murdoch

At last Murdoch broke the sequence with an ugly stroke – lucky, says one report – for a single off the final ball, taking him to the unfamiliar terrain of Peate at the Gasworks end. It was just after 1.00, so that 14 overs had been bowled in 17 minutes.

Over 35: Peate to Murdoch

A maiden.

Over 36: Barlow to Bannerman

A maiden.

Over 37: Peate to Murdoch

No runs came from the first three balls. It was 1.06. Murdoch faced the 64th delivery of his innings and, to it, went back and played on to a great cheer. The ball would have hit the wicket if he'd missed it.

Of the stand of 15, he had made 13, playing 'with extraordinary care and steadiness, and his departure was an evident relief to the English team'.[10]

Australia 21 – 2.

The giant Bonnor emerged and *that* got a different kind of cheer – all big hitters in all eras excite a particular, almost primitive, anticipation – which lasted until he reached the wicket and took guard. As he did, the fielders dropped back to accommodate the hitting.

Over 38: Barlow to Bannerman

A maiden.

Over 39: Peate to Bonnor

Bonnor was nearly bowled by the first ball. Off the third, he announced himself by driving Peate hard and straight for a single, but it wasn't Bonnor's sort of situation or wicket: dig for victory. Bannerman negotiated the final ball without scoring off it.

Over 40: Barlow to Bonnor

At just after 1.11, Barlow conjured a fast one which kept low and hit the middle and off. It was the second ball of the over. Australia 22 – 3. Bonnor had been in five minutes and faced six balls. Horan came to the wicket and didn't score off the final two balls.

Bonnor – but it wasn't his day.

Over 41: Peate to Bannerman

A maiden.

Over 42: Barlow to Horan

Horan took a single from the first ball, working in onto the leg-side. Bannerman didn't score off the second but cut the third late through the slips for 3. He hadn't scored since 12.30 and faced 61 deliveries since. Bannerman's motives are not clear. He may have reasoned that he could give the innings its backbone and, in the modern phrase, the other batsmen could play off him. He may have been held prisoner by the defensive nature of his technique and was simply hanging on. He may have concluded that if both ends were open the innings might become a rout. Whatever it was, it was about to go wrong.

Over 43: Peate to Bannerman

He negotiated the first two balls but prodded the third to Grace who, 'rushing in' from point, made a magnificent left-handed catch to a special cheer, a mingling of salute to the Old Man and jubilation. It meant that, at 1.18 and just 70 minutes into the great match, England were moving to what seemed a strong position.

Australia 26 – 4.

Giffen came to the wicket and negotiated the final ball.

Over 44: Barlow to Horan

Horan on-drove the final ball for a couple.

Over 45: Peate to Giffen

A maiden.

Over 46: Barlow to Horan

A maiden. Giffen and Horan were visibly nervous, visibly inhibited. That was unusual because, as Grace once wrote, 'as a batsman Giffen never gave me the impression of being troubled with nerves. He was perfectly cool and collected on all occasions, and it made little difference whether he went in first man or later in the innings. He had great patience as well, and watched the ball very closely; and his hitting was good all round.'[11] Giffen and Horan set themselves to survive and that, inevitably, led back to the trench warfare.

Over 47: Peate to Giffen

Giffen took a single from the second ball on the leg-side. Horan played the final two balls safely enough.

Over 48: Barlow to Giffen

A maiden.

Over 49: Peate to Horan

A maiden.

Over 50: Barlow to Giffen

Giffen had a single from the last ball to make Australia 30 at 1.29. It had taken 79 minutes.

Over 51: Peate to Giffen

A maiden.

Over 52: Barlow to Horan

The first ball bowled Horan, striking the leg-stump bail. It was 1.32.

Australia 30 – 5.

Horan's innings lasted 20 minutes and 20 balls. Blackham came to the wicket and negotiated the last three deliveries.

Over 53: Peate to Giffen

Giffen was beaten by the first ball. The second was, as one source puts it, 'beautiful, breaking through him and hitting the top of the wicket'.

Australia 30 – 6.

Giffen's innings lasted 17 minutes and 20 balls. 'The collapse of six such wickets for 30 runs caused as much astonishment as delight. The wicket was very slow but the bowling of Peate and Barlow was superb, not one batsman having ventured to take a liberty with it.'[12] Aggression: Garrett came in and Ulyett was moved to silly mid-on so that, with Grace looming at point, they would intimidate. Garrett negotiated the final two deliveries and Peate, zealous as all bowlers are, drew applause for a sharp piece of fielding off his own bowling.

Over 54: Barlow to Blackham

A maiden.

Over 55: Peate to Garrett

Garrett 'soon let out at the slows',[13] hitting the second ball above Ulyett's head for a single.

Over 56: Barlow to Garrett

A maiden.

Over 57: Peate to Blackham

A maiden.

Over 58: Barlow to Garrett

Garrett on-drove the third ball for 2.

Over 59: Peate to Blackham

Blackham spooned the first ball towards the slips but it fell short. He took a single from the second. Garrett on-drove the third for 2. The intimidation, or field adjustment, almost worked because at one moment Ulyett fielded the ball and had a shy from mid-off to try and run Blackham out. The ball went wide. That made the Australian total 36, at 1.45.

They had taken 95 minutes to get there, but now Blackham and Garrett began a partnership which threatened to tilt the match away from England.

Over 60: Barlow to Blackham

A maiden.

Over 61: Peate to Garrett

Garrett jumped out and 'slogged' Peate's second ball for 3, and Blackham 'somehow or other' snicked the third on the leg-side for 2. He was lucky to get away with it. Australia had reached 40 at 1.49, lunch 11 minutes away.

Over 62: Barlow to Garrett

A maiden.

Over 63: Peate to Blackham

Blackham took a single from the first ball, and Garrett off-drove the second for 2. It would have been a boundary if Read hadn't run fast enough to cut it off.

Over 64: Barlow to Blackham

Blackham either on-drove or pulled the final ball for 3 (the contemporary reports are contradictory). This was now the only free scoring of the whole innings, and, with lunch approaching, Hornby decided to make a double bowling change. First Steel, with his tapering handlebar moustache and tricky medium-pace deliveries, replaced Peate at the Gasometer end.

Over 65: Steel to Blackham

It was five minutes to two and fine rain fell. A maiden. Ulyett now resumed at the pavilion end.

Over 66: Ulyett to Garrett

A maiden.

Over 67: Steel to Blackham

Blackham took a single from the first ball; Garrett negotiated the next three.

Over 68: Ulyett to Blackham

A maiden, and the bell rang for lunch. That was 2.00 and in the 110 minutes of the session Australia had dug out 48 runs for the loss of the six wickets (Blackham 8, Garrett 10). Peate and Barlow dictated the pace and direction of the whole morning. Of their first 20 overs each, most had been maidens.

As the players ate their lunch, the sky became threatening but rain held off. The crowd was so great that 'despite the efforts of police and others, the boundary of the playing ground was not kept quite free from the encroachment of spectators. During the day, and lunch time especially, hundreds wearying of standing and obtaining only glimpses of the play, grew bold, coming beyond the boundary, squatted on the grass, and there remained. More than once it happened that the ball was driven in their midst and although they would jump up to let it roll, yet of course the fielder could not get at it as if the space had been clear. Thus a "drive" was sometimes counted for four ... when the ball might have been thrown back as three runs.'[14]

Play resumed at 2.45, Peate bowling to Garrett from the Gasometer end.

Over 69: Peate to Garrett

Garrett seemed to be reluctant to get back into the trench warfare or was perhaps disappointed that he had gone in before lunch. He lifted the final ball to Read, fielding between straight and long-off, and Read made a comfortable catch as the batsmen crossed. Garrett's innings lasted 25 minutes and 38 balls.

Australia 48 – 7.

Boyle came to the wicket.

Over 70: Barlow to Boyle

Boyle hit the second ball to Hornby at mid-on, but he couldn't quite catch it, and drove the fourth for a single.

Over 71: Peate to Boyle

Boyle took a single from the third ball to bring up the Australian 50, five minutes after the resumption. It had taken almost two hours.

Over 72: Barlow to Boyle

Boyle survived the first two balls, but the third – fast – got through, reared and flicked a bail off. His innings lasted five minutes and seven balls.

Australia 53 – 8.

Jones came to the wicket, and Blackham must have realised, with only Spofforth to follow, trench warfare was no longer the right tactic. The problem was as it had been all day: how do you break out of it?

Over 73: Peate to Blackham

A maiden.

Over 74: Barlow to Jones

A maiden.

Over 75: Peate to Blackham

Blackham played the first three balls and did try to break out. With rain falling and heavy cloud overhead threatening a heavy downpour, he cut the final ball for 4, only the second of the whole innings. As the ball crossed the boundary it kept Jones on strike.

Over 76: Barlow to Jones

A maiden, the heavy rain holding off.

Over 77: Peate to Blackham

Blackham took a single off the third ball.

Over 78: Barlow to Blackham

Blackham drove the second ball straight back past Barlow to the pavilion boundary. It seems he felt, however gallantly Jones was holding on, he wouldn't be able to hold on much longer. Blackham survived the third ball but skied the fourth to Grace at point, who stepped back and caught it easily. The ball must have achieved some altitude because the batsmen crossed before Grace made the catch. That was just after 3.00. Blackham's innings lasted 40 minutes and 55 balls.

Australia 59 – 9.

It had been a brave, as well as dogged, innings by Blackham. At one point during it, he 'received a hard blow, apparently on his side, from Barlow's bowling and lay writhing on the ground with Mr Grace standing over him for a minute or more, but he pluckily mastered his pain'.[15]

Spofforth came to the wicket and, because it had been the last ball of the over and the batsmen crossed, had strike immediately.

Over 79: Peate to Spofforth

Spofforth on-drove the final ball to the boundary.

Over 80: Barlow to Jones

Jones survived the first three balls but struck at the fourth, sending it to Barnes at third man who made the catch.

Australia all out 63.

It was 3.07, and the innings had lasted 133 minutes.

'Enthusiasm appeared to be unbounded. It was counted a great privilege, when the ball came among the spectators, to advance on the ground and throw it back, and when the Australians were out, and the horse and roller came on the scene, a desperate rush was made for all quarters of the ground to the immediate vicinity of the wickets and after the retiring players.'[16]

The 63 was the Australians' lowest score in their 30 matches so far. Barlow (5 for 19 from 31 overs) had been the main tormentor, with Peate (4 for 31) offering consistent, insistent support.

Spofforth described it as a 'sorry show... and were most disappointed. I might speak for myself, and say I was disgusted and thought we should have made at least 250.'[17]

Giffen was more temperate in language and judgement. 'Dicky Barlow's bowling was responsible for our downfall; we ought to have made at least 100.'[18]

Barlow and Grace were given a tremendous ovation when they appeared down the pavilion steps at 3.30. Barlow took guard and prepared to face Spofforth from the Gasometer end. Blackham stood behind the stumps, Bonnor at slip, Jones at cover slip, Murdoch at point, Bannerman at forward point, Garrett in the covers, Massie mid-off, Boyle short mid-on, Giffen long-on, Horan short-leg. Spofforth had three men in an arc around the off-side and, like England, that clearly would be his line of attack.

Over 1: Spofforth to Barlow
The first ball went for two byes, and the next Barlow stroked to the on-side for a single. Grace negotiated the next two so that England were already 3 for no wicket and, with their extraordinary strength in depth – Hornby, Barlow's usual opening partner at Lancashire, at number 10 – they'd make the Australian 63 look puny, and they'd do that quickly.

Over 2: Garrett to Barlow
Garrett bowled from the pavilion end, Blackham behind the stumps, Bonnor at slip, Murdoch at point, Bannerman at forward point, Giffen in the covers, Horan third man, Spofforth mid-off, Massie deep mid-off, Jones in the deep behind the bowler, Boyle short mid-on – the off-side attack again. A maiden.

Over 3: Spofforth to Grace
The Doctor drove the first for a single, and Barlow negotiated the next three.

Over 4: Garrett to Grace
A maiden.

Over 5: Spofforth to Barlow
And now the England openers began to move the score along despite some sharp fielding by Garrett at cover point which drew applause. Barlow took a single from the first ball, and Grace a single from the second.

Over 6: Garrett to Grace
The Doctor took a single from the first ball, and Barlow hit the next to square-leg. They ran 2. He on-drove the final ball for 3 so that England reached 10 in even time, and the Australian total was coming more and more into perspective, only 53 away now.

Over 7: Spofforth to Barlow
A maiden.

Over 8: Garrett to Grace
Grace took a single from the second ball, and Barlow played the over out.

Over 9: Spofforth to Grace
The Doctor tried to 'make free' with the final ball, a leg-stump yorker, and it

bowled him. That may have been the turning point in the whole match because it was low scoring, Grace had made a feast of runs for a generation and even 40 or 50 from him here would have put the match beyond Australia's reach, but his portly figure was making its way back to the pavilion after 20 minutes, 23 balls and four singles: not a feast but starvation.

England 13 – 1.

Over 10: Garrett to Barlow
A maiden.

Over 11: Spofforth to Ulyett
The first ball almost bowled Ulyett, and he gave a stumping chance – a hard one, evidently – from the second. He was almost bowled again by the third or fourth ball. Now with Grace gone the nervous time began, especially with Ulyett looking so vulnerable to Spofforth.

Over 12: Garrett to Barlow
A maiden. Nor could Barlow have been calming the gathering nerves because on such a wicket England needed to keep the score moving. They'd seen what had happened to the Australians who, once they were trapped in their trenches, hadn't been able to find a way out of them.

Over 13: Spofforth to Ulyett
Ulyett began to settle. He drove the first ball for a single, Barlow didn't score from the second but sent the third into the leg-side for 2. They stole a single from the final ball, so sharp that Barlow might have been run out sprinting to the bowler's end to complete it, but the England score *was* moving again.

Over 14: Garrett to Barlow
Barlow kept the score moving with a single from the second ball, again into the leg-side.

Over 15: Spofforth to Barlow
Spofforth tilted the match again and at the right moment from an Australian point of view. Barlow looked increasingly dangerous, and Ulyett looking increasingly settled. Barlow played at the first ball and sent a catch to Bannerman at forward point. Bannerman was standing close – the Grace intimidation? – and the catch was described variously as clever, splendid and neat.

England 18 – 2.

Barlow's innings lasted half an hour and 23 deliveries. Lucas came to the wicket.

Over 16: Garrett to Ulyett
Ulyett drove the third ball in front of point to the boundary, getting the first real cheer of the innings for a stroke rather than cheers of relief: this was the first boundary of the innings. He took a single from the final ball to make the score 23 in half an hour. The Australian total lay only 40 runs away.

Over 17: Spofforth to Ulyett
No run came from the first ball but 4 byes – all run – from the second. Ulyett took a single from the last.

Over 18: Garrett to Ulyett
No run came from the first ball but a leg bye from the second brought Lucas onto strike and the scoring slowed again.

Over 19: Spofforth to Ulyett
A maiden.

Over 20: Garrett to Lucas
Lucas took a single from the first ball to get off the mark, a powerful drive which was cut off, and Ulyett played the over out.

Over 21: Spofforth to Lucas
A maiden.

Over 22: Garrett to Ulyett
Ulyett took a single and Lucas played the over out.

Over 23: Spofforth to Ulyett
A single from the third ball brought the England total to 32, reaching comfortably towards the Australian total and bringing a crisis for Murdoch.

Over 24: Garrett to Ulyett.
A maiden. Somewhere among it Ulyett almost hit Garrett to Spofforth at mid-on: not a catch.

Over 25: Spofforth to Lucas
Lucas smacked the first ball through the unguarded square-leg area for 4, only the second boundary of the innings and the sixth of the match.

Over 26: Garrett to Ulyett
Ulyett kept the score moving with an on-drive for 2 from the first ball and played out the rest of the over.

Over 27: Spofforth to Lucas
The match seemed to tilt more and more heavily towards England. Lucas took a single from the second ball, Ulyett a single from the third, Lucas a single from the fourth. Spofforth now switched to the pavilion end.

Over 28: Spofforth to Lucas
Under the rules of the time, Spofforth was entitled to bowl consecutive overs to change ends. Evidently this happened not infrequently. The Laws said 'no bowler shall bowl more than two overs in succession'. Spofforth bowled a maiden. That allowed Boyle to come on at the Gasometer end, this Boyle who was 'right arm, medium pace, generally round the wicket, and broke [the ball] slightly both ways'.[19]

Over 29: Boyle to Ulyett
Ulyett 'rushed' out to meet the first ball and struck it down to long-on for 2

then played the rest of the over out – but now he'd got the taste for giving 'Old Boyley' some treatment.

Over 30: Spofforth to Lucas
A busy, bustling over, Lucas taking a single from the third ball, then a no-ball, then Ulyett taking a single from the last.

Over 31: Boyle to Ulyett
Another bustling, busy over, Ulyett 'rushed' out to the first ball again and struck it to long-on for another 2, took a single from the third ball to bring him back on strike against Spofforth.

Over 32: Spofforth to Ulyett
A maiden.

Over 33: Boyle to Lucas
A maiden.

Over 34: Spofforth to Ulyett
Ulyett played the first two balls without scoring but drove the third to the on-side for a 2 to bring up England's 50. That was 4.30. Ulyett played a similar shot to the final ball, taking his own score to 22, the highest in the match so far.

Over 35: Boyle to Lucas
A maiden, and somewhere amid all this Murdoch was warmly applauded for the fifth or sixth time for good fielding at point.

Over 36: Spofforth to Ulyett
Ulyett snicked the first ball down the leg-side for 3 – a lucky shot which evidently might have gone anywhere. Lucas played the rest of the over out, but England were now 56, just seven runs behind and with eight wickets in hand.

It must have seemed more than a promising position, especially against Australians who had never beaten England in England: it must have seemed to be moving towards impregnability.

Over 37: Boyle to Ulyett
A maiden.

Over 38: Spofforth to Lucas
A maiden.

Over 39: Boyle to Ulyett
Ulyett took a single from the first ball, and Lucas played the over out.

Over 40: Spofforth to Ulyett
Ulyett, and there is some unanimity about this, had simply become too confident, especially in going up the wicket to punish Boyle. He didn't score from the first ball, didn't score from the second but, and there is great unanimity about this, too, made a terrible misjudgement to the third in taking

on Spofforth with another of his rushes. He completely missed the ball, and Blackham stumped him no bother at all.

Bell's Life admonished Ulyett. 'To this piece of rash cricket I certainly attribute a good deal of England's subsequent misfortune. The only real chance that a batsman had on such a wicket was to get his eye in, and Ulyett had got his in, and he certainly ought to have kept steady, and played the strict game.'

The Times admonished him, too, for being 'a little too venturesome'.

The Daily Telegraph wrote of how he 'would persist in running out at dangerous deliveries, and in the end in following these tactics he missed Spofforth and had his bails whipped off by Blackham'.

Ulyett's innings lasted 55 minutes and 59 balls.

England 57 – 3.

Lyttelton came to the wicket. It was just after 4.40.

Over 41: Boyle to Lucas
Lucas took a single off the second ball, and Lyttelton played the over out.

Over 42: Spofforth to Lucas
A maiden. The game began to tighten.

Over 43: Boyle to Lyttelton
A maiden. That was 4.49.

Over 44: Spofforth to Lucas
A maiden.

Over 45: Boyle to Lyttelton
A maiden.

Over 46: Spofforth to Lucas
A maiden.

Over 47: Boyle to Lyttelton
Lyttelton took a single from the second ball, at 4.56. It was the first run for 24 deliveries. In a match of such precious runs and intense psychology, each constantly feeding off one another, there was a tilting again and this time clearly away from England.

Over 48: Spofforth to Lyttelton
A maiden.

Over 49: Boyle to Lucas
Lucas was caught at the wicket off the second ball, and that *did* tilt the match.

England 59 – 4.

Lucas's innings lasted 65 minutes and 64 balls. It was 5.00 and Lucas had been batting since a few minutes before 4.00. Studd came to the wicket, this Studd whose 'bats, which were specially made for him, had handles one inch longer than the usual length, but his wrists were so powerful that they could easily cope with the extra strain thrown upon them.'[20] His first ball 'whipped' past him, and he survived the next.

Over 50: Spofforth to Lyttelton

Lyttelton took a single from the first ball, only his second run in 20 minutes. Spofforth pitched the ball a long way outside Studd's off stump and it cut back, so much even Studd was surprised, rose and flicked the off bail. 'The batsman was utterly surprised at finding he was out.'[21]

England 60 – 5.

Studd's innings, such as it was, lasted two minutes and the three balls. No record seems to survive of what he did with the second ball he received – whether he hit it or not – but the powerful wrists and long bat handle hadn't helped much. Read came to the wicket, loudly cheered all the way as a Surrey player, and took a single from his first ball.

Over 51: Boyle to Read

Read on-drove the third ball for 2 towards 10 minutes past five, making England 63. It had taken an hour and 40 minutes: Australia had taken 33 minutes longer.

Over 52: Spofforth to Lyttelton

The first ball reared, flicked Lyttelton's glove, and he was caught behind.

England 63 – 6.

Lyttelton's innings lasted 25 minutes and 24 balls – for two singles. The crowd fell silent.

Barnes came to the wicket and restored their voices by hitting a single from the final ball to haul England into the lead. It was scant consolation after being 57 for 2, and knowing they would have to bat last on a wicket which might by then be anything.

Over 53: Boyle to Barnes

Barnes hit the final ball to the boundary at deep square-leg, restoring the crowd voices even more.

Over 54: Spofforth to Read

Spofforth struck Read a hard blow in the ribs, and although the batsmen took a leg bye from the second ball and Barnes played out the last two there was a short break for Read's injury. Nor had Spofforth finished with him.

Over 55: Boyle to Read

Read took a single from the third ball to make England 70.

Over 56: Spofforth to Read

A maiden. Aggression: Spofforth started to work Read over, hitting him on the knee and then the elbow.

Over 57: Boyle to Barnes

Boyle broke the first ball back, and it bowled Barnes.

England 70 – 7.

Barnes's innings lasted nine minutes and 12 balls. Steel came to the wicket and the light had begun to fade. One report describes it as 'very bad'. He on-drove the final ball for 2, and the game began to tilt back towards England.

Over 58: Spofforth to Read

Singles from the third and final balls kept the score moving and already, despite Spofforth's hostility and accuracy, the batsmen looked as if they could establish some sort of command. In response to this, the Australian bowling tightened again.

Over 59: Boyle to Steel

A maiden.

Over 60: Spofforth to Read

A maiden.

Over 61: Boyle to Steel

Steel took a single from the third ball. That was 5.30, and it made England 75. They had toiled two hours almost to the minute to get them.

Over 62: Spofforth to Steel

A maiden, so the batsmen had been restricted to one run in four overs.

Over 63: Boyle to Read

Read late cut the final ball cleanly through the slips for 3.

Over 64: Spofforth to Read

By now the light was 'wretched', but Read could see all right, because he negotiated the first three balls and on-drove the fourth to the boundary amid great cheering: only the third boundary of the innings.

Over 65: Boyle to Steel

Steel touched the second ball down to fine leg, and they ran 3.

Over 66: Spofforth to Steel

Steel placed the first ball neatly into the on-side – almost square – and they ran 3 again. Read played the over out. Murdoch saw the danger clearly: in a match of such low scoring that every run assumed an importance of its own, another few minutes of this and England would have constructed a dangerous lead. The crowd were cheering every run taking England further ahead. At 5.41 Murdoch replaced Boyle with Garrett.

Over 67: Garrett to Steel

Steel cut the second ball past point to the boundary and loud cheering greeted it.

Over 68: Spofforth to Read

Read negotiated the first three balls and on-drove the fourth to the boundary – very loud cheering greeted that. England had reached 96, danger rising all around Murdoch. Read and Steel were accomplished batsmen, now accelerating, Hornby still to come and a lead of 33 already. If he did any sort of mental arithmetic, Murdoch calculated that 17 wickets had fallen so far at an average of 7.7 runs each. At that rate it would take four Australian wickets just to overhaul the 33.

Over 69: Garrett to Steel

Garrett rescued Murdoch and Australia. Steel came forward to the second ball – wide – and seemed to be trying to pull it. He dragged it on to his stumps.

England 96 – 8.

Steel's innings lasted 22 minutes and 26 balls. Hornby, always popular, came to the wicket to a great ovation, light rain falling to compound the light. He played the over out.

Over 70: Spofforth to Read

Read cut the first ball for 3, and Hornby took a single from the fourth to bring up the 100 at 10 minutes to six 'amidst the most deafening applause'.[22]

Over 71: Garrett to Hornby

Hornby took a single from the third ball – a lucky stroke, evidently – and, because Read didn't score from the fourth, Hornby had strike. It was a fatal moment.

Over 72: Spofforth to Hornby

The first ball was fast enough to beat Hornby and strike the leg-stump.

England 101 – 9.

Hornby's innings lasted five minutes and seven balls. Peate came to the wicket and survived the second ball but spooned the third to mid-off where Boyle took the catch. That was seven minutes to six. England had taken two hours and 20 minutes to make their 101.

On this darkening, damp evening the players must have been happy to go off knowing they wouldn't be coming back until the next day, and knowing that both sides had everything to play for.

Read, 19 not out after an heroic innings of 54 minutes and 45 deliveries, was cheered all the way back to the pavilion. He'd earned it, but as he made his way there even he might have been contemplating what Spofforth (7 for 46) would do in the second innings on a wicket which had to be worse.

All the other England players, peering out over the Oval as the Australians walked back and the great crowd began to disperse, must have been wondering that, too – and wondering just what a lead of 38 might really be worth.

Notes

1. *A History Of Cricket*, H.S. Altham and E.W. Swanton.
2. *With Bat And Ball*, Giffen.
3. *The Badminton Library: Cricket*, Steel and Lyttelton.
4. *The Evening News*, London.
5. *The Daily Telegraph*, London.
6. Ibid.
7. Pardon in *Bell's Life*.
8. *Cricket*, Grace.
9. Giffen op cit.
10. *The Manchester Guardian*.
11. Grace op. cit.
12. *Manchester Guardian*.
13. *Daily Telegraph*.
14. *Daily Chronicle*, London.
15. Ibid.
16. Ibid.
17. *The Story Of Australian Cricket*, Egan.
18. Giffen op. cit.
19. Grace op. cit.
20. *Cricket With The Kangaroo*, G.F. McCleary.
21. *The Manchester Guardian*.
22. *The Daily Telegraph*.

29 August 1882

HEAVY RAIN fell in the morning between 9.30 and 10.30, increasing to a downpour for a few minutes at 10.00. Despite this, 'there was at this hour almost a complete belt of spectators round the field of play, who, protected by umbrellas, macintoshes & coats maintained their positions throughout all discomfitures'. One estimate put their number at several thousand, a sort of foundation to the day because the crowd grew to 19,593 paying.[1]

The Daily Chronicle, a London newspaper, set the scene:

'The attendance of spectators was even more numerous than on the day previous, and was, on the whole, respectable in quality. The larger portion were apparently persons of the middle-class, though of course there was a number of the rougher element about. Of boys there were not a few, but their interest in the game, which, so to speak, made everybody kin, kept them attentive and sedate, and even invested them with temporary dignity, as they, with more or less practical knowledge, criticised the character of the play. Comparatively few ladies were present. Not a small number of clergymen and ministers were among the spectators and observing the law of the occasion, dismissed for a time being the cares of their calling, lighted up a cigar perhaps, and were absorbed in the play.

'Every vantage point from which the play was to be seen was sure to be occupied. Persons were seen creeping about under the stands, looking at the field through the crevices. Some had brought with them stools whereon they stood in the promenade behind the deep row of onlookers over whose heads a good view was thus obtained. Men were visible at points about the neighbouring gas works, while the roof of an adjacent public house was crowded with spectators.'[2]

The rain stopped by 11.00, the clouds broke up and the sun came out.

The pitch was still too wet to consider starting at the advertised time, 11.30, and the *Bell's Life* reporter wrote he arrived 'just upon that time [...] and one look at the ground was sufficient to convince me that for an hour or two the bowlers would be at a serious disadvantage. The heavy roller had only made bad worse.'

England finally emerged from the pavilion at 12.07, the amateurs coming out first again, and the crowd got in the mood by cheering Bannerman and Massie all the way to the wicket. Ironic cheers?

Barlow felt that Hornby made an elementary tactical error because 'he went out in my judgment a bit too soon on the second day. The ground was wet, and Peate and I could not stand, while the ball was like soap. I had to get the groundsman to fetch a spade to get the mud out of the bowling holes, so that I could fill them up with sawdust.'[3]

One report says 'the creases were plentifully bestrewed with sawdust'.

It meant that for a short, precious interlude, and for the first time in the match, the conditions favoured the batsmen. Brilliant, daring Hugh Massie saw his chance and would not be afraid to take it. He was 28 and wore a handlebar moustache that drooped. He was, according to Grace, 'one of the best fellows that ever visited England'. Teammate Giffen gives this assessment of his armoury:

'Massie made nearly all his runs with off strokes, the best of them a cover hit which would send the ball like a streak to the boundary, but he frequently got out in attempting this stroke. He might, on the whole, have been inclined to undue rashness, but then it was due to his temperament. He could no more refrain from having a bang than the moth can keep away from the flame that singes its wings.'[4]

Barlow opened the bowling from the pavilion end.

Over 1: Barlow to Bannerman

Bannerman cut the first ball for 2 and 'fluked' the fourth through the slips for another 2. One source describes the wicket as 'moist', another that occasionally balls 'kicked awkwardly' but generally 'held their course' and were not breaking as much as the day before.

Over 2: Ulyett to Massie

Massie drove the second ball deep into the off-side, Read giving frantic chase and cutting the ball off before it reached the boundary. The batsmen turned for the third run: a risk. Both were vulnerable. Read returned the ball to Lyttelton who broke the stumps with Bannerman just home. If Read had thrown to the other end, Massie was a long way out...

Over 3: Barlow to Massie

Massie cut the fourth ball over point's head and it ran away towards the boundary but, the outfield wet, slowed and Barnes almost overtook it. The crowd cheered Massie. He had scored 7 from six balls and was making a statement: 'while the wicket is easier I will attack'.

Over 4: Ulyett to Bannerman

A maiden, and perhaps Bannerman was making a statement to Massie: *I'll keep the other end secure while you attack.*

Over 5: Barlow to Massie

Massie clipped the fourth ball in front of square-leg for 3, making the score 14. 'Massie saw his opportunity and made the most of it. His game was to hit, and hit he did with a power and brilliance that perhaps no one else in the two 11s could have equalled. There was no suspicion of nervousness or hesitation about his play. He got nearly every ball in the middle of the bat, and treated the spectators to the only piece of really rapid cricket that was seen in the match.'[5]

Over 6: Ulyett to Massie

Massie was almost bowled twice, the first of them 'as nearly as possible' without actually being bowled to a ball on the leg-side. Massie took a single from the last ball.

Over 7: Barlow to Massie

A maiden.

Over 8: Ulyett to Bannerman

Bannerman took a single from the third ball, and Massie didn't score from the fourth.

Over 9: Barlow to Bannerman

A maiden, but Bannerman wasn't looking completely secure. He'd mishit a couple.

Over 10: Ulyett to Massie

Massie smacked the second ball to the square-leg boundary and that made Australia 20, scored in a mere 17 minutes. Massie took a single from the fourth ball to keep strike.

Over 11: Barlow to Massie

Massie hauled the third ball to the square-leg boundary, to applause. Hornby faced a crisis. Much more of this and Massie would have taken the match away, especially since the wicket would be getting more and more difficult as it dried. He took Ulyett off.

Over 12: Peate to Bannerman

A maiden. Hornby took Barlow off.

Over 13: Studd to Massie

Massie went after Studd immediately, driving him to the boundary in front of the stand to the right of the pavilion from the first ball. 'The next ball would

75

certainly have travelled for a like addition, but the Cantab [Studd] just succeeded in stopping it, a circumstance which brought forth ringing cheers from the spectators' – Massie had straight driven it powerfully.[6]

Over 14: Peate to Bannerman

A maiden.

Over 15: Studd to Massie

Massie took a single from the third ball.

Over 16: Peate to Massie

Massie lifted the first ball to the on-side boundary, almost straight.

Over 17: Studd to Bannerman

A maiden.

Over 18: Peate to Massie

Massie off-drove the first ball to the boundary so hard that it went deep into the spectators standing there, and now the Australians were level – Massie 33 of the 38 – at 12.45. Bannerman, playing the solid, supporting role, was 'comparatively inactive'.[7] Massie took a single from the third ball.

Over 19: Studd to Massie

Massie plundered the last ball, straight driving it to the boundary, bringing up the 40 (43, actually) and getting loud applause.

Over 20: Peate to Bannerman

Bannerman cut the first ball dangerously through the slips for 2 and cut the third ball for 2 as well. The crisis for Hornby deepened. He took Studd off.

Over 21: Barnes to Massie

Massie hit the first ball long, hard and directly into Lucas's hands at long-off. To general astonishment and dismay, he spilled it. 'The hit was a pretty hard one, but Lucas got the ball in his hands, and ought to have held it [...] the whole team looked downcast.'[8] They'd run a single, and Bannerman cut the fourth ball for 2. That was the 50 up in 35 minutes, and the crowd applauded warmly.

Over 22: Peate to Massie

As if to celebrate his escape, Massie pumped the first ball to the off-side boundary over Hornby's head. He mishit the second, which looped towards the slips, and drove the third for 2. Steel, like a terrier, cut it off before it reached the boundary.

Over 23: Barnes to Bannerman

A maiden. Hornby took Peate off.

Over 24: Steel to Massie

Massie took a single from the second ball, and Bannerman played the over out, although he almost gave a chance to forward point.

Over 25: Barnes to Massie

Massie took a single from the third ball.

Over 26: Steel to Massie

Massie laid about Steel, hitting him for two 2s to square-leg from the third and fourth balls. That was just before 1.00 and, in direct contrast to the whole of the rest of the match, Massie had 50 in 47 minutes with eight boundaries. Bannerman had limped to 11.

Over 27: Barnes to Bannerman

A maiden.

Over 28: Steel to Massie

Massie reasoned[9] that Steel was starting to bowl well and needed to be knocked out of the attack. He didn't score from the first ball but struck the second to the deep square-leg, which it reached with Barlow in hot and vain pursuit.

Massie thought one more boundary would knock Steel out of the attack, and he sprang out to the third ball intending to send it, like the second, to the square-leg boundary. It was faster. He missed it and it plucked the leg stump out of the ground.

Australia 66 – 1, a lead of 28.

It was 1.05 and Massie, with a combination of bravery and luck, had turned the match. His innings lasted 57 minutes and 60 balls, and he'd scored nine 4s, two 3s, three 2s and seven singles. The crowd showed their appreciation in full measure.

Murdoch understood that the wicket might remain easy enough for hitting for a little while longer and sent Bonnor in rather than himself: half an hour of *him* could take the match completely away from England.

When Massie reached the Australian dressing room, 'disappointed', he told Spofforth 'he was very sick, because he had no right to hit at the ball'.[10] Giffen, who would be batting himself soon enough, paid this tribute:

'…fortunately for us we had the man for the moment in Hugh Massie. Never on a slow wicket have I seen a batsman do a grander bit of hitting. Only for 20 minutes or so was the pitch really easy, but in that time Massie had got his eye in, so that when the ball did begin to bite he could bang away with as great certainty as before. It is worth noting that the only fair, genuine chance given during the great match came from Massie's bat, and it cost England 17 runs… At last A.G. Steel came on and bowled Massie, but our hitter had given us a chance in the game.'[11]

That is an astonishing statement, made more astonishing because it is entirely accurate: Lucas had dropped the only real chance of the whole match. The final ball of Steel's over flew past Bonnor's bat.

Over 29: Barnes to Bannerman

A maiden.

Over 30: Steel to Bonnor

Bonnor drove the second ball to the on-side, Hornby mis-fielded, and they ran 2.

Over 31: Barnes to Bannerman

Bannerman placed the third ball neatly behind point for 2, and that made Australia 70 at just after 1.10. Ulyett replaced Steel, Hornby no doubt fearful of what havoc Bonnor might wreak with all his giant reach, all his awesome strength. Ulyett would know what to do.

Over 32: Ulyett to Bonnor

The fourth ball was on a length, fast and broke a little. It took Bonnor's middle stump clean out of the ground to a great roar. Ulyett had known what to do.

Australia 70 – 2, a lead of 32.

Bonnor's innings lasted nine minutes and nine balls. Murdoch came to the wicket to steady everything and was warmly applauded on his way.

Over 33: Barnes to Bannerman

Bannerman skied the fourth ball to Studd at deep mid-off and the roar for that was louder than for dangerous Bonnor: Bannerman's dismissal opened a big door. The innings was suddenly falling apart.

Australia 70 – 3, a lead of 32.

Bannerman had made a prudent 13 from 69 balls in an hour with no boundaries. Hornby called up Peate to replace Ulyett, reasoning that Horan might be more vulnerable to spin. *The Evening Standard* reported that the English bowling 'just now was being changed with consummate judgement, according to the different styles of the batsmen'. The *Bell's Life* reporter noted 'We are beginning to see how strong Horan is with fast bowling, just as we have discovered that a first-rate ball of great pace is the thing to get rid of Bonnor.' Peate, of course, was slow and could be tantalising. Murdoch had strike, however.

Over 34: Peate to Murdoch

The second ball was a long hop, and Murdoch smote it square to the boundary.

Over 35: Barnes to Horan

Horan's tactic seems to have been to hold on and support Murdoch. He took a single from the first ball of the over, and they ran 2 byes from the next then Murdoch took a single from the fourth.

Over 36: Peate to Murdoch

A maiden.

Over 37: Barnes to Horan

Horan took a single from the final ball.

Over 38: Peate to Horan

Horan spooned the first ball – 'puzzling' – gently and low into Grace's hands at point.

Australia 79 – 4, a lead of 41.

Horan's innings lasted 10 minutes and seven balls. Giffen came to the wicket and spooned his first ball to Grace precisely as Horan had done.

Australia 79 – 5.

The cheering was growing in depth and volume, not least because Peate was on a hat-trick. Blackham came to the wicket, but Peate bowled him a 'dreadful' long hop which went to the long-leg boundary. Blackham didn't score off the fourth.

Over 39: Barnes to Murdoch

A maiden, although one ball rose so far that Murdoch did well to play it down.

Over 40: Peate to Blackham

Blackham took a single from the first ball, and Murdoch took a single from the third, but Blackham almost sent a catch to the slips from the fourth. It went 'dangerously' near Steel.

Over 41: Barnes to Murdoch

Murdoch took a single from the first ball, and Blackham played the over out.

Over 42: Peate to Murdoch

Murdoch used his feet and on-drove the first ball for 2, on-drove the third to the same place in the same way, but the fourth just missed the stumps after Peate beat him comprehensively. It ran away for 4 byes and that made the Australians 90 at just after 1.40.

Over 43: Barnes to Blackham

Blackham took a single on the leg-side from the second ball, and Murdoch on-drove the third for 3. Blackham took a single from the fourth just as a shower, which briefly became heavy, sent them scurrying to the pavilion and lunch quarter of an hour early, Australia 99 – 5, a lead of 61 (Murdoch 14, Blackham 7). The match hung in the most delicate balance, made even more tantalising because to evaluate such a lead in such a tight match was impossible. In that sense nothing had changed since the close of play on Monday. The same questions had to be asked, and the answers were still elusive. Who could know – including Murdoch and Hornby – what 61 really meant? Murdoch, however, must have reasoned that he could win or lose the match himself when he resumed his innings.

During the interval more rain fell, but not heavy.

Play resumed at 2.45, the rain gone, the sun shining brightly. The bowling would be from the Gasometer end.

Over 44: Peate to Blackham

The first ball beat Blackham and the second beat him, too. He left the third alone, played at the fourth and was finely caught low down outside the off stump by Lyttelton.

Australia 99 – 6.

Blackham's innings lasted 13 minutes and 12 balls. Jones came to the wicket and moved to what was now, the over completed, the non-striker's end.

Over 45: Barlow to Murdoch

A maiden.

Over 46: Peate to Jones

A maiden, but Jones was 'looking anything but comfortable'.

Over 47: Barlow to Murdoch

Murdoch took a single to square-leg to hoist the 100 at just after 2.50. That was loudly applauded. Jones played the over out.

Over 48: Peate to Murdoch

A maiden.

Over 49: Barlow to Jones

Jones cut the second ball for 2 to get off the mark – a fluky shot – just in front of cover and cut the next, also in front of cover, to the boundary.

Over 50: Peate to Murdoch

Murdoch on-drove the first ball for a single, and Jones played the over out.

Over 51: Barlow to Murdoch

A maiden.

Over 52: Peate to Jones

A maiden. Jones, interested only in survival, was playing no attacking shots and concentrating on covering his wicket. Once, somewhere in the midst of all this, he was almost run out.

Over 53: Barlow to Murdoch

Murdoch straight-drove the last ball for 2, Ulyett cutting it off before it reached the boundary.

Over 54: Peate to Jones

A maiden. The wicket was deteriorating, and quickly.

Over 55: Barlow to Murdoch

A maiden.

Over 56: Peate to Jones

A maiden.

Over 57: Barlow to Murdoch

Murdoch on-drove the second ball for 3, making Australia 110, and Jones played the over out. That was 3.12.

Over 58: Peate to Murdoch

Murdoch on-drove the third ball for a single. Hornby realised that not only was Murdoch now well set but Jones, despite his difficulties, was surviving. He'd bring on Steel for Barlow at the pavilion end, see what that would do.

Over 59: Steel to Murdoch

Murdoch didn't score from the first ball and was fortunate to get away with the second which he lofted into the leg-side. Short-leg would have caught it – if there had been one. They ran the single. Wicketkeeper Lyttelton sprinted but the ball was too far away for him to catch. Lyttelton fielded the ball and threw it to Grace who stood at the stumps.

Once Jones had made his ground he 'strayed' out of the crease – one report suggested he'd gone out to pat the wicket in the traditional way – thinking that the ball was dead. It wasn't. Grace caught the ball, broke the wicket and appealed. Here was controversy, the only such in the whole match. Umpire Bob Thoms gave Jones out, as he was bound to do, but it provoked some salty comments from the Australians in the crowd. Charles Pardon wrote in *Bell's Life*: 'It was reported to me that Thoms, on being appealed to, answered "If you claim it, sir, out!"' The reporter thought this 'unlikely' and vowed to find out afterwards.

The English daily newspapers were restrained.

The Manchester Guardian described the dismissal as happening 'in a rather curious fashion' and did not explore the ethics or legality.

The Times described the incident factually: 'With the score at 113, Mr Murdoch hit a ball to leg, which was fielded by Mr Lyttelton, who threw it at the wicket; the object was missed, and the ball went to Dr Grace, who as Mr Jones was out of his ground, put the wicket down, the batsman being adjudged run out.'

The Daily Telegraph wrote that Jones 'walked out of his crease, whereupon the leather, not being considered dead, was taken by W.G. Grace, who put down the batsman's wicket'.

Spofforth described it as 'an unfortunate incident' but 'it seemed to put fire into the Australians'.[12]

None of them mentioned Murdoch's obvious rage or his demonstrating it visibly. Lord Hawke, then beginning his career with Yorkshire, remembered how Grace said 'I taught the lad [Jones] something', but also how the incident generated a great deal of ill-feeling at the time.

Jones had played a valiant innings, clinging on through 28 deliveries and exactly half an hour for his 6 of the 15 partnership.

Australia 114 – 7, a lead of 76.

Spofforth came to the wicket and played out the over.

Over 60: Peate to Murdoch

Murdoch hit the first ball into the on-side and they ran 3, bringing – dangerously – Spofforth down on to strike. He survived the second and third balls, but the fourth beat and bowled him middle stump.

Australia 117 – 8, a lead of 79.

Spofforth's innings had lasted only three minutes and four balls. The innings was melting away from Murdoch whatever he did. Garrett came to the wicket.

Over 61: Steel to Murdoch

Murdoch drove the third ball, but Ulyett, moving fast, saved the boundary and confined them to a single.

Over 62: Peate to Murdoch

Murdoch drove the first ball into the off-side for 2, bringing up the 120 at 3.22.

Over 63: Steel to Garrett

Garrett drove the first ball strongly between Studd at cover and Hornby at extra cover. Hornby, nearest the ball, set off in pursuit, but Studd, 'knowing that Hornby could not throw'[13] set off after *him*. The batsmen ran 2 and Garrett, 'seeing it was Hornby and knowing that he could not throw, called for another run.' Hornby seized the ball and 'jerked' it to Studd, who threw to Lyttelton, poised behind the stumps. As the ball arched through the overcast sky to him, Murdoch was running frantically to make his ground. Lyttelton caught the ball perfectly and, 'amidst the greatest excitement'[14] broke the wicket with Murdoch a couple of feet from safety.

Australia 122 – 9, a lead of 84.

It must have seemed a decisive moment, perhaps the decisive moment. Murdoch had come to the wicket when the total was 70, and of the 52 added during his innings he had made 29 of them from 55 deliveries in one hour and 10 minutes of toil. *Bell's Life* wrote that Murdoch had given 'an admirable display of sound defensive cricket on a wicket getting more difficult every minute'. Those five final words were a counter-balance to the bleakness of the scoreboard.

Giffen felt that 'if one praises Massie's hitting, what can be said of Murdoch's batting? Long before he had completed the putting together of his 29 the wicket was as difficult as any bowler could wish. W.L.M. demonstrated then how great a batsman he really was...'[15]

Boyle came in to face the second ball of the over. He stabbed at it, popping it up, and was almost caught. The third ball bowled him.

Australia all out for 122.

It was 3.26 and this immensely strong English batting side needed a mere 85. When Steel and Peate returned to the pavilion, 'they were surrounded by a most enthusiastic and cheering crowd'.

Bell's Life summed up the innings, and the situation. Sixty-six of the runs 'or more than half, were made in the first 55 minutes, and made, too, while the wicket was wet, and certainly much less difficult than it either had been on Monday or became as Tuesday progressed. Of the 56 runs made by the last nine wickets, Murdoch [...] made 29, and not one of the other batsmen played with an approach to confidence. They all seemed to realise the high quality of the bowling, to be impressed with the closeness of the fielding, and to hold in something more than respect the difficulty of the ground [pitch]. Lyttelton's wicket-keeping had all through been magnificent. He stood up to Ulyett and Barnes with unflinching courage, and of the six byes that were given four were from the ball of Peate, who so nearly bowled Murdoch. It appeared to me that both Murdoch and Lyttelton thought this ball had actually hit the wicket. Of the six English bowlers tried, Peate was the most successful, and Barlow the least. The former never seemed easy to play, and his eight wickets in the match for 71 runs was a performance worthy of the reputation of the best of English bowlers.'

Much was happening in the pavilion. In the Australian dressing room Spofforth, assessing the wicket, insisted 'this thing can be done'.

'As we excitedly discussed our chances during the interval', Giffen remembered, specifically referring to England getting the runs, 'Spofforth said they wouldn't. Spoff's faith in himself and Murdoch's cheery assurance inspired the rest of us, and we filed out of the dressing-room to make the effort of our lives.'[16]

In the England dressing room Hornby made a decision, still mysterious, to alter the batting order. That can only have added an element of uncertainty and betrayed, even, a lack of confidence. Hornby himself would open with Grace, Barlow at 3. The middle order remained unchanged but, and it's not clear when, Hornby scrambled the lower order so completely that only Peate batted in the same place in both innings: number 11.

Studd caught the mood. 'The weather was cold. We sat in the Committee Room, and the windows were shut because of the cold. Except that such strange things happen in cricket, none of us dreamed we could be beaten.'[17]

Bell's Life summed it up neatly.

'All sorts of opinions were expressed as to England's chances of making the runs. Superficial critics, men of sanguine temperament, and probably imperfect knowledge, had no doubt England would easily win, but there were plenty of pessimists who knew, or thought they knew, that the forthcoming

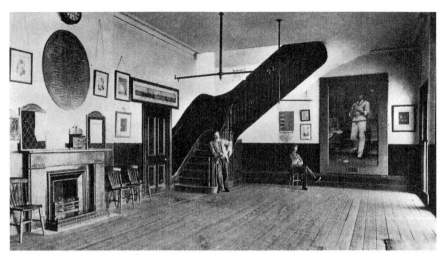

This is the Long Room, undated. Did the sorry procession of England batsmen pass this way on their way to the wicket? (Courtesy of Surrey County Cricket Club)

trial was beset with difficulties, and that if England won at all, it would only be after a very desperate fight. These men made full allowance for the worn and treacherous condition of the wicket, which they knew to be in precisely the state to suit Spofforth, and many of them knew, also, from long experience as players or spectators, how hard it was to make runs at the pinch of a game, how it is always the batting side which monopolises the nervousness, and how extraordinarily well the famous Colonial eleven finish an uphill game.'

At 3.45 the Australians came out. 'Amidst almost breathless anxiety, the spectators watched the Colonials enter the field.'[18]

'There was a good deal of speculation as to who would start the innings, and a lot of applause greeted Grace and Hornby as they walked down the Pavilion steps to commence it.'

This was immediately after the Australians.

Spofforth would begin from the Gasometer end, to Grace. He was more than a great bowler, he was thoughtful about every aspect of his art. Variation, he would say, 'is not the slightest use unless you learn to hide it. The sole object in variation is to make the batsman think the ball is slower or faster than it really is. ... I have always considered the best plan is to hold a small portion of the ball and get the impetus that sends the ball forward from one side. By doing this your arm will go through the air just as swiftly for a slow ball as for a fast one, which is very apt to mislead the batsman, and it has another advantage, that the ball is likely to break. This kind of variation requires a great deal of practice so as to get the pitch accurate, but with careful study success is sure to come.'[19]

Grace and, in a moment, Hornby, would not only face this but a familiar word of the era, 'break'. Spofforth describes that 'Spinning the ball, or what is commonly known as break, is the principal means of getting wickets a first class bowler uses, and no one can possibly be a "crack" bowler unless he can "turn the ball". There are many degrees of break. [...] The off-break [...] is effected in two ways, by finger-spin and by "cut". The latter is the method the writer most frequently adopted. By cutting I mean getting the force that propels the ball on its journey from one side without any twisting action of the fingers.'[20]

That Spofforth 'had instructions to put on the pace was made evident by Blackham standing back several yards'. Spofforth would reveal 'during my visits to England with the Australians, no one, not even the members of my own side, could tell when I was [going to bowl] fast, slow or medium, and that prince of wicket-keepers, Blackham, always received a signal what to expect.'[21]

He prepared to implement his philosophy. 'Always be on the offensive; directly you are on the defensive the batsman is on good terms with himself. Nothing worries a batsman more than always trying to get him out, instead of waiting for him to make a mistake.'

Grace prepared to face Spofforth's 'terrifying' action because 'he came up to the wicket, a long, lean man' – 6ft 3in – 'all arms and legs, and all apparently making amazing evolutions. His actual bowling was intensely difficult and most disconcerting.'[22]

Grace knew the action well of course, describing it as 'high and fairly fast'. Grace knew, too, that 'most dangerous deliveries from Spofforth were those at medium pace which, when he was in form, he could pitch where he liked. Whether he broke six inches or two feet, so wonderful was his command of the ball that if it beat the batsman it invariably hit the wicket. His very fast ones were generally Yorkers, which were delivered without any apparent alteration of pace.'[23]

Blackham settled behind the stumps. His reactions were so fast that he could position himself close to them, take the ball and have the bails off in one movement, but even he wouldn't stand up to The Demon.

Over 1: Spofforth to Grace

A maiden, Spofforth bowling fast – at a 'terrific rate' – and Blackham unusually standing a long way back.

Over 2: Garrett to Hornby

Hornby, known for 'throwing' his left leg across the wicket as the bowler bowled so that the stumps could no longer be seen, confronted Garrett's 'beautifully easy action'. He could make the ball 'come quickly off the pitch'

Spofforth bowling to Grace, as depicted by *The Illustrated and Dramatic News*.

and make it break both ways, whose tactic was 'pegging away on a good length'.[24] Hornby drove the third ball into the on-side for a single. Grace drove the next ball for another.

Over 3: Spofforth to Grace

Grace cut the third ball for a single. Blackham came up to the stumps: if Spofforth intended to blast Grace out, he'd overwhelm Hornby with guile – but Hornby worked the fourth on to the leg-side for another single.

Over 4: Garrett to Hornby

A maiden.

Over 5: Spofforth to Grace

Grace pushed the second ball just in front of himself, and they scampered a single to the delight of the crowd. Hornby played the over out.

Over 6: Garrett to Grace

Grace might have been caught and bowled – it fell just short of Garrett – and then took another cheeky single from the third ball, and the crowd loved it. The Australians 'were fielding like cats'.[25] Hornby took a single from the last ball.

Over 7: Spofforth to Hornby

Hornby played the first ball brilliantly through the slips to the boundary – 'cut it very prettily' – and snicked the last ball for a lucky 2 on the leg-side. That made England 13.

Over 8: Garrett to Grace

Grace took a single from the third ball.

Over 9: Spofforth to Grace

Grace took a single. The next ball beat Hornby and hit his off stump.

England 15 – 1, 70 to win.

Hornby's innings lasted 16 minutes and 16 balls. Barlow, regarded as one of the safest batsmen in England, came to the wicket and Spofforth beat him: a fast ball breaking in and, although Barlow managed to touch it with the bat, it hit middle and off.

England 15 – 2.

Ulyett came to the wicket and negotiated the fourth ball. It gave Spofforth the unusual distinction of bowling each ball in the over to a different batsman. The Australian mood had now changed to we will win this.[26]

Over 10: Garrett to Grace

Grace drove the fourth ball deep into the on-side, and Jones cut it off a yard in front of the wall of spectators. They ran 3 'amid a good deal of cheering'.[27]

Over 11: Spofforth to Grace

Grace on-drove the third ball high but safe for 2 to make the score 20 at 4.09, 65 to win.

Over 12: Garrett to Ulyett

A maiden.

Over 13: Spofforth to Grace

Grace drove the first ball to the on-side boundary. It may well be that this was the boundary *The Daily Chronicle* described:

'As the day previous, the boundary of the field was overpassed some yards by spectators reposing and sitting on the grass. As often as the ball was driven their way they would rise and make a line for its progress; but this succession did not offer all the advantage of clear space. In one instance it was understood that an urchin – from mistaken motives of kindness, no doubt – presumed to arrest the ball as it was finishing its course boundary wards. It was just possible, so some thought, that it might have been fielded at three runs; but as there was little doubt that if it had been left alone by the aforesaid urchin, the force which it was impelled by Mr Grace would have carried it to the boundary, the drive counted for four. It might be added that from the press box there was visible a commotion among the crowd just where the urchin had performed his rash exploit, and it looked as if somebody was being roughly handled and turned out.'

Grace on-drove the third ball for 3 to 'loud and general cheering'.[28] The fourth was a no ball.

Over 14: Garrett to Grace
Grace took a single from the first ball, Ulyett a single from the last. That brought 30 up – 55 to win – at 4.15.

Over 15: Spofforth to Ulyett
A maiden.

Over 16: Spofforth to Grace
Spofforth changed to the pavilion end, bowling consecutive overs as he had done in the first innings. Grace drove the second ball into the off-side for 2. Boyle came on at the Gasometer end, with his right-arm, medium pace.

Over 17: Boyle to Ulyett
Ulyett drove the first ball back so hard that it hurt Boyle's fingers. Ulyett took a single from the second, and Grace played the over out.

Over 18: Spofforth to Ulyett
Ulyett took a single from the second ball, and Grace played the over out.

Over 19: Boyle to Ulyett
Ulyett took a single from the second ball, and Grace struck the fourth high and handsome to the leg-side boundary. The match tilted towards England and in another four balls would tilt further still.

Over 20: Spofforth to Ulyett
Ulyett hit the first ball to the leg-side boundary and took a single from the third with a lofted off-drive. Grace cut the last ball for 2, making England 46, only 39 to win.

Over 21: Boyle to Ulyett
Ulyett took a single from the second ball, and Grace played the over out.

Over 22: Spofforth to Ulyett
Ulyett took a single from the first ball, then Grace brought up the 50 at 4.35, with a 'good hit' to the on-side, 35 to win.

'This hard, free hitting raised the hopes of the spectators very high. Ulyett had not, perhaps, played in particularly good form, but he had scored fast. Grace, despite two or three lofty hits, had played first-rate, plucky cricket, and looked like stopping till the match was won. Spofforth scarcely got a ball past his bat, and the popular belief that the 'demon' was his master appeared as if it would be falsified. Few among the spectators could have thought when 50 went up after 55 minutes' play, and with only two wickets down, that the defeat of England was impending. Those who, at the start, had given most weight to the difficulties of the English task began to see that, but for some extraordinary collapse, the batting side must win. The Australians themselves could hardly at this time have thought of victory. Two grand players were in, and well set, and there were six first-class batsmen to follow, while only 30 [35] runs were wanted to win the match.'[29]

Giffen, in the field, remembered 'the hitting of the Champion [Grace] and Ulyett changed the complexion of the game, which then appeared to be drifting away from us. Ulyett did not bat particularly well, but W.G.'s innings was a masterpiece.'[30]

Over 23: Boyle to Grace

A maiden.

Over 24: Spofforth to Ulyett

Ulyett negotiated the first ball but the second was delivered at such pace that he could do nothing but snick it low down to Blackham outside the off stump.

England 51 – 3, 34 to win.

Ulyett's innings lasted 32 minutes and 26 balls. He'd hit the one boundary. Lucas came to the wicket.

Over 25: Boyle to Grace

Grace cut the first ball for 2, but, to the third, played a drive he didn't get hold of properly, and it went high to Bannerman at mid-off for an easy catch. If Grace had hit the ball a yard either side of Bannerman that might have altered everything – and brought him a boundary – but he hadn't. The Australians could barely contain themselves.

England 53 – 4, 32 to win.

Grace's innings lasted 55 minutes and 54 balls. Lyttelton came to the wicket.

Over 26: Spofforth to Lucas

Lucas turned the first ball to leg for a single, leaving the next three balls to Lyttelton. 'Every ball was watched with the keenest anxiety. A fast delivery very near Mr Lyttelton's bails travelled away for 3.'[31] That was the last ball, and he'd snicked it, and had no idea where it was going.

Blackham, who stood up to Spofforth's bowling.

Over 27: Boyle to Lyttelton
A maiden.

Over 28: Spofforth to Lucas
A maiden, but, as it seems, Lucas gave Murdoch a half chance at point off his glove.

Over 29: Boyle to Lyttelton
Lyttelton got the fourth ball away for 2 on the leg-side.

Over 30: Spofforth to Lucas
A maiden.

Over 31: Boyle to Lyttelton
Lyttelton took a single from the third ball to make the score 60 at three minutes to five amid cheering.

Over 32: Spofforth to Lyttelton
Lyttelton struck the second ball to the leg-side boundary to 'an outburst of applause' and took a single from the third. That made the score 65, 20 to win, but the wicket was drying and bumpy, Spofforth and Boyle were breaking the ball in from a perfect length and the Australians were still fielding like terriers, especially Bannerman. More than that, some Spofforth balls reared. Lyttelton and Lucas had a nasty choice: take a risk, with all that that might entail, to try and score even a single or simply defend and defend. It was 5.00 and the long afternoon was going to get much, much longer.

Over 33: Boyle to Lyttelton
At 5.01, a maiden.

Over 34: Spofforth to Lucas
At 5.03, a maiden, although one source described it as 'a very nasty over'.

Over 35: Boyle to Lyttelton
At 5.05, a maiden.

Over 36: Spofforth to Lucas
At 5.06, a maiden.

Over 37: Boyle to Lyttelton
At 5.08, a maiden.

Over 38: Spofforth to Lucas
At 5.10, a maiden.

Over 39: Boyle to Lyttelton
At 5.12, a maiden.

Over 40: Spofforth to Lucas
At 5.13, a maiden.

Over 41: Boyle to Lyttelton
At 5.15, a maiden.

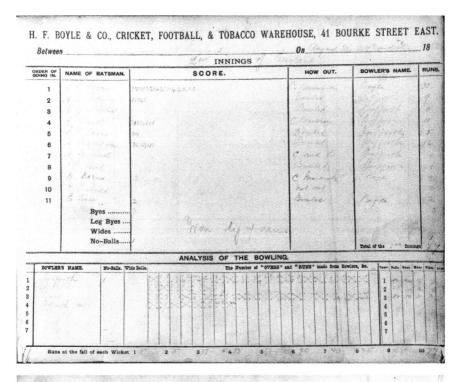

The original Australian scorebook.

Over 42: Spofforth to Lucas

At 5.17, a maiden.

Over 43: Boyle to Lyttelton

At 5.19, a maiden.

Over 44: Spofforth to Lucas

At 5.20, a maiden. Surrey secretary C.W. Alcock wrote that Blackham had 'no one behind him' – no long-stop – and if he missed a ball or two it might bring disaster, but he didn't.

Over 45: Boyle to Lyttelton

Was it now that Spofforth whispered something to Murdoch and Bannerman, out of hearing of both batsmen? Spofforth said 'Mis-field a hit if you can, give Lucas a single and that will bring Lyttelton to face me'. At 5.22, Lyttelton negotiated the first ball from Boyle and scored a lucky single on the leg-side from the second. Bannerman mis-fielded it, 19 to win, but Lyttelton would have 'the dark background of the pavilion behind that deadly arm' of Spofforth.[32] Lucas played the over out.

Over 46: Spofforth to Lyttelton

At 5.23, a maiden.

Over 47: Boyle to Lucas

At 5.25, a maiden. Was it now that Hornby said something to Studd? 'Then came the time,' Studd remembered, 'when the best English batsmen played over after over and never made a run. If I remember right, something like 18 to 20 overs were bowled without a run, maiden after maiden. They got out, and Hornby on his own account began to alter the order of going in. He asked me if I minded and I said "No". Then things began to change and a procession began. Of course Hornby told me he was holding me in reserve.'[33]

Over 48: Spofforth to Lyttelton

At 5.27, a maiden.

Over 49: Boyle to Lucas

At 5.29, a maiden.

Over 50: Spofforth to Lyttelton

At 5.30 Lyttelton negotiated the first ball but the second, coming from that dark background and deadly arm, broke through and hit the top of the middle stump.

England 66 – 5, still 19 to win.

Lyttelton's innings had lasted 50 minutes and 55 balls. Steel came to the wicket, his nerves tormenting him. Was he the batsman, as one Australian remembered, whose 'lips were ashen grey and his throat so parched that he could hardly speak' as he made his way to the wicket?[34] *The Manchester Guardian* judged that the Australians had 'totally demoralised' England and

That deadly arm. These classic shots by George Beldam in *Great Bowlers And Fielders: Their Methods At a Glance* give some idea of what the England batsmen faced.

added: 'So very nervous and uncertain became the batting that Mr Steel, whose style is commonly most finished, played his first two balls from Spofforth as clumsily as a novice.' He 'shaped very badly'.[35]

Over 51: Boyle to Lucas

At 5.34 Lucas chopped the first ball, slow, very late through the slips to the boundary to an explosion of cheering, 15 to win. Lucas had not scored since the 26th over at 4.47. He had faced, and survived, 44 balls between the two scoring strokes.

Over 52: Spofforth to Steel

At 5.35 Steel played a 'wretched' stroke to the first ball, deceptively slower and 'sucking' him forward. He spooned it to Spofforth for an easy catch and bowled.

England 70 – 6, still 15 to win.

Steel had been in for some four minutes, and Spofforth had struck a profound psychological blow. Giffen remembered how we 'gradually tightened our hold on the game; and the moment, I fancy, it was really clinched was when Steel was dismissed without scoring. So long as he remained, we could not feel perfectly safe. The situation was one of those trying ones in which I think the batsmen invariably appear at a disadvantage.'[36] Read came to the wicket.

One spectator[37] described Spofforth's bowling:

'With his long, puzzling run and lightning deliveries rendered indiscernible by a background of shifting heads, moving white paper and cards, mixed up with wafted tobacco smoke, no wonder the batsmen were utterly incapable of playing his balls, and had to take their chance at a blind block or hit. I have no doubt that if each of the batsmen were asked they would say they could not see the delivery of at least three balls out of the "demon's" overs.'

'Among the enormous mass of spectators, the majority of whom were not of the ordinary kind but cricketers from various parts of the country, the excitement became if possible more marked.'[38]

Was it now, as legend insists, that the old man in the pavilion began to gnaw the handle off his umbrella or had he already started?

Was it now, as 'Buns' Thornton[39] said, that Studd was found 'walking round the pavilion with a blanket round him'. It seems unlikely: Studd has placed himself in the Committee Room watching through closed windows because of the cold, and it's more likely he was walking round and round there, wearing the blanket simply because the cold afternoon *was* cold.

Read had the over to play out. His selection for the match 'was admittedly something of an experiment. He has played two or three lucky innings lately,

'Buns' Thornton.

but these do not make a cricketer any more than two or three swallows make a summer.'[40] He negotiated his first ball, but the second – the third of the over – bowled him middle and off stump. The Australians gathered and 'exhibited to the full their increasing delight'.[41]

England 70 – 7, still 15 to win.

With Read's dismissal 'a change came over the scene. While the Colonists could not help betraying their glee the spectators became downcast and silent, the silence being only broken by some involuntary outburst of admiration at the fine fielding and bowling. Still there was hope even yet.'[42] Barnes was cheered to the wicket and drove the ball to long-on for 2, 13 to win.

Giffen records that, as the crisis deepened, a gentleman in the pavilion said 'If only they would play with straight bats they would be sure to get the runs,' to which the lady with him said 'Would they really? Couldn't you get them some?'

Over 53: Boyle to Lucas

At 5.40 a maiden. Murdoch confessed later the only fear he had was that a batsman would have a go at Boyle – a few lusty blows would settle the match – with the unstated implication that nobody would be having a go at Spofforth.

'It is impossible to describe the state people were in just before the end of the game. Men who were noted for their coolness at critical moments were shaking like leaves – some were shivering with cold – some even fainted. At times there was an awful silence. And all the while Blackham was standing up to Spofforth with the utmost calmness, taking him as easily and certainly as if he was bowling slow, instead of at a tremendous pace. A slight mistake might have lost his side the match, but he worked like a machine.'[43]

Over 54: Spofforth to Barnes

At 5.42 the third ball went for 3 byes, bringing Lucas down to the pavilion end and the deadly arm for the first time since the 44th over, 10 to win. The 'faces of the vast ring brightened'.[44] Lucas looked the man to win it, this Lucas 'against whom no charge of nervousness could be made, and who had played cool, steady cricket for a long time, and stopped many better balls than those that had taken wickets.'

He played on.

England 75 – 8, still 10 to win.

He was so annoyed with himself he 'lifted his bat and struck the dead ball'.[45] His innings lasted 65 minutes and 55 balls for the boundary and a single. The Australians gathered again. Studd came in and moved to the non-striker's end.

Over 55: Boyle to Barnes

At 5.45 Barnes fended at the first ball and it flipped up to Murdoch, close in, off his glove.

England 75 – 9, still 10 to win.

Barnes's innings lasted six minutes and five balls.

It must have seemed a long journey as the Yorkshireman with the strong, solid face, swept back hair and drooping moustache came down the pavilion steps. Edmund Peate moved down the corridor between the ranks of men severely dressed in the Victorian way – long coats, top hats, bowler hats. He had his orders: 'block, leave the scoring to Studd'. He came out on to the pitch and he was very alone. He made the long journey and the 20,000 watched every step he took, and wondered.

He took guard, Boyle, ball in hand, waiting.

He struck his first ball, the second of the over, to square-leg for 2, 8 to win, 7 to tie. Was there consternation in the pavilion that he'd disobeyed orders? Was Hornby protesting 'What's the man doin'? What's the man doin'?' to anyone who'd listen. Was Grace stroking his beard and muttering under it? Two runs were only useful if Peate didn't risk getting more. Studd could possibly win the match, but Peate could certainly lose it.

Boyle ran up and bowled the third ball of the over. Peate missed it. Did he play a shot at all? If he did, what sort was it? Defensive? Trying for more runs? None of the reporters recorded this, no doubt because at that instant it didn't seem relevant. It might have been, especially if he did take a risk, because that would explain why he did what he did in the next few seconds – which shaped the future of cricket.

The scorers put a dot in the scorebooks.

Boyle ran up and bowled the final ball of the over.

The crowd fell silent.

As the ball came towards him Peate flailed at it: the simple, crude movement of the tail ender. The ball struck the stumps.

It was 5.48 on the long, cold afternoon.

A great yell went up, the one Grace never forgot.

The crowd, suddenly released from all their agonies, came on.

'The victorious cricketers were charged in all directions by a demonstrative multitude that were soon swarming over the field and clamouring in front of the Pavilion for the appearance of Spofforth, of Murdoch and the other Australians. As, responding to the distinctive calls, each came and stood upon the steps, thousands of hats, sticks or umbrellas were enthusiastically waved, and loud shouts of applause were repeated. Mr W.G. Grace and other prominent members of the England team were also called for.'[46]

'The scene when the game finished can hardly be described. The reaction after the severe tension of the last half-hour left the spectators almost paralysed. The effect in many ways was not without its comic side. In the high pressure of such a sensational finish, it is said that the reporters, whose duty it was to telegraph to the evening papers, were so overcome as to forget to transmit the result.'[47]

One source says that the result had a devastating effect in the Surrey club's office 'upon the members of the committee and some of their friends'. Secretary Alcock 'sat down on the edge of the huge iron safe and buried his head in his hands, eyes seemingly oblivious to everything.' He recovered his composure and, for some unremembered reason, had to go to the Press Box. As he made his way there 'I recognised the form of an old habitué of the Oval on one of the seats in the stand. He was leaning over the seat, and touching him on the back I asked him if there was anything the matter with him. "Oh no," was his reply "only I don't know whether to cry or be sick".'[48]

A spectator, George Eber Spendler of 191 Brook Street, Kensington, 'complained to a friend of feeling unwell and left the seat he had for some time occupied. Scarcely had he done so when he fell to the ground, and blood commenced to flow freely from his mouth. He was at once conveyed to a room adjoining the Pavilion, where he was examined by several medical men, amongst whom was Dr Jones, the president of the Surrey Cricket Club, who pronounced life extinct, the cause of death being attributed to a ruptured blood vessel.'

Down all these years there's been a claim that someone died of a heart attack during the final, desperate half hour. One spectator did – Spendler – but afterwards.

The *Bell's Life* reporter found his way into the Australian dressing room a few minutes after the game when 'Hornby, Lyttelton, Earl Darnley, and others were congratulating Murdoch and his men upon the success. Spofforth said he could not possibly have had a wicket that suited him better. I know that that was the case, and I know also that the Australians behaved with modesty and good taste, and that the Englishmen took their beating with a good grace. They freely acknowledged that [...] Spofforth's bowling had been about the finest ever seen in a cricket field. A great deal has been said about the nervousness of some of the English batsmen. I saw it, and I regret it.'[49]

The *Bell's Life* reporter had another task. He'd felt Umpire Thoms hadn't said 'if you claim it, sir, out!' over the controversial Jones-Grace dismissal in the Australian innings. The reporter 'took the first opportunity of asking Thoms what he really did say, telling him at the same time what I had heard. He, as I expected, denied having said anything more than the necessary word. 'Out!' Thoms told me the point was a very simple one, the ball was not dead, and the batsman was run out. If Grace, instead of going up to the wicket and putting off the bails, had thrown at the stumps and missed them, the batsman could, and probably would, have run again, and then every one would have said what a smart thing the Australians had done. Jones did a foolish, thoughtless thing in going out of his ground, and he paid the penalty of rashness. Grace did what he was perfectly justified in doing, and there can be no doubt the run out was legal and fair. It was in my hearing called "Cricket, but dirty." I can't agree in this opinion. It may not have been a particularly courteous or generous action, and if England had won a close match we should never have heard the last of the matter. The thick-and-thin supporters of Australian cricket would have talked about sharp practice, and ungentlemanly play, and there would probably have been some revival of the old ill-feeling. I don't mean that the Australians themselves would have been weak enough to make a serious complaint as to an action which

The issue of *The South London Gazette* after the match.

SUDDEN DEATH AT THE OVAL.—Immediately after the conclusion of the Australians' innings in the match at Kennington Oval on Tuesday afternoon, one of the spectators, named Spendler, who had journeyed up from Eastbourne to be present at the match, fell down, blood at the same time issuing freely from his mouth and nostrils. He was at once carried off the ground and examined by several medical men, amongst whom was Dr. Jones, the president of the Surrey County Cricket Club. After a brief examination he was pronounced to have died from congestion of the lungs, accelerated by the bursting of a blood vessel. An inquest was held on Thursday, when evidence to the above effect was given, the widow of the deceased adding that he had had a cough some little time, and had been in the habit of expectorating blood. A verdict of "Death from natural causes" was returned.

HAWKSTONE HALL.—A meeting was held in this hall on Monday evening in connection with the various temperance societies associated with Christ Church. The Rev. Newman Hall, LL.B., in introducing Mr. Jenkyn Ingram, the editor of the *Fireman*, said that the worst fire raging in the country was the fire of strong drinks, which had destroyed many a home, many a heart, and many a character. They were trying to put out the fire with temperance. Mr. Jenkyn Ingram then delivered an interesting lecture on "Fires, firemen, and fire engines," remarking that history told them that all kinds of men had been acquainted with fire, a knowledge of the use of it being the practical distinction between man and brute. After detailing the methods of producing fire in use amongst the ancients and the general causes of fires in dwellings, the lecturer traced the progress made in the manufacture of fire extinguishing appliances. Interesting experiments with asbestos cloth were made, and a working could not be attacked on any but sentimental grounds. But Murdoch expressed his disapproval openly in the field, and was evidently angry, and we all know how strong sentiment is, and how easily a grievance grows and spreads.'

Grace contented himself by saying 'Well, well, I left six men to get thirty odd runs and they couldn't do it.'

Giffen reflected that 'A bit of fearless hitting might have snatched the game from us, but after Lyttelton and Lucas went, none of the great English batsmen could muster up the courage to have a bang, and, considering the magnificent way in which Spofforth was bowling, there was some excuse for them.

'I remember on our way to England, Spoff had figured in a fancy dress ball as Mephistopheles; but, aided by art on that occasion, he did not look half the demon he did when at the Oval on that Tuesday afternoon he sent in those marvellous breaks, almost every one of which, if it had passed the bat, would have hit the wicket.'[50]

Peate was asked why he played the way he had and replied 'I couldn't trust Mr Studd.' He must have meant it ironically, and whether he said it at all – or to whom – is not clear. What seems much more likely is that, at the supreme moment and after waiting for two hours, he lost his judgement or he lost his nerve – or both.

The final irony, of course, is that if he had not done that, if he'd found a way through the final three deliveries of the 55th Australian over and Studd had taken care of the endgame – as he was eminently capable of doing by ability and temperament – we'd have a wonderful match enshrined in cricket history and nobody would ever have heard of The Ashes.

Notes

1. *The Times,* London.
2. *The Daily Chronicle,* London.
3. *40 Seasons Of First Class Cricket,* R.G. Barlow, 1908, Manchester.
4. *With Bat And Ball,* Giffen.
5. Pardon in *Bell's Life.*
6. *The Daily Telegraph,* London.
7. Ibid.
8. Pardon op. cit.
9. *The Story Of Australian Cricket,* Egan.
10. Ibid.
11. Giffen op. cit.
12. Egan op. cit.
13. *C.T. Studd Pioneer And Cricketer,* Norman P. Grubb.
14. *The Daily Telegraph.*
15. Giffen op. cit.
16. Ibid.
17. Grubb op. cit.
18. *The Daily Telegraph.*
19. *Great Batsmen, Their Methods At A Glance,* G.W. Beldam and C.B. Fry.
20. Ibid.
21. Ibid.
22. *Recollections And Reminiscences,* Lord Hawke.
23. *Cricket,* Grace.
24. Ibid.
25. *The Daily Telegraph.*
26. Giffen op. cit.
27. *The Manchester Guardian.*
28. Pardon in *Bell's Life.*
29. Ibid.
30. Giffen op. cit.
31. *The Daily Telegraph.*
32. *A History Of Cricket,* Altham and Swanton.
33. Grubb op. cit.
34. Quoted in Altham.
35. Pardon in *Bell's Life.*
36. Giffen op. cit.
37. *Cricket: A Weekly Record Of The Game.*
38. *The Manchester Guardian.*

39. Charles Inglis Thornton had a nickname – 'Bun and Jam' – at Eton after an incident when, while fielding during a match, he bought one from a vendor and a high catch came to him. He either swallowed the bun or put it in his pocket (see Lord Harris article, www.cricinfo.com). Thornton played for Cambridge University, Kent and was a big hitter like Bonnor.

40. *The Manchester Guardian.*

41. Pardon in *Bell's Life.*

42. *The Manchester Guardian.*

43. *Surrey Cricket,* The Rt. Hon. Lord Alverstone and C.W. Alcock.

44. *The Manchester Guardian.*

45. Ibid.

46. *The Daily Chronicle.*

47. Alverstone and Alcock, op. cit.

48. Ibid.

49. Pardon in *Bell's Life.*

50. Giffen op. cit.

AUSTRALIA first innings

A.C. Bannerman	c Grace b Peate	9
H.H. Massie	b Ulyett	1
W.L. Murdoch	b Peate	13
G.J. Bonnor	b Barlow	1
T.P. Horan	b Barlow	3
G. Giffen	b Peate	2
J.Mc. Blackham	c Grace b Barlow	17
T.W. Garrett	c Read b Peate	10
H.F. Boyle	b Barlow	2
S.P. Jones	c Barnes b Barlow	0
F.R. Spofforth	not out	4
	Extras (b1)	1
	Total	63

1/6, 2/21, 3/22, 4/26, 5/30, 6/30, 7/48, 8/53, 9/59, 10/63

	O	M	R	W
Peate	38	24	31	4
Ulyett	9	5	11	1
Barlow	31	22	19	5
Steel	2	1	1	0

ENGLAND first innings

R.G. Barlow	c Bannerman b Spofforth	11
W.G. Grace	b Spofforth	4
G. Ulyett	st Blackham b Spofforth	26
A.P. Lucas	c Blackham b Boyle	9
Hon. A. Lyttelton	c Blackham b Spofforth	2
C.T. Studd	b Spofforth	0
J.M. Read	not out	19
W. Barnes	b Boyle	5
A.G. Steel	b Garrett	14
A.N. Hornby	b Spofforth	2
E. Peate	c Boyle b Spofforth	0
	Extras (b6, lb2, nb1)	9
	Total	101

1/13, 2/18, 3/57, 4/59, 5/60, 6/63, 7/70, 8/96, 9/101, 10/101

	O	M	R	W
Spofforth	36.3	18	46	7 (1 nb)
Garrett	16	7	22	1
Boyle	19	7	24	2

AUSTRALIA second innings

A.C. Bannerman	c Studd b Barnes	13
H.H. Massie	b Steel	55
G.J. Bonnor	b Ulyett	2
W.L. Murdoch	run out	29
T.P. Horan	c Grace b Peate	2
G. Giffen	c Grace b Peate	0
J.Mc. Blackham	c Lyttelton b Peate	7
S.P. Jones	run out	6
F.R. Spofforth	b Peate	0
T.W. Garrett	not out	2
H.F. Boyle	b Steel	0
	Extras (b6)	6
	Total	122

1/66, 2/70, 3/70, 4/79, 5/79, 6/99, 7/114, 8/117, 9/122, 10/122

	O	M	R	W
Peate	21	9	40	4
Ulyett	6	2	10	1
Barlow	13	5	27	0
Steel	7	0	15	2
Barnes	12	5	15	1
Studd	4	1	9	0

ENGLAND second innings

W.G. Grace	c Bannerman b Boyle	32
A.N. Hornby	b Spofforth	9
R.G. Barlow	b Spofforth	0
G. Ulyett	c Blackham b Spofforth	11
A.P. Lucas	b Spofforth	5
Hon. A Lyttelton	b Spofforth	12
A.G. Steel	c & b Spofforth	0
J.M. Read	b Spofforth	0
W. Barnes	c Murdoch b Boyle	2
C.T. Studd	not out	0
E. Peate	b Boyle	2
	Extras (b3, nb1)	4
	Total	77

1/15, 2/15, 3/51, 4/53, 5/66, 6/70, 7/70, 8/75, 9/75, 10/77

	O	M	R	W
Spofforth	28	15	44	7 (1 nb)
Garrett	7	2	10	0
Boyle	20	11	19	3

AUSTRALIA WON BY SEVEN RUNS

4

THE SPORTSMA[N]

CRICKET.

FIXTURES FOR AUGUST.

30—OVAL, ENGLAND V. AUSTRALIA
30—Aldershot, Free Foresters v. The Division
30—Dorking, Guildford v. Dorking
30—Liverpool, Liverpool v. Oxton
30—Lord's, M.C.C. and Ground v. Birmingham and District
30—Ongar, Ongar v. Mr Tween's Eleven
30—Tufnell Park, Holloway United v. Old Buxtonians
31—Bexley, Surrey Club and Ground v. Bexley
31—Chester, Chester v. Chester College
31—Oval, South of the Thames Licensed Victuallers v. Lavender Hill Tradesmen
31—Tufnell Park, Hampstead United v. Dartmouth Park
31—Tunbridge Wells, Australians v. United South of England

GREAT MATCH AT THE OVAL.

ENGLAND v. AUSTRALIA.

VICTORY OF THE AUSTRALIAN ELEVEN.

EXCITING FINISH.

(BY OUR SPECIAL REPORTERS.)

"ADVANCE, Australia," may fairly be blazoned on the colours of our visitors after the concluding scenes of the above great match at the Oval yesterday. If pluck and determination, combined with consummate skill, deserve success, then do the Colonial team deserve, and that fully, the laurels they have gathered on many a well-fought field. It was a matter for surprise to many lovers of the game, in spite of the acknowledged fact of a difficult wicket, that the display of our representatives with the willow on Monday was so poor. Nearly every one of them had done wonders against the most difficult of bowling, and on the most uncertain of grounds, many a time and oft previously. How came it, then, that out of such an eleven only four were able to reach double figures? whilst in their second venture—well it might be advisable to drop a veil over the second if that were possible, but under the circumstances it is not. True the amounts completed by the visitors were not particularly large, and they left anything but a difficult task for their opponents. How did the latter avail themselves of their chance? W. G. Grace played up like a man, and added a dashing thirty-two, whilst he was ably seconded on what there is no wish to disguise was a bad wicket by Ulyett, but as to the rest, with the exception, perhaps, of the Hon. A. Lyttelton, they simply collapsed. When the close drew near and their task was but a light one, 19 runs only to be scored for five wickets, they simply lost their nerve, and stood up to be knocked down, metaphorically speaking, like so many ninepins. All their brilliant services in the field were thrown away, and the skill of the bowlers wasted, simply because they had not the nerve to play pluckily at a critical point in the game. Men who at Portsmouth fought skilfully and well went down before the bowling of Spofforth and Boyle like so many tailors' dummies, and when the end came England had lost the victory, which at one time was easily within their grasp, by seven runs. All honour to the victors, whose performance in the field and with the leather was simply masterly. Never disheartened by the near prospect of defeat, they played up manfully, and with as much coolness and confidence as though they were achieving an easy task. Well, they have their reward. An Australian eleven has, for the first—and let us hope it will be the last—time, decisively beaten a picked eleven of all England. There should be no cavilling about this matter. Our side were as ably chosen, and probably as representative, as could possibly be gathered together. In the light of previous performances they ought to have won, and that right easily; but as it turned out, the closeness of the finish was too much for their poor nerves, and they failed lamentably. Otherwise, the game was a grand one. Most certainly our side showed equal cleverness in the field and destructiveness with the leather to their rivals, and had they only kept cool and collected to the end they must have won. We would not for one moment detract from the fulness of our visitors' measure of success. True, the margin between victory and defeat was but small; but it was sufficient. All Australia will ring with the prowess of her sons, and once more the old country must take a back seat. No matter how many further defeats the Colonials may have in store ere returning to the land of the kangaroo

but 29 to give success, a regular rot set in. Lyttelton and Lucas held up their sticks for a long time, although for few runs; but after them "the deluge." Down went the defenders one after the other, until, amidst almost breathless excitement, Peate's wicket fell, and Australia had vanquished England by *seven runs*. It may here be mentioned that at the last meeting between similar representative teams two years ago, England won by five wickets, after a game remarkable for the grand innings of W. G. Grace (one hundred and fifty-two) and Murdoch (one hundred and fifty-three, not out). On that occasion five of the team who scored victory yesterday took part, Murdoch, Bannerman, Blackham, Boyle, and Bonnor, Spofforth being ill at the time. Amongst the chief engagements which have yet to be fulfilled by our visitors are a couple of matches against Shaw's Australian team at Holbeck and the Oval respectively, Nottingham, and a United Eleven at Tunbridge to-morrow (Thursday). Their match list extends nearly up to the end of next month, but even should defeat still await them they will find ample consolation in the fact that they have lowered the standard of "All England."

On the drawing of the stumps overnight, it will be remembered both sides had just completed an innings each, the Englishmen, who certainly had the worst of the light, overtopping their adversaries' poor score of 63 by 38. This number, however, on recommencing was generally considered to be more than neutralised by the advantage the Colonists had in the wicket, and not a few people expressed their confidence in their ultimate ability to win. A morning's rain having given way to sunshine, a resumption of the game was soon effected with the Australians sending in first, as before, Bannerman and Massie, to whom were opposed as bowlers the Lancastrian, Barlow, and Ulyett. Unlike their opening efforts on Monday, the two batsmen quickly got to work. In fact, Barlow's very first delivery Bannerman cut sweetly for a couple. Massie, in response, off-drove the Sheffielder most magnificently, but the hit only resulted in a trio, Maurice Read running a considerable distance in the out-field, and returning the ball with such precision that "Alec." was nearly run out. In the Lancashire representative's next over Massie cut a delivery in grand style to the boundary for four, and soon afterwards on-driving the same bowler, the 20 went up at 12.30. Prior to this Massie despatched Ulyett to the leg boundary, and although his associate was content with singles, the rate of scoring was evidently too fast for the English captain, who, at 25, decided upon trying a different mode of attack, the two slow bowlers, Peate and Mr Studd, superseding the fast performers. The Yorkshireman opened with a maiden over, but his *confrère* was not so fortunate, as from his first delivery Massie, continuing his brilliant batting career, added another on-drive for four. The next ball would most certainly have travelled for a like addition, but the Cantab just succeeded in stopping it, a circumstance which brought forth ringing cheers from the spectators. Hereabouts Peate, who had sent up two unproductive overs, was faced by Massie, but no sooner had this occurred than the Victorian lifted him to the on boundary. All this time Bannerman was comparatively inactive, still at a quarter to one his side had rubbed off the balance against them. At a terrific rate Massie went on slogging again, and after driving Peate to the off for four he turned his attention to the other performer, and fairly mastered the bowling. Mr Studd, after proving very expensive, at length gave way to Barnes at 47, and from the latter's very fast delivery Massie should have been caught deep behind the wicket by Mr Lucas. At this period the Victorian had contributed thirty-eight, and his escape was all the more galling to the Englishmen, for he continued hitting away at a wonderfully fast pace. Twice in one over Bannerman cut Peate for two, and very rapidly the scores were raised to 56, when Mr Steel superseded the Yorkshireman. As a set-off against the slow rate of scoring on Monday, when it took an hour and a half to make 36 runs, yesterday in two-thirds of that time the 50 were elevated, but this was all due to the efforts of Massie, who made fifty-five out of 66, and then, amidst a perfect outburst of applause he was bowled leg-stump. On returning the partisans of the Cornstalk were loud in their praises of his efforts, and really his innings was a fine one, consisting as it did of no fewer than nine fours, two threes, three twos, and the rest singles. Bonnor came in first wicket down, and although Mr Steel was bowling remarkably well, Mr Hornby very wisely decided upon putting on Ulyett to the big hitter, who only just improved upon his opening exhibition and was then clean bowled, centre stump, by the Sheffielder. As expected, the giant's dismissal was the signal for a great outburst of English cheers, and when Bannerman fell at the same figure—three for 70—the demonstrations were renewed again and again. "Alec" was caught at cover-point by Mr Studd, and when he returned the cracks, Murdoch and Horan, became associated. Deciding upon another mode of attack to these batsmen, the English captain's judgment was soon again to the fore, as, after Murdoch had smacked Peate nearly square for four, that bowler had the immense satisfaction of seeing Mr Grace capture Horan and Giffen from two successive deliveries, standing close in at point. Thus it was that the fourth and fifth batsmen fell at 79, and as the first wicket did not retire until 66 runs had been added the early successful hopes of the Colonials had been, as it were, in a few overs dashed to the ground, the glorious uncertainty of the game never being more clearly demonstrated than on the present occasion. Blackham next came in to aid his captain, and immediately on his arrival he put a veto on the possibility of Peate performing "the hat trick" by cracking that bowler's following delivery round to leg for four. In response Murdoch, after being nearly bowled by Peate, got Barnes away for a single, and off-driving the other trundler for one more next over four byes sent the 90 up at 1.45. Presently the Antipodean captain managed to cut Barnes in his well-known style for a trio, but just as the scores denoted a single this side of the century a shower caused an adjournment, lunch being partaken of meantime. During the interval it rained, but not much, and punctually at 2.45 play was resumed, the attendance at this stage being about equal to that on the first day. Blackham, who

nomen of "demon," and no mistake. Full score and analysis subjoined:

AUSTRALIA.	1st inn.		2nd inn.
*A. C. Bannerman, c Grace, b Peate	9	c Studd, b Barnes	13
H. H. Massie, b Ulyett	1	b Steel	55
*W. L. Murdoch, b Peate	13	run out	29
*G. J. Bonnor, b Barlow	1	b Ulyett	2
T. Horan, b Barlow	3	c Grace, b Peate	2
G. Giffen, b Peate	2	c Grace, b Peate	0
*J. M'C. Blackham, c Grace, b Barlow	17	c Lyttelton, b Peate	7
T. W. Garrett, c Read, b Peate	10	not out	2
*H. F. Boyle, b Barlow	2	b Steel	0
S. P. Jones, c Barnes, b Barlow	0	run out	6
F. R. Spofforth, not out	4	b Peate	0
Bye	1	Byes	6
Total	—63	Total	—122

ENGLAND.	1st inn.		2nd inn.
Barlow, c Bannerman, b Spofforth	11	b Spofforth	0
*Dr. W. G. Grace, b Spofforth	4	c Bannerman, b Boyle	32
Ulyett, st Blackham, b Spofforth	26	c Blackham, b Spofforth	11
*Mr A. P. Lucas, c Blackham, b Boyle	9	b Spofforth	5
*Hon. A. Lyttelton, c Blackham, b Spofforth	2	b Spofforth	12
Mr C. T. Studd, b Spofforth	0	not out	0
Read, not out	19	b Spofforth	0
*Barnes, b Boyle	5	c Murdoch, b Boyle	2
*Mr A. G. Steel, b Garrett	14	c and b Spofforth	0
Mr A. N. Hornby, b Spofforth	2	b Spofforth	9
Peate, c Boyle, b Spofforth	0	b Boyle	2
Byes 6, l b 2, n-b 1	9	Byes 3, n b 1	4
Total	—101	Total	—77

* Played in England v. Australia, September, 1880.

ANALYSIS OF THE BOWLING.

AUSTRALIANS.—FIRST INNINGS.

	o.	m.	r.	w.		o.	m.	r.	w.
Peate	38	24	31	4	Barlow	31	22	19	5
Ulyett	9	5	11	1	A. G. Steel	2	1	1	0

SECOND INNINGS.

	o.	m.	r.	w.		o.	m.	r.	w.
Barlow	13	5	27	0	Studd	4	1	9	0
Ulyett	6	2	10	1	Barnes	11	5	15	1
Peate	21	9	40	4	Steel	7	0	15	2

ENGLAND.—FIRST INNINGS.

	o.	m.	r.	w.		o.	m.	r.	w.
Spofforth	36.3	18	46	7	Boyle	19	7	24	2
Garrett	16	7	22	1					

Spofforth bowled one no ball.

SECOND INNINGS.

	o.	m.	r.	w.		o.	m.	r.	w.
Spofforth	28	15	44	7	Boyle	20	11	19	3
Garrett	7	2	10	0					

Spofforth bowled a no ball.

Umpires: Thoms and Greenwood.

We subjoin a list of results of the engagements of the Colonials to date:

May 15, at Oxford, v. Oxford University. Won by nine wickets.
May 18, at Brighton, v. Sussex. Won by an innings and 355 runs.
May 22, at Twickenham, v. Orleans Club. Drawn; 44 runs ahead, one wicket to fall.
May 25, at Oval, v. Surrey. Won by six wickets.
May 29, at Cambridge, v. Cambridge University. Lost by six wickets.
June 1, at Manchester, v. Lancashire. Won by four wickets.
June 5, at Bradford, v. Yorkshire. Drawn. Yorkshire wanted 87 runs, with seven wickets to fall.
June 8, at Nottingham, v. Notts. Drawn. Nottingham wanted 126 runs, with nine wickets to fall.
June 12, at Derby, v. Derbyshire. Won by an innings and 109 runs.
June 19, at Sheffield, v. Yorkshire. Won by six wickets.
June 22, at Oval, v. GENTLEMEN OF ENGLAND. Won by an innings and 1 run.
June 26, at Chichester, v. United Eleven. Won by an innings and 263 runs.
June 29, at Leicester, v. Leicestershire. Won by 74 runs.
July 3, at Northampton, v. Northamptonshire. Won by an innings and 80 runs.
July 6, at Lord's, v. Middlesex. Won by eight wickets.
July 10, at Lord's, v. M.C.C. and Ground. Drawn. M.C.C. 164 runs ahead on first innings.
July 13, at Dewsbury, v. Yorkshire. Drawn. Yorkshire 52 runs ahead; nine wickets in second innings still to fall.
July 17, at Bradford, v. Yorkshire. Won by 47 runs.
July 20, at Middlesbrough, v. Yorkshire. Won by seven wickets.
July 24, at Gosforth Park, v. Northumberland. Won by an innings and 6 runs.
July 27, at Edinburgh, v. Gentlemen of Scotland. Won by an innings and 18 runs.
July 31, at Liverpool, v. Liverpool and District. Drawn. Australians wanting 4 runs to win, with nine wickets still to fall.
August 3, at Clifton, v. Gloucestershire. Won by an innings and 159 runs.
August 7, at Canterbury, v. Kent. Won by seven wickets.
August 10, at Kennington Oval, v. PLAYERS OF ENGLAND. Lost by an innings and 34 runs.
August 14, at Derby, v. An Eleven of England. Drawn; the Colonials requiring 38 to win, with five wickets still to fall.
August 17, at Portsmouth, v. Cambridge University Past and Present. Lost by 20 runs.
August 21, at Taunton, v. Somersetshire. Won by an innings and 19 runs.
August 24, at Clifton v. Gloucestershire. Drawn. Colonials had four wickets in second innings to fall, and were 157 ahead.
August 28, at Kennington Oval, v. ENGLAND. Won by 7 runs.

Matches won, 19; lost, 3; drawn, 8. Total, 30.

The following is an outline of the future arrangements of the Colonials:

To-morrow the return match is commenced against the United Eleven, whom, it will be remembered, suffered a crushing single-innings defeat at Chichester in June last. The venue on this occasion is Tunbridge Wells, where a cricket week is at present being held, and of which it will form the fixture for the latter part of the week.

The English team, at the time of writing, has not been definitely announced, but we understand that a good eleven has been got together.

From Tunbridge the Antipodeans journey to Nottingham, where, on Monday next, they commence the return

THE MANCHESTER GUARDIAN, WEDNESDAY, AUGUST 30, 1882.

THE STATE OF IRELAND.

A "MOONLIGHT" OUTRAGE.

A telegram from Carrick-on-Shannon reports that shots ere fired by "Moonlighters" on Sunday night into the ouse of a farmer, named Gillooly, at Drumshan, county eitrim. Gillooly rushed out with a gun, and fired two hots at the attacking party, who then retreated. They ad only been gone a few minutes when a police patrol ame up, but failed to capture any of them.

THE IRISH CONSTABULARY AGITATION. EXCITEMENT AT LIMERICK.

Telegraphing late on Monday night, our Limerick correspondent says:—The Limerick people have practically ecome their own policemen, as a large majority of the onstabulary quartered in the city have refused to go on uty. The greatest excitement prevails in the William-reet Barrack, which, to prevent any more serious consequences, has been locked on the Inspector General and ie men, who have become almost completely demoraised at what they look on as the arbitrary dismissal of ieir five comrades. Colonel Bruce is stopping at ruise's Hotel, and at half-past two o'clock this ternoon he was rather startled by the hasty rival of an orderly, who informed him that of the men had refused to do their duty and id tendered their resignations. The Inspector General immoned them at the barracks and addressed them; it the men refused to withdraw their resignations. ie Inspector General was finally obliged to withdraw the County Inspector's office, as the men would arcely give him a hearing, and they cheered for the b-constables who had resigned. A meeting was to be ld this evening, and it was expected many more would ad in their resignations. In Cork the members of the rce have not become infected with the spirit of insubordination which appears to have strongly manisted itself in Limerick. Everything is quiet here, d the men even go to the extent of disapproving of e proceedings in Limerick. The following additional rticulars have transpired with reference to the proceedgs at the William-street Police Barracks to-day. Subnstable Patrick Coffey, who sent in his resignation is morning after the dismissal of the other five subnstables, had it accepted within an hour, when he is paid off, and left the William-street Police Barracks iid the cheers of the men. The men on duty in the eets having heard the circumstance, quitted their ats, and to the number of forty handed in their signations. Colonel Bruce, the Inspector General, is sent for, and appealed to the men not to act stily. In reply to questions put to him, he denied at the five men were dismissed for their connecn with the late agitation for increased pay, but for usal to obey orders, their transfer having been decided owing to the action taken by the constabulary New Pallas. At that station troops have been artered in the barracks for some time past, and the lice objected to messing with the soldiery. They morialised for their removal from the constabulary rracks, or else they would send in their resignations. e Limerick men were held to blame for this, and hence order for their transfer. One of the sub-constables d this could not be, as Sub-constable Guiry was not tioned in the city at all, but at Kilmurry, some les distant. Thereupon Colonel Bruce appealed to sub-constables who had handed in their resignations not to act hastily, and under the circumnces the sub-constables decided to continue on ty. It is feared, however, that they will act on eir resignations, and that other men in Limerick d different parts of Ireland will follow their exple. Telegrams are arriving from all parts of Ireland omising to contribute to a fund for the dismissed nstables. The excitement among the men has grown a white heat. Colonel Bruce, in view of the gravity the situation, remains in Limerick. Late to-night 58 b-constables paraded in the William-street Police rracks and proceeded to the county inspector's office, ere they handed in their resignations. The Inspector neral, Colonel Bruce, who was present, begged the en not to act so rashly, but they continued obdurate, d stated, after several appeals, that unless the five dissed men were reinstated they would lay down their ms within three days. It was semi-officially conveyed to e dismissed sub-constables that if they memorialised the rd Lieutenant they would more than probably be nstated, but this they refused to do. Telegrams from rk, Belfast, Derry, Waterford, Athlone, Clonmel, d other constabulary centres have arrived, stating at unless the men are reinstated they will resign *en asse*. Five sub-constables in lieu of those dismissed rived in Limerick to-night for duty, and were coldly ceived by the local men, whose determination to resent e dismissal of their comrades is hourly increasing. bscription lists have been already opened for the dissed constables, and the same has been done in nearly ery police barrack throughout Ireland. So the teleams received this evening state. Only a few policeen were seen on duty to-night, the main body keeping barracks.

The following circular has been issued from Dublin stle:—"Inspector General.—With reference to the recent ansfer of certain members of the force from Limerick other counties, which was ordered by you, with his cellency's sanction, for the good of the service, withit cause assigned, I am directed by his Excellency to form you that, as an impression appears to have got road in the force that such transfer was in the nature punishment for the connection which these men had ith the recent agitation for an increase in pay, pension, c., his Excellency authorises you to state to the force iat such was not the case, but that the transfer was itirely due to circumstances connected with the force Limerick which occurred subsequently to this agitaon, and which, in his Excellency's judgment, entirely istified the order given.—R. G. C. HAMILTON."

CORK, TUESDAY EVENING.

Matters remain almost without change in respect to

CRICKET.

ENGLAND v. AUSTRALIA: DEFEAT OF ENGLAND.

If the first day of this match was fertile in surprises, yesterday's play completely eclipsed it. Rarely has there been such a failure of brilliant batting talent. The bowling had throughout been surprisingly fine and had nonplussed the batting of each side in turn, but when the England innings opened with only 85 runs to win, nothing seemed more certain than that the Colonials would suffer a crushing defeat. After the stand made by Mr. Grace and Ulyett the betting was at enormous odds. The crowd, numbering upwards of 20,000 persons, was wrought up to a pitch of intense excitement, and every hit, however small, was enthusiastically cheered. The Australians, however, never bated a jot of hope and courage. Bowling and fielding were superb. With only four wickets down and but 20 runs wanted to win, everything seemed dead against them. Spofforth and Boyle strained every nerve, and 12 maiden overs followed in succession. The defence, however, was stubborn against this splendid bowling, the batsmen being Mr. Lucas and Mr. Lyttelton. At last Mr. Lyttelton made a single. More maidens followed, and then Spofforth clean bowled Mr. Lyttelton. Still, with 19 runs to win and only half the wickets down everything seemed favourable to England. But the Colonists, whose play cannot be too much praised, had totally demoralised their opponents. So very nervous and uncertain became the batting that Mr. Steel, whose style is commonly most finished, played his first two balls from Spofforth as clumsily as a novice. A maiden succeeding, Mr. Steel had to face the same fatal antagonist, and the second ball he played straight into the bowler's hands. Among the enormous mass of spectators, the majority of whom were not of the ordinary kind, but cricketers from various parts of the country, the excitement became if possible more marked. Maurice Read, the Surrey professional, who played a good innings on the first day, succumbed to the second ball. The placing of him in the eleven was admittedly somewhat of an experiment. He has played two or three lucky innings lately, but these do not make a cricketer any more than two or three swallows make a summer. With his dismissal a change came over the scene. Whilst the Colonists could not help betraying their glee the spectators became downcast and silent, the silence being only broken by some involuntary outburst of admiration at the fine bowling and fielding. Still there was hope even yet. Seven wickets were down for 70, and Barnes having joined Mr. Lucas two more runs were added and there was a bye for three. The faces of the vast ring of spectators brightened and they looked on with breathless interest. Then Mr. Lucas played a ball from Spofforth on to his wicket; such was his chagrin that he lifted his bat and struck the dead ball. He had been at the wickets since the score stood at 51, and although he had put together but five runs, he had made a brilliant defence. The next comer was Mr. Studd—whose antecedents warranted the belief that he would make a respectable stand. He had not, however, the opportunity. An easy catch at point got rid of his partner Barnes, and Peate, who followed, was easily bowled by Boyle. Five wickets had fallen in three-quarters of an hour. Thus the Australians won by seven runs, a fitting reward for their superb bowling and fielding and their remarkable pluck.

The innings closed on the first day with an advantage to England of 38 runs, the Australians having scored 63 and England 101 for a complete innings each. Rain fell heavily between half past nine and half past ten yesterday morning, and play could not be begun until ten minutes past twelve o'clock. The second innings of Australia was commenced by Bannerman and Massie, to the bowling of Barlow and Ulyett. In the first over Bannerman hit Barlow for a couple of twos, and then Massie drove Ulyett for three, the ball being finely returned and the wicket being very smartly put down. Having got to the opposite wicket Massie cut Barlow for four, and played the same bowler to square leg for three. Two singles were made, and then Massie hit Ulyett round to square leg for four. In this way the score reached 25, and a double change of bowling was tried, Peate going on in place of Ulyett, and Mr. C. T. Studd taking the ball from Barlow. Peate bowled a maiden, but Massie at once drove Mr. Studd for four—a splendid hit down to the stand by the right of the pavilion. Just after this Massie made two fours off Peate, the balance of runs on the first innings thus being hit off without the loss of a wicket. Massie now drove Mr. Studd splendidly for four, and Bannerman cut Peate twice for two. At 47 Barnes was put on in the place of Mr. Studd, and off his first ball Massie was missed at long off by Mr. Lucas, a mistake which cost England no end of trouble. At the time of the let off Massie had made 38, and just afterwards he drove Peate to the on for four. With the score at 56 Mr. Steel was tried at Peate's end, he being the sixth bowler who had gone on in about three-quarters of an hour. Massie hit him for two twos and a four, and then, in jumping out to drive, had his leg stump knocked out of the ground. Out of 66 runs scored for the first wicket Massie had made no fewer than 55, his splendid hitting having quite altered the appearance of the match. He made his runs at the rate of exactly one a minute, his figures being nine fours, two threes, three twos, and seven singles. No one could have played pluckier or more spirited cricket. Now came a remarkable turn in favour of England. Bonner went in and Ulyett took the ball from Mr. Steel. The wisdom of the change was quickly proved, for with the score at 70 a very fast ball from the Yorkshireman sent Bonner's middle stump clean out of the ground. Murdoch then joined Bannerman, but before another run had been scored the latter hit a ball into mid-off's hands. Horan became Murdoch's partner, and Peate resumed in place of Ulyett, Mr. Hornby changing bowling just now with consummate judgment, according to the different styles of the batsmen. Peate

Grace, who hit Boyle past point for two, and was immediately afterwards out to an easy catch at mid-off. He had played a capital innings of 32. With exactly 32 runs wanted to win Mr. Lyttelton faced Mr. Lucas. Mr. Lyttelton played Spofforth to leg for four, and one or two singles made it 20 to win. Mr. Lyttelton was clean bowled by Spofforth. Then followed the succession of disasters detailed above, the colonists finally winning by seven runs at a quarter to six o'clock.

Bowling analysis:—

	Overs.	Maidens.	Runs.	Wickets.
Spofforth	28	15	44	7
Garrett	7	2	10	0
Boyle	20	11	19	3

Spofforth bowled a no ball.

Score—

First innings.	Australians.	Second innings.	
Bannerman c Grace b Peate	9	c Studd b Barnes	13
Massie b Ulyett	1	b Steel	55
Murdoch b Peate	13	run out	29
Bonnor b Barlow	1	b Ulyett	2
Horan b Barlow	3	c Grace b Peate	2
Giffen b Peate	2	c Grace b Peate	0
Blackham c Grace b Barlow	17	c Lyttelton b Peate	7
Garrett c Read b Peate	10	not out	2
Boyle b Barlow	2	b Steel	0
Jones c Barnes b Barlow	0	run out	6
Spofforth not out	4	b Peate	0
Extras	1	Extras	6
Total	63	Total	122

First innings.	England.	Second innings.	
Barlow c Bannerman b Spofforth	11	b Spofforth	0
W. G. Grace b Spofforth	4	c Bannerman b Boyle	32
Ulyett st Blackham b Spofforth	26	c Blackham b Spofforth	11
A. P. Lucas c Blackham b Boyle	9	b Spofforth	5
Hon. A. Lyttelton c Blackham b Spofforth	2	b Spofforth	12
C. T. Studd b Spofforth	0	not out	0
Read not out	19	b Spofforth	0
Barnes b Boyle	5	c Murdoch b Boyle	2
A. G. Steel b Garrett	14	c and b Spofforth	0
A. N. Hornby b Spofforth	2	b Spofforth	9
Peate c Boyle b Spofforth	0	b Boyle	2
Extras	9	Extras	4
Total	101	Total	77

GENTLEMEN OF LINCOLNSHIRE v. GENTLEMEN OF NOTTINGHAMSHIRE.

First innings.	Lincolnshire.	Second innings.	
P. H. Toynbee c Foljambe b Milner	6	b Miles	0
W. Toynbee c Barlow b Milner	4	not out	20
S. F. Hood b Oates	30	b Miles	2
J. R. Sutton b Oates	5	st Dalpin b Miles	6
F. O. Amcotts c Milner b Oates	0		
Rev. C. Harrison run out	3	not out	22
A. G. West b Hutchinson	16		
G. W. Cole c Hewitt b Milner	19	b Miles	0
L. D. Marsden b Oates	25		
W. Parke not out	22	lbw, b Barlow	15
M. Sidthorp b Barlow	6		
S. Barrett b Mills	11		
Extras	23	Extras	7
Total	162	Total	66

Nottinghamshire.	
W. C. Oates b Cole	119
W. C. Tonge b West	43
S. Miles b Parke	23
Huntsman b Cole	6
Foljambe c Barrett b Cole	4
Milner b Cole	11
Barlow b Parke	18
Machin b Amcotts	5
Rev. —. Miles b Cole	7
Hutchinson not out	56
Hewitt c Toynbee b Parke	20
Rev. —. Dalpin c Sutton b Cole	13
Extra	12
Total	337

LANCASHIRE v. MIDDLESEX.

To the Editor of the Manchester Guardian.

Sir,—I was surprised to see in the report of this match that no comment at all was made on the decision which gave Mr. C. T. Studd stumped out in the second innings. I do not think that any good cricketer who was in a position to see well at the time could possibly have come to any other conclusion but that the decision was a most incorrect one. There are, of course, numbers of cases in which opinions may differ as to whether a player be in or out, as, for instance, in the case of Mr. G. B. Studd in this very innings, who was given run out by the same umpire, though he himself and a number of other people thought he was decidedly in; but when the point is a fine one it is only fair to suppose that the umpire ought to be the best judge as to whether a batsman be in or out. In Mr. C. T. Studd's case, however, I do not think there could be two opinions among those who were in a position to see. The bat was grounded fully one second before the ball was knocked off. I have taken a keen interest in cricket all my life, and was watching Mr. Studd's play most carefully. I was in an excellent position to see, and I don't think I ever in the whole course of my life saw so incorrect a decision given. I was surrounded by some very warm partisans of the Lancashire team, and the universal feeling round me seemed one of great regret at such a decision being given. There is no doubt that the decision gave great dissatisfaction to the Middlesex eleven, and also to some warm supporters of the Lancashire team. I don't mean to say for a moment that the umpire gave what he knew to be an unfair decision, but still I maintain most positively that the decision was a most incorrect one, and I know, too, that many good cricketers are of the same opinion.—I remain, &c.,

FRED. G. MILNER.

LANCASHIRE CRICKET.

To the Editor of the Manchester Guardian.

Sir,—I have this morning perused with very great amusement the letter signed "H. J. Brown." I am of opinion that that gentleman can have had but very little experience in *cricketing, especially in the bowling department*, and that he is therefore not qualified to set himself up as a judge of the game. Crossland's averages in the principal matches of the season are fully equal to those of any other English fast bowler, and his style of delivery, though undoubtedly peculiar, has never been challenged by an umpire. Mr. Brown's suggestion that "an umpire has to get the best part of his living by umpiring, and is therefore not likely to object," is the most absurd remark ever uttered on this question, and one not likely to be endorsed by the cricketers of to-day. I hope that next season we shall again see Crossland in such form as he has shown during the past season.—I am, &c. ONE INTERESTED.

Eccles, August 29, 1882.

To the Editor of the Manchester Guardian.

Sir,—Kindly give me space for a few words in reply to H. J. Brown's letter in Saturday's issue. I don't know if he forms his ideas on talks and rumours, but he is very wide of the mark in most of his statements. He says, "It appears Crossland has not been selected to play for his 'county.'" I presume he means "country," as every cricketer knows he has been playing for his "county" all the season. Again, he says "that it is rumoured that the Australians would object to him on the ground of his unfair delivery." Why did not they object to him when he played against them for Lancashire and Liverpool? Not having done so then, can they do so now? With regard to him being "heavily punished" by them I think the letter signed "Impaul" in to-day's *Guardian* clearly proves the contrary, as 14 wickets for 135 runs in the two matches is quite the opposite to "heavy punishment." H. J. Brown "maintains" that Crossland's delivery is a "throw," and that "he gets his wickets by brute force." Who made H. J. Brown a judge of fair bowling? Is he more capable of forming a judgment than "the powers that be" at the Marylebone Club, Crossland having played at Lord's several times without being objected to. Again he says "he was surprised Mr. Hornby was not in the team," and yet he goes on to say "he does not think him worth his place." Perhaps he will be more surprised now he knows that Mr. Hornby is not only in the team, but is captain of it. Unfortunately Mr. Hornby's batting has not been quite so brilliant this year for his county, he having played his best innings outside his county engagements. If H. J. Brown will go carefully into Mr. Hornby's analysis for all the first-class matches he has played in I think the result will prove to him that Mr. Hornby still can "wield the willow" with great effect, and that no team can be representative without the popular Lancashire captain.—I am, &c. AN OLD CRICKETER.

Manchester, August 28, 1882.

THE FRENCH ATLANTIC CABLE.

On Monday morning the Telegraph Construction Maintenance Company's steamer Scotia, engaged pairing the French Atlantic cable, put back into mouth from the Atlantic the second time in two mo When, in May last, the Scotia left London she h board some 4,000 tons of cable stored in her for aft tanks. About 1,000 miles from Brest the cabl connected, and the vessel returned to within 400 of Brest to make good "a fault." Upon this work taken in hand it was found that the American end cable was again broken, and testings demonstrated the accident had occurred 20 miles east of the or breakdown. Buoying the cable, the Scotia came Plymouth, shipped coals and provisions, and left. cable off Brest was spliced, and the Scotia sough new fault. This was discovered, but considerable t was experienced in the endeavours to repair it. cable has several times chafed at the bottom and p with the result that, after a month's work, affairs r practically as before. One end is now buoyed; the is at the bed of the sea. During the operations 140 of cable have been paid out.

THE LOSS OF THE ROYAL GEORG

Yesterday was the hundredth anniversary of the greatest disasters in the annals of the British the loss of the Royal George. On the 29th of A 1782, the ship was careening at Spithead, and m her guns being on one side and some of her upper being open, a sudden gust of wind caught the and the catastrophe is only too well known—th went down "with all her crew complete." Nearly 60 perished, including Admiral Kempenfeldt. Captain horn, who escaped, was subsequently tried by court-m for negligence in the careening operation, but w quitted. The Royal George was a fine ship of 108 and was the principal vessel in Lord Howe's fleet. schemes were subsequently proposed for raisin vessel, but none were adopted. In 1839 some po of the vessel and its cargo were detatched by gunp and brought to the surface, but except for that di ance it still remains embedded where it sank.

A Press Association telegram says the buri the remains of C. Kickham, one of Stevens's " Executive" was attended with significant circumst The remains were removed to Thurles on Sunday but the Archbishop of Cashel's permission to allo coffin to rest in the Cathedral during the nigh refused, and at Mullinahane next day no priest att to perform the funeral ceremony.

DESTRUCTIVE STORM AT HASTINGS.—A vi storm visited Hastings yesterday, inflicting damage. Eight large ropewalks, with their co were entirely swept away, and others were under by the action of the waves. Large portions of the were also carried away, and the roads near the for were rendered impassable in places through the sweeping over them.

Sir Erasmus Wilson, at a meeting of Governors of the Margate Royal Sea Bathing Infir on Monday, handed over the key of the magnificen wing of the infirmary, to be named the Erasmus wing, which he has built at a cost of over £30,000. wing includes two large day-rooms and four dormi each to contain 16 beds, with a swimming bath c of containing 15,000 gallons of sea water.

HIGH TIDE AT SOUTHPORT.—Yesterday noon the tide at Southport rose to a great heigh washed over the north end of the promenade wit siderable force. The boats in the channel were in d of being washed away, but only one has been repor having been taken from her moorings. The pier s well. It was computed that at high water there not have been fewer than 10,000 persons on the menade watching the tide.

The *Morning Post* states that on Friday last Charlotte Cadogan, daughter of Mr. Frederick and Adelaide Cadogan, met with an accident which c her to be dreadfully burnt. For some hours her lif despaired of, but she at last rallied, and under th of Mr. Oscar Clayton and Mr. Heckman is, it is hoped, in a more favourable state. Miss Cad recovery, if happily it takes place, must be accomp by severe suffering, and will be of long duration.

REDUCTION OF FARM RENTS IN FORFARSHI Agricultural depression, as evidenced by falling re still felt in Forfarshire. The farm of Longbank Forfar, has just been let at £375. Twenty years was let at £500, and latterly was held at £450. Lad another farm on the Logie estate, has just been £285. The previous rent was £420. Rather tha mit to the reductions, the Right Hon. W. E. Baxt taken into his own hands a large farm on his est Kincaldrum, and Sir Thomas Monro, of Linderti followed the same course in respect of one of his farms, the Kirkton of Kingoldrum.

THE MORTALITY RETURNS.—The Regi General reports that the annual rate of mortalit week, in 28 of the largest English towns, average per thousand of their aggregate population. The Derby was 13; Bristol, 15; Halifax and Londo Birkenhead and Brighton, 19; Cardiff, Norwich, L ter, and Portsmouth, 21; Sheffield and Bradford Blackburn, 23; Bolton, 24; Huddersfield, 25; Ol Plymouth, Sunderland, and Preston, 27; Liverpool tingham, Newcastle, and Leeds, 28; Manchester Birmingham, 29; Wolverhampton, 31; Salford, 32; 34. The rate in Edinburgh was 16, Glasgow 1 Dublin 23.

SHOCKING AFFAIR IN BROUGHTON.—A half-past five on Monday evening, a man named Gerrald, 67 years of age, living at 18, Thompson-s Broughton, entered the Irwell Inn, Broughton Bridg proceeded to the bar parlour. He called for some to drink, and was served by the waiter. About a qu past seven the discharge of a pistol was heard, a going into the bar parlour the landlord found Gerrald had shot himself with a pistol. His righ was completely blown off. Dr. Pinder was at once for, and on the arrival of that gentleman's assi (Mr. Williams) Gerrald was taken to the Salford Hospital and Dispensary. The man was still alive y day, but in a very critical condition. The lan states that Gerrald was perfectly sober when he w the Irwell Inn.

THE NEW KEEPER OF THE CROWN JEW Major General George Dean-Pitt, C.B., upon whom Majesty has been pleased to confer the appointme Keeper of the Jewels in the Tower of London, place of the late Colonel John Cox Gawler, was about the year 1821, and entered the army in 1839, obtained a lieutenancy in the 80th Regiment in became captain in 1849, was promoted to major in lieutenant colonel in 1865, and colonel 1870. In 18 raised, organised, and trained the Victorian Volu Force, and on the renewal of the war in New Zeal 1863 he was commissioned by the Colonial Governme raise local corps to aid the troops. In a very short tim succeeded in raising upwards of 2,000 men, for w service he was promoted to an unattached majority. the end of 1863 he was appointed assistant ...

ENING STANDARD, TUESDAY, AUGUST 29, 1882.

TO-DAY'S POLICE.

BOW-STREET.

...an, giving the name of George Webb, aged 27, ...ing himself as an interpreter, was charged with ... placing himself at Charing-cross and exposing ...unds and deformities, for the purpose of obtain-...ns, and with assaulting the police. —About three ...on Monday afternoon the Prisoner was seen by ...a, the Mendicity Society's officer, to place himself ...orway at Charing-cross. Seeing himself watched ...he pulled up his coat sleeve and exposed ...ot from the wrist to the elbow of his right arm, ...hich blood was issuing. His fingers had been ...ated. He was seen to receive money, and then ...went up to him, and asked him to go to the ...g-cross Hospital. He refused, but with the ...ce of Police-constable 33 A B he was conveyed ...I transpired that he had been taken there a few ...previously by Police-constable Honour, 17, ...whose attention had been drawn to ...in Lincoln's-inn-fields, where he had ex-...his arm in a similar manner, and had ...himself to the ground as if he were in ...On his way to the hospital he pretended to have ...of fits. Upon arriving there his arm was attended ...erupon he pulled off the bandage and threw it ...surgeon's face. In consequence of this the ...ties declined to admit him on the second occasion, ...was taken to King-street Police-station, and ...uently by the advice of the divisional surgeon to ...dmaier Hospital. His arm was again bandaged, ...he was being taken back to the police-station he ...very violent, tried to tear the bandages off ...and also assaulted a constable by kicking him ...verily on one of his legs. He was then charged, ...was found he was drunk. Mr. Vaughan said he ...are some inquiries made about the Prisoner, as ...could win the result of accidents of course in ...ht that it should be attended to, but if it had ...aised by some other means to excite compassion ...cene deserved no pity. From what he had ...he was disposed to think that the Prisoner was ...ll desirous for recovery. —He was remanded to ...ase of Detention for the surgeon there to report ...case.

WORSHIP-STREET.

...Tythe, a dealer, was charged, on remand, with ...been concerned in stealing two cases of books, ...perty of Messrs. Pickford and Co., the carriers, ...he height of the 11th inst., a constable of the G-...o, on duty in Tabernacle-row, saw two men ...ig a barrow, and finding that he was looking at ...rew it up at the door of a doctor's stable, and ...e Prisoner speaking loudly to the other man, ...im to go near the public-house close by, ...all the stablemen to get the keys. This ...went off, but did not return. The con-...tten went to the Prisoner, who was standing ...rom the barrow, and asked him what the sacks ...barrow contained. The Prisoner said, " Corn, ...a doctor's horse." The constable, however, ...to look, but the Prisoner refused to return to ...ro-r, and when the constable pressed it, ran ...Chase was given; the Prisoner struck at the ...le with a piece of iron, and the constable drew ...I and tipped the Prisoner, who then arrest-...The sacks were found to contain 123 pairs of ...which subsequently proved to have been stolen ...ssrs. Pickford, and formed part of two cases ...e consigned by merchants in London to customers ...country. The cases were stolen from Messrs. ...d's, but how or in what way could not be traced. ...al evidence was given as to the possession and ...hip of the goods, which were valued at about 40l. ...and it was also shown that a sum of 7l. 10s. in ...ssides silver and copper money, was found on the ...r. He applied that might be given up to ...t, alleging that it was her money, given him to ...svent-garden Market. —Mr. Beard opposed the ...tion, and Mr. Saxtby paid the judge at the trial ...order it to be applied towards the expenses of the ...tion. —The Prisoner was committed for trial.

HAMMERSMITH.

...am Newell and John Pooley, a coal-dealer, ...in Hammersmith, were charged with furious ...and causing damage to a bath chair, the pro-...r a lady named Jamieson. —On Monday after-...rs. Jamieson was riding in the bath chair on the ...t in the Grove, Hammersmith, when the ...cabs came along in a van. Newell driving ...fast. The van, which was driven on ...pavement, caught the wheel of the ...chair and damaged it. The van then ...along the Beadon-road, and Pooley was seen ...the horse with a whip. A constable called ...Prisoners to stop, but they took no notice and ...n, the horse going at the rate of ten miles an ...The constable accosted a cab and followed ...he van, which was stopped in the Kensington-...It was proved that Newell was drunk and ...Pooley had been drinking.—The Prisoner ...said the horse and van belonged to ...The horse was in the habit of going to ...wharf in the Grove, and while they were ...it turned sharply round the corner, and the van ...n to the pavement. —Mr. Sheil said he had a ...med to send the Prisoners to gaol, as they might ...lled the lady, though the bath-chair had no right ...the pavement. He fined each Prisoner 40s., ...dered Pooley to pay 12s., the amount of the ...e, in addition; both to be imprisoned for one ...in default.

CLERKENWELL.

...ries Frederick Treherne, refusing his address and ...ion, was charged with burglariously breaking ...a house, No. 44, St. Augustin's-road, Kentish ...and stealing therefrom two coats, a silver spoon, ...schaum pipe, and other articles, the property of ...er. Ellen R. Winter, 28, a married woman, ...nd-street, Camden Town, was charged with ...ng the property, knowing it to have been stolen. ...traced by the police that during the past fort-...eveml small burglaries have been committed in ...orthern suburbs of London. On Saturday the ...ner was found at an early hour in the ...ing in some enclosed premises near the ...ator's house; which had previously been ...into. He was taken into custody and ...st before the magistrate at the inst. The prisoner were ...t by Detective-sergeants Miller and Allcock, of ...division, who on searching the premises found ...'roecutor's stolen property, and a number of ...s which were believed to be the proceeds of six or ...other burglaries. It was stated that all the pro-...can be seen on application at the Kentish Town ...station.—The Prisoner Winter accounted for the ...sion of the property by saying that her brother ...ft it, having purchased it at a public sale.—Both ...ers were remanded for further inquiries.

MANSION HOUSE.

...rles Moorhouse, a printer's labourer, was charged, ...mand, with a serious assault upon his wife, Esther. ...ppeared that the Prisoner and his wife had, at ...

THIS DAY'S CRICKET.

ENGLAND V. AUSTRALIA.

To everyone interested in cricket, the details of yesterday's cricket at the Oval must by this time be thoroughly familiar, and it is needless to go over the same ground again. Briefly, it may be said that the wicket was very difficult, the bowling surprisingly fine, and the batting very nervous and uncertain. It has often been said that high-class batting goes for very little on a bad wicket, and we certainly think that two ordinary country teams on the same ground and against the same bowling would have made as many runs as were scored by the picked Elevens of England and Australia. As readers will readily remember, an innings was completed on each side, Australia scoring 63 and England 101. Thus the day closed with an advantage to England of 38 runs.

TWENTY-PAST TWELVE.

Rain fell heavily between half-past nine and half-past ten, and the original intention of commencing play before twelve o'clock had to be given up. It is generally felt that everything will depend upon the ground. If the wicket should remain easy for a couple of hours the Australians will have an innings advantage, as it is sure to be terribly difficult in the latter part of the day, unless indeed there come more rain. By ten minutes past twelve the fieldsmen were in their places, and a minute or so later the second in-nings of Australia was commenced by Bannerman and Massie, to the bowling of Barlow (pavilion end) and Ulyett. In the first over Bannerman hit Barlow fora couple of twos, and then Massie drove Ulyett for three, the ball being finely returned and the wicket very smartly put down. Having got to the opposite wicket, Massie cut Barlow for four, and played the same bowler to square-leg for three. At this point our report left. Score, 14 for no wicket.

TWENTY TO ONE

Two singles were made, and then Massie hit Ulyett round to sharp leg for four. Another single followed, and Massie sent Barlow to square leg for another four. In this way the score reached 28, and a double change of bowl-ing was tried, Peate going on at the Gasworks end in place of Ulyett, and Mr. C. T. Studd taking the ball from Barlow. Peate bowled a maiden, but Massie at once drove Mr. Studd for four—a splendid hit down to the Stand by the right of the Pavilion. Just after this Massie drove Peate for four, making 34. Massie then hit Peate for another four, and the balance of runs on the first innings was hit off without the loss of a wicket. Massie has made 33.

TWO O'CLOCK (LONDON TIME).

Massie now drove Mr. Studd splendidly for four, and Bannerman cut Peate twice for two. At 47 Barnes was put on in the place of Mr. Studd, and off his first ball Massie was missed at long off by Mr. Lucas—a mistake which might have cost England no end of trouble. At the time of the let off, Massie had made 38, and just afterwards he drove Peate to the on for four. With the score at 56, Mr. Steel was tried at Peate's end, he being the sixth bowler who had gone on in about three quarters of an hour. Massie hit him for two twos and a four, and then in jumping out to drive had his leg stump knocked out of the ground. Out of 66 runs scored for the first wicket, Massie had made no fewer than 55, his splendid hitting having quite altered the appearance of the match. He made his runs at the rate of exactly one a minute, his figures being nine fours, two threes, three twos and seven singles. General applause greeted his retirement, and the cheering was thoroughly deserved, for no one could have played pluckier or more spirited cricket. One wicket for 66. Now came a remarkable turn in favour of England; Boonor went in, and Ulyett took the ball from Mr. Steel. The wisdom of the change was quickly proved, for with the score at 70 a very fast ball from the Yorkshire-man sent Bonnor's middle stump clean out of the ground. Murdoch then joined Bannerman, but before another run had been scored, the latter hit a ball into mid-off's hands. Three wickets for 70 was very different to one for 66, and the English Eleven looked delighted. Horan became Murdoch's partner, and Peate resumed in place of Ulyett, the English bowling just now being charged with consummate judg-ment, according to the different styles of the batsmen. Peate bowled a long hop, which Murdoch hit to leg for four, and then off two successive balls from the same bowler Horan and Giffen were caught at point. Four and five for 79. These disasters for the Austra-lians were naturally received with enthusiastic cheers. Blackham joined Murdoch, and at once hit Peate to leg for four. A bye went for the same number, and with various small bits the score reached 99. Then at about ten minutes to two; rain stopped the game, which will not be resumed until after luncheon. The Australians are 61 runs to the good with five wickets to fall. Score :—

AUSTRALIA.

A. C. Bannerman, c Grace, b Peate	9
H. H. Massie, b Ulyett	1
W. L. Murdoch, b Peate	13
G. J. Bonnor, b Barlow	1
T. Horan, b Barlow	2
G. Giffen, b Peate	2
J. M'C. Blackham , c Grace, b Barlow	17
T. W. Garrett, c Read, b Peate	10
H. F. Boyle, b Barlow	2
S. P. Jones, c Barnes, b Barlow	0
F. R. Spofforth, not out	4
Bye	1

THIS DAY'S SPORTING.

HUNTINGDON RACES.

HUNTINGDON, TUESDAY.

The KIMBOLTON WELTER HANDICAP of 5 sovs each for ... starters, with 15l. added ; winners extra ; One mile. ...

Mr. Leopold de Rothschild's PETTALLION, by Hambout—...tum Gish, 4 yrs, 9st 9lb .... W adell ... (1) Mr. G. Chetwynd's THE GILDER, 4 yrs, 7st 11lb..... Wood ... (2) Lord Calthorpe's RUNNYMEDE, 4 yrs, 7st 9lb...... Lynham ... (3) ... Count F. de Lagrange's CORDON, 3 yrs, 6st 11lb ... Morris ...

Betting —7 to 4 agst the first even on Kimbolton, 6 to 2 ...first 4 to 1 agst Petterlion, 100 to 30 agst The Gilder, 10 to 1 agst ...Pawtie. The first ran away like a steam company, but on settling...this piaces The Gilder drew clear of the others, of whom Petter-...lion was the whippier in two, where fairly in the line for home, he ... came away and won easily by a length and a half ; bad third.

RAMSAY PLATE.

Serge	1
Florence	2
Radanne	3

Also ran :—Dabra and Terror.

PROGRAMME FOR 5TH DAY.

3 0—The FITZWILLIAM SELLING STAKES. Peel Course ...
  • Runnymeae, 6 yrs
  • Coniston, 4 yrs

3 30—The PEEL HANDICAP. Five furlongs.
  • 2 Maghiun, 5yr 1 | 13 Kaldaborn, 4 yr | 7 The Donner...
  • 6 Baronmfm. 5yr | 7 Humble, 3yrs | ...
  • 9 Brenhmore, a | 12 Maid of | 7 Knrths, 5yrs
  • 4 Morella, 3yr | ... | 9 Dutch Agnes, 3yr
  • 5 Tower and | 22 Effie, 4 yrs | 3 yrs
  • ... | 5 Quest, 6 yrs | 2 Lennel, 4yrs
  • 8 Squire, 4 yrs | 4 Fontin, 4 yrs | 5 Nuremere, 3yr
  • 6 Fernwind Lad, | 1 Beantie, 3 yr | 9 Candy May, 3y
  • 4 yrs | 7 Missner, 5yrs | 6 Lady Mag, 3y
  • 5 Petterlean, 4 y | 7 Beatus, 4 yrs | 7 Flywer, 6yrs
  • 9 Scottilonne, 5 | 6 D ly Perkinot | 3 yrs
  • 7 Ti Danan, 5 yrs | ... | ...

4 0—The PORTHOLME CUP. Five furlongs, straight.
  • 10 4 Lady Chelma- | 9 5 Tower and | 9 Sunnistan. 3 yr
  • 4 yrs | 7 Cordon. 4 yr | Beagul, aged
  • 9 Fenctus, 4 yr | 3 Psycho, 3 yrs | 11 Lars, 2 yrs
  • ... | 6 Korlla, 3 yrs | 11 Constanttn, 3 y

4 30—The APETHORPE SELLING STAKES. Five furlongs ...and 120 yards.
  • a Cumberland, 4 yrs | 3 Dickins, 7 yrs
  • ... | Each to be sold for 50l

5 0—The HINCHINGBROOK PLATE. Six furlongs.
  • 9 1 Dwarow | 8 9 Persius | 5 6 Lad Eche-...
  • 7 9 Highland | 5 Thereord | ... | quar—Vax-...
  • Chief | 8 The Dundn | Star Bell
  • 1 Gloucester | ... | 8 Moity
  • 4 Poluria | 5 Orlens | 5 Homespup
  • 4 Queen of the | 9 Creil Craven | 6 Musitle
  • 6 Holly | 5 Druid | 8 Ferra Atma
  • 9 Erminie | 9 Dennno | 9 S P by Adven-...
  • 9 Father Frost | 5 Abaco | turer—Marie
  • 9 Bla lisle | 6 Madame Gar- | Galatea
  • ... | fleld | 4 Delinde
  • 8 Suterah | 9 S Lawn

HUNTINGDON, MONDAY NIGHT.

The following horses have arrived :—Carnillan, Oneta, Cumber-land, Cider, Maglcian, Morcedo, Merlt, Nicosia, Oatmeal, Suart, Sunnyburn, Terrier.

A large number of horses engaged are trai ed at Newmarket, and will arrive to-morrow (Tuesday) morning.

ADDITIONAL ARRIVALS Lowing1 Lad, Ermine, Maid of Orleans, Enthusiasm, Huntbason, Dunno, Tower and Sword, Florence, Lociot, Perisonu, Lady Chelmsford, Effie, Minster, Sperts, Psyche, Lady May, Vesper Bell Slly, Polaris, Kuhleborn, Lende, Radanne, Salrep, Lava.

WEYMOUTH MEETING.

PROGRAMME FOR THIS DAY.

2 0—A HUNTERS' HURDLE-RACE PLATE. Two miles, ...over eight flights of hurdles.
  • 2 Entomaria, 5 y | La Sienna, aged | Gluton, 6 yrs
  • a Danlease of Glou- | Bitter aged | Quickstep, aged
  • cester, aged | Stargazer, aged | Stargazer, 4 yrs
  • Arkamo, 4 yrs

2 35—The SELLING HURDLE RACE. Two miles.
  • a Sidonus, aged (901) a Matfort, 5 yrs 60l) a Glondorah(c4l 000
3 10—A HURDLE-RACE HANDICAP. Two miles.
  • 7 Ruther, aged | a 11 11 Lady | Jaro a 15 (2? Miles May,
  • 12 Wetminster, | ... | flute One- | 3 yrs
  • 1 yrs | ... | half aged
  • 12 Quadroon, | a 17 Roanof Kan- | a 10 7 Kaipool, 3 yr
  • ... | tnek, aged | ...

3 45—A SELLING HUNTERS' HURDLE-RACE PLATE. Two ...miles over eight flights of hurdles.
  • a Duchess of Glou- | Fortuna, 4 yrs | a Regalia, 4 yrs
  • cester, aged | a Glutton, 6 yrs | a Isaac o Kan, 5 yr
  • Bitter, aged | a Stargazer, 4 yr | a Dantry, 4 yrs
  • 2 Entomaria, 5 y | ... | a Hase Hill, 4 yrs
  • a Marsehee, 4 yrs | Riwha, aged | Vagrant, 4 yrs
  • a Newhridge II., 5 y | a Farina, 4 yrs | ...
  • A LOCAL HUNTERS' RACE did not fill.

Tower and Sword having been improperly entered in the Perl Handicap, the Stewards have decided he cannot run.

LATEST SCRATCHINGS.

OUT OF ALL ENGAGEMENTS AT HUNTINGDON.—Castillion and Red King.

OUT OF GREAT YORKSHIRE HANDICAP.—Purosbeary and Bonaparte.

OUT OF FEVERIL OF THE PEAK PLATE, DERBY.—Red Hose. OUT OF DERBY ENGAGEMENTS.—Alltohate and Hornpipe. OUT OF DONCASTER NURSERAL DERBY.—Santfotaol.

THIS DAY'S CITY INTELLIGENCE.

QUARTER-PAST ELEVEN.

Owing to the progress of the Settlement, business in the Stock Markets is very quiet, and the only movement of importance is a further improvement in Turkish Bonds. Consols are steady; at 99½ to 99¾ for money, and 99½ to 99¾ for the account. Among Home Railways, Metropolitan is ½ higher, and Brighton Deferred, Chatham Ordinary, and South-Eastern A ½ but Sheffield Deferred shows a decline of ⅜, and Caledonian, North-Western, and North Eastern of ¼. In Foreign Bonds, Turkish A, B, and C have risen; ditto Six per Cents. of 1865, 1869, and 1873 ¼ and ditto General Debt and Italian Five per Cents. ⅛ but Egyptian Unified, Domain, and Daira are ¼ lower, and Russian of 1873 ⅝. Among American Railways, Wabash Preferred Shares show a rise of 1, Illinois ⅛ and Erie ½; but Pennsylvania have receded ½.

It is announced that the half-yearly interest due September 1st on the Charlow-Kremenenberg (now Charkoff and Nicolajeff) Railroad Loan for 1,716,000l., guaranteed by the Imperial Russian Government will, together with the Bonds drawn for repayment, be paid on and after that date at the counting house of Messrs. J. Henry Schröder and Co.

The total traffic receipts of the Manchester, Sheffield, and Lincolnshire Railway Company's railways and canals (exclusive of joint-lines), from the 1st July to August 20, 1882, amounted to 253,129l., as compared with 255,061l. from 1st July to August 21, 1881. The total expenses, including rents, tolls, duty, &c. (exclu-sive of joint lines), from 1st July to August 20, 1882, were 133,180l., as against 125,521l. from 1st July to August 21, 1881. The receipts and expenses for the corresponding period of 1881 include one day more than the current period. In order to make a correct comparison for an equal number of days, the figures for the one day should be added to those above shown for 1882, which may be estimated at 8250l. for receipts, and 2600l. for expenses. The receipts and expenses in the current period include those of the Trent and Ancholme Line, which is now vested in the Manchester, Sheffield, and Lincolnshire Railway. Allowing for the extra day, the receipts show an increase of 22,318l., and the expen-...

THE DAILY TELEGRAPH, WEDNESDAY, AUGUST 30,

voice of Graziella pre-
that her father's boat
ks, and demanding help.
ie main was "laughing"
serve "None but a mad-
To launch a boat in such
themselves. In despair
zo: "Thou hast often
save my father, and I
man is not surprised
me thy cross as true
ceives the bauble and
follows, watched by all
visible to us; watched,
for the convent bell
ious women are heard
to which the villagers
keeps all informed as to
ventura. At length the
," makes further prayer
dent ends with "three
musical treatment of
oticeable for sustained,
d vigour. There is no
ers on the one hand,
meness on the other.
the chorus when
help is measured in
poser intends here, per-
indifference of an un-
h the keen emotions of
ke. The "Miserere"
ribed as powerful. Its
elaborate, and the diffi-
on were assuredly not
tion of the bell, which
s in every bar. Sir
good a musician to be in
barrassed by his own
claims rank among dis-
ather rescued, Graziella
ankfulness, when Renzo
companied by Alonzo,
student. Graziella at
father with the claim
thus leading up to an
approved operatic style—
r her individual feeling
of a less lively emotion
Graziella is thankful,
ropaternal, Alonzo love-
pathetic. The piece is
e masses of vocal har-
om the entrance of the
however, by the lighter
nd the charm of true

e second scene, Alonzo
gers at Procida, "held
loveliness of matchless
t she may yet be his.
vs—one which will fulfil
l be often heard apart
e is nothing in the work
than "When first this
r more certain of wide
ended, Graziella enters,
urge his suit, first of all,
feminine weakness, de-
"a student of humble
th the Count Lavagna."
surprise in store. We
l the vow that binds her
nit a moment later that
ee, would be Alonzo's.
airly sprung upon us, as
o happens to overhear
bout to go away despair-
io in which he pleads,
etimes when the sun
ocean;" Graziella on
breathe his name
time of day; while
with "wild commotion,"
the ruin of his hopes;
ng forward to a better
l realms above." This
numbers the work con-
written, full of expres-
very page the stamp of
its close, Alonzo is about
steps from his hiding-
t obliging manner, that
iella's heart he will not
ng to seek death on the
irit he formally releases
vow, and, while the
e melody used when
he generously observes,
ay'st thou glide smiling
." Naturally the lovers
away happy, leaving
from his breast and be
'The shipwrecked heart"
some out of the cantata,
er its purpose sufficiently
t invite particular obser-
now enters, learns from
ed, and grants his most
t the wedding of Gra-
t take place. But the
nother must first be ob-
Venice. The agreeable
l to anything, offers to
ther before seeking death
brings on a quartet
racters, after which the
ilors' chorus, "Up with
artet—"Sweet Graziella,
btless be popular, since it

ziella), Madame Patey (Abbess), Mr. Lloyd (Renzo), Mr. King (Alonzo), and Mr. Campion (Zennaro). In such hands they were safe, and the audience applauded one and all, demanding an encore for the "Shipwrecked Heart," (Mr. Lloyd), and "Our lives are like the stormy ocean" (Madame Patey). No less honourable, if less honoured, were Mr. King's delivery of "When first this lonely shore I sought," and Madame Roze's execution of "Lovers' vows." At the close Sir Julius received hearty applause from every part of the hall. The second part of the programme contained a number of miscellaneous selections, conspicuous amongst which were Mr. F. Cowen's "Language of the Flowers," "Deeper and deeper still," capitally sung by Mr. Maas, and warmly applauded, "Ocean, thou mighty monster" (Miss Anna Williams), and the overture to "Benvenuto Cellini."

ENGLAND V. AUSTRALIA.

The match at Kennington Oval yesterday ended, not only in a surprise, but also in a scene of excitement scarcely, if ever, equalled on any cricket ground. Notwithstanding the threatening appearance with which the morning opened, such was the public interest awakened by the first day's play that by ten o'clock some thousands of persons were gathered at the enclosure, and as the day wore on the crowd increased until there were, it is believed, at the close of the match, not far from twenty-five thousand spectators; and assuredly it may be said that all the elements were present to sustain the interest in the play from the beginning to the end. We ventured yesterday to say that the Colonials had played an exceedingly uphill game with such spirit as to give fine proof of their quality, and that although the English team had 38 runs in hand on the first innings the issue was still an open one. How well the Australians deserved this praise was shown when they went in for their second innings. The wicket was even more decidedly against the batsman and in favour of the bowler than on the previous day. Nevertheless, our visitors nearly doubled their score, making 122 as against 63. There was, perhaps, some slight falling off in the English bowling. Barlow—who bowled almost the whole of the preceding afternoon with remarkable steadiness and success, taking five wickets for only 19 runs—was less effective, and even Peate did not succeed as he had in the first innings in the long succession of maiden overs which made his analysis so striking. Still, on the whole, the bowling was remarkably good, especially in the latter part of the Australian innings. It will be seen by the score that only three of the Colonials reached double figures, including Massie's fine achievement of 55, the highest individual total of the match. Two noteworthy incidents marked the Australian innings. The first of these showed the strictness with which the game was played. Murdoch and Jones were together, when the captain made a hit to short leg. Mr. Lyttelton, the wicket keeper, fielded, and threw in the ball, which was received by another member of the team and dropped at the wicket. The ball, however, was not "dead"—the wicket-keeper having for the moment only acted as fielder, and Jones, forgetting this important fact, left his ground, and Mr. Grace, observing the movement, instantly picked up the ball and removed the bails. There was some momentary complaining on the part of sympathisers with the Colonists, but no kind of protest was made, or was, indeed, possible. The second incident followed shortly afterwards, when Murdoch, having made a fine drive to the off, was attempting a second run—on the strength of the fact that Mr. Hornby, who was fielding, would be unable to throw in on account of an injury to his arm. This calculation proved unsound. Mr. Hornby passed the ball to Mr. C. T. Studd, who threw it to Mr. Lyttelton, and so very smartly closed the Australian captain's innings for an admirably played 29. A neater or more expeditious piece of fielding has rarely been seen.

In the end the whole Australian team was disposed of for 122 runs, thus leaving the home side 85 to win. This for one of the most perfect batting elevens the country could select seemed no great feat, and the odds were supposed to be largely in their favour. Dr. W. G. Grace and Mr. Hornby opened the innings, their appearance at the wickets being the signal for hearty cheering. Both played with considerable animation, but when the score had reached 15 the Lancashire captain was bowled by Spofforth for 9. Barlow, one of the steadiest batsmen in England, followed, but was immediately bowled also by "the demon," as he is called, for 0. Ulyett followed, and for a while the spell of the Colonial bowling seemed to have been broken. Runs came with fair rapidity; 20, 30, 40, 50 were successively exhibited on the board, and the hopes of an English triumph rose high. At length Ulyett gave a chance to Blackham, who never misses one, and Mr. A. P. Lucas took his place. There were thus three wickets down and 34 runs were required. But the overthrow of Ulyett was a great encouragement to the Australians, and when very soon afterwards Dr. Grace was caught by Bannerman at mid off—having made 32 out of a of making a little over 20 runs. It cannot be said that either side was favoured by luck. The wicket, which was moist at the outset but afterwards dried somewhat, was equally difficult for both. Except one apparently easy chance missed by Lucas, when Massie had scored 38, it could not be said that the contest was materially influenced in this direction. Indeed, so far as circumstances went, the Australians had most to withstand, as from the very beginning the chances against them seemed little short of overpowering. But they never desponded for an instant, and struggled to the end with a determination, a cheerfulness, and a coolness, withal, which extorts the highest admiration. Massie's innings of 55 was batted with a freedom and confidence which had no parallel on the other side, and his efforts were ably supplemented by those of Murdoch and Bannerman. None of the others, however, made a stand, and all were at length out for 122. The English bowling was not so successful as on the previous day, and the fielding was less close. When they assumed the defensive only Dr. W. G. Grace rose to the importance of the occasion, and he played in truly champion form for his 32. Spofforth's bowling, however, was simply marvellous, and the fielding was truly beyond praise. So fine, however, was the form shown by the visitors, and so well did they deserve their victory, that at the close they were accorded round after round of cheering by the multitude who were plainly disappointed by the result.

It was not till five minutes past twelve that play commenced, although the start had been fixed for half-past eleven. With 38 to put on before being on an equality with their antagonists, the Australians commenced their second innings with Massie and Bannerman. Barlow and Ulyett led off the bowling, and the batsmen quickly got to work. In fact, Barlow's very first delivery Bannerman cut for a couple. Massie, in response, drove the Sheffielder magnificently, but the hit only resulted in a 2, Maurice Read running a considerable distance in the out-field, and returning the ball with such precision that Bannerman was nearly run out. In the Lancashire representative's next over Massie cut a delivery in grand style to the boundary for 4, and soon afterwards driving the same bowler, the 20 went up at 12.30. Prior to this Massie despatched Ulyett to the leg boundary, and, although his associate was content with singles, the rate of scoring was evidently too fast for the English captain, who at 25 decided upon trying a different mode of attack, the two slow bowlers, Peate and Mr. Studd, superseding the fast performers. The Yorkshireman opened with a maiden over, but his *confrère* was not so fortunate, as from his first delivery Massie, continuing his brilliant hitting career, added another on-drive for 4. The next ball would most certainly have travelled for a like addition, but the Cantab just succeeded in stopping it, a circumstance which brought forth ringing cheers from the spectators. Hereabouts Peate, who had sent up two unproductive overs, was faced by Massie; but no sooner had this occurred than the Victorian lifted him to the on boundary. All this time Bannerman was comparatively inactive; still, at a quarter to one, his side had rubbed off the balance against them. At a terrific rate Massie went on hitting, and, after despatching Peate to the off for 4, he turned his attention to the other performer, and fairly mastered the bowling. Mr. Studd, after proving very expensive, at length gave way to Barnes at 47, and from the latter's very fast delivery Massie should have been caught deep behind the wicket by Mr. Lucas. At this period the Victorian had contributed 38, and his escape was all the more galling to the Englishmen, as he continued hitting away at a wonderfully fast pace. Twice in one over Bannerman cut Peate for two, and very rapidly the scores were raised to 56, when Mr. Steel superseded the Yorkshireman. As a set-off against the slow rate of scoring on Monday, when it took an hour and a half to make 36 runs, yesterday in two-thirds of that time the 60 was elevated, but this was all due to the efforts of Massie, who made 55 out of 66, and then, amidst a perfect outburst of applause, he was bowled leg-stump. On his retirement the partisans of the Australian were loud in their praises of his efforts, and really his innings was a fine one, consisting as it did of no fewer than nine 4's, two 3's, three 2's, and the rest singles. Bonnor came in first wicket down, and although Mr. Steel was bowling remarkably well, Mr. Hornby very wisely decided upon putting on Ulyett to the big hitter, who only just improved upon his opening exhibition, and was then clean bowled, centre stump, by As expected, his dismissal was the signal for a great outburst of English cheers, and when Bannerman fell at the same figure—70 for three—the demonstration was renewed again and again. Bannerman was caught at cover-point by Mr. Studd, and when he retired Murdoch and Horan became associated. Deciding upon another mode of attack to these batsmen, the English captain's judgment was soon again fully demonstrated, as, after Murdoch had sent Peate nearly square for 4, that bowler had the satisfaction of seeing Mr. Grace capture Horan and Giffen from two successive deliveries, standing close in at point. Thus it was that the fourth and fifth batsmen fell at 79, and as the first wicket did not fall until 66 runs had been added, the early hopes of the Colonials had been, as it were, in a few overs, dashed to the ground, the glorious uncertainty of the game never being more clearly demonstrated than on the present occasion. Blackham next came in to aid his captain, and immediately on his arrival he put a veto on the possibility of Peate performing the "hat trick" by getting that bowler's following delivery round to leg for 4. In response Murdoch, after being nearly bowled by Peate, got Barnes away for a single, and off-driving his *confrère* for one more. Next over four byes sent the 90 up at 1.45. Presently the Antipodean captain managed to cut Barnes in his well-known style for a trio; but, just as the scores denoted a single this side of the century, a shower caused an adjournment, lunch being partaken of in the meantime. During the interval it rained, but not much, and punctually at 2.45 play was resumed, the attendance at the time being about equal to that on the first day. Blackham, who had a total of seven to his credit, had first of all to oppose Peate, but in antagonising that performer he had met more than his match, as from the Yorkshireman's fourth delivery he was splendidly taken at the wicket low down by Mr. Lyttelton. Jones now issued forth, and on his arrival Barlow opposed the Antipodean captain. More successful than when he opened the innings, the Lancastrian started this time with a maiden over, but soon after this Murdoch caused the elevation of the third figure with a single. Replying to his captain, the new-comer hit Barlow neatly for a couple, and then the next ball he sent in a similar direction for double that number, Murdoch managed to drive Barlow to the on for a couple, and six balls subsequently he repeated the hit for one more, whereupon Mr. Steel

the bowling of Spofforth, who fairly justified his cognomen of "demon." Full score:

AUSTRALIA.

A. C. Bannerman, c Grace, b Peate	9	c Studd, b Barnes	13
H. H. Massie, b Ulyett	1	b Steel	55
W. L. Murdoch, b Peate	13	run out	29
G. J. Bonnor, b Barlow	1	b Ulyett	2
T. Horan, b Barlow	3	c Grace, b Peate	2
G. Giffen, b Peate	2	c Grace, b Peate	0
J. M'C. Blackham, c Grace, b Barlow	17	c Lyttelton, b Peate	7
T. W. Garrett, c Read, b Peate	10	not out	2
H. F. Boyle, b Barlow	2	b Steel	0
S. P. Jones, c Barnes, b Barlow	0	run out	6
F. R. Spofforth, not out	4	b Peate	0
B	1	B	6
Total	63	Total	122

ENGLAND.

Barlow, c Bannerman, b Spofforth	11	b Spofforth	0
Dr. W. G. Grace, b Spofforth	4	c Bannerman, b Boyle	32
Ulyett, st Blackham, b Spofforth	26	c Blackham, b Spofforth	11
A. P. Lucas, c Blackham, b Boyle	9	b Spofforth	5
Hon. A. Lyttelton, c Blackham, b Spofforth	2	b Spofforth	12
C. T. Studd, b Spofforth	0	not out	0
Read, not out	19	b Spofforth	0
Barnes, b Boyle	5	c Murdoch, b Boyle	2
A. G. Steel, b Garrett	14	c and b Spofforth	0
A. N. Hornby, b Spofforth	2	b Spofforth	9
Peate, c Boyle, b Spofforth	0	b Boyle	2
B 6, l b 2, n b 1	9	B 3, n b 1	4
Total	101	Total	77

ANALYSIS OF THE BOWLING.

AUSTRALIANS—First Innings.

	O.	M.	R.	W.		O.	M.	R.	W.
Peate	38	24	31	4	Barlow	31	22	19	5
Ulyett	9	5	11	1	A. G. Steel	2	1	1	0

Second Innings.

Barlow	13	5	27	0	Studd	4	1	9	0
Ulyett	6	2	10	1	Barnes	12	5	15	1
Peate	21	9	40	4	Steel	7	0	15	2

ENGLAND.—First Innings.

Spofforth	36.3	18	46	7	Boyle	19	7	24	2
Garrett	16	7	22	1					

Spofforth bowled a no ball.

Second Innings.

Spofforth	28	15	44	7	Boyle	20	11	19	3
Garrett	7	2	10	0					

Spofforth bowled a no ball.

Umpires—Thoms and Greenwood.

Immediately after the conclusion of the innings of the Australians, one of the spectators—whom it was afterwards ascertained was George Eber Spendler, of 191, Brook-street, Kennington—complained to a friend of feeling unwell, and left the seat he had for some time occupied. Scarcely had he done so when he fell to the ground, and blood commenced to flow freely from his mouth. He was at once conveyed to a room adjoining the Pavilion, where he was examined by several medical men, amongst whom was Dr. Jones, the president of the Surrey Cricket Club, who pronounced life extinct, the cause of death being attributed to a ruptured blood-vessel.

HANTS v. SUSSEX.

At Portsmouth, yesterday, this match was concluded, and resulted in a victory for the visitors by an innings and 21 runs. Score:

SUSSEX.

R. T. Ellis, c Underdown, b Armstrong	4	E. J. M'Cormick, b Longman	17
H. Whitfeld, c Hill, b Young	58	C. A. Smith, c Seymour, b Bencraft	61
A. H. Trevor, c Seymour, b Armstrong	13	Tester, b Young	8
H. Phillips, c Leat, b Tuck	31	Hide, b Young	2
W. Humphreys, b Young	4	Seneschal, not out	3
Rev. F. F. J. Greenfield, c Young, b Bencraft	11	B 19, l b 4, w 2	25
		Total	227

HAMPSHIRE.

Tuck, c Greenfield, b Hide	4	run out	5
C. R. Seymour, c Greenfield, b Hide	18	c Humphreys, b Tester	19
A. Andrews, b Seneschal	0	st Phillips, b Humphreys	14
Leat, b Seneschal	0	b Humphreys	0
E. Hall, b Seneschal	3	c Trevor, b Tester	10
G. H. Longman, l b w, b Humphreys	8	b Humphreys	44
G. Underdown, b Seneschal	11	c Tester, b Seneschal	9
A. H. Wood, b Seneschal	23	b Humphreys	5
R. Bencraft, b Seneschal	2	b Seneschal	4
Young, c Smith, b Tester	6	c Phillips, b Humphreys	0
H. Armstrong, not out	0	not out	9
Byes 3, l b 1	4	Byes 3, l b 2	5
Total	81	Total	125

STATE OF IRELAND.

Our Limerick correspondent telegraphs last night:

All the sub-constables who tendered their resignations yesterday have withdrawn them at the request of the inspector-general. Colonel Bruce is still in Limerick, and the action of the men to-day is the reverse of what it was yesterday. They have decided on confining their agitation for the present to a memorial to the Lord-Lieutenant, praying for the reinstatement of the five sub-constables who were dismissed yesterday. Late last night some sixty sub-constables threatened to resign forthwith, and even went so far as to tender their resignations, but to-day more prudent counsels seem to prevail. The memorial asks the Lord-Lieutenant to reinstate the dismissed sub-constables on the grounds that they could not be held responsible for the threatened resignation of the police at New Pallas, owing to soldiers being lodged and messed with them in the barracks, that the order of transfer gave no time whatever for them to make due preparations, &c. The memorial is signed by sixty-seven sub-constables, is most respectful in tone, and expresses the unswerving loyalty of the men and their regret that anything should occur to disturb the harmonious relations which have hitherto prevailed in the force, and which have only been disturbed by the undue interference of certain special resident magistrates.

A largely attended meeting of the members of the Cork police force was held yesterday, at which resolutions were adopted strongly condemning the action of the authorities towards the six Limerick sub-constables, opening a subscription list on their behalf, and deciding to postpone present action until the result of the inquiry now being held is made known. This course will probably be followed by the remainder of the police in Ireland. In the meantime a good many members of the force contemplate resigning and emigrating.

The authorities at Dublin Castle believe the constabulary agitation has subsided, and that the dismissal of the five men at Limerick has had the effect of teaching their comrades the wisdom of awaiting the result of the committee of inquiry at present taking evidence concerning their grievances.

THE BRITISH ASSOCIATION.

The construction of a channel tunnel was discussed yesterday in the Geological Section, presided over by Mr. R. Etheridge, F.R.S. The section was largely attended, and the discussion was of a highly interesting character.—Professor Boyd Dawkins introduced the subject in a verbal statement on the geology of the Channel bed; and he was followed by Mr. C. K. de

The Mysterious Urn

AUSTRALIANS discovered what had happened two days later. *The Age* in Melbourne had a column devoted to foreign news, which in effect meant news of the British Empire. Britain was fighting in Egypt and one item, datelined Alexandria, 29 August, said: 'The British troops are suffering greatly from the effects of the great heat and some cases of sunstroke have occurred in the ranks.'

The item below, with the same dateline, said a prominent Egyptian 'factotum' had been 'taken prisoner and is now in Sir Garnet Wolseley's camp'.

The item below that was about serious fighting between Turkey and Greece, then an item about the Irish constabulary. 'Many ... stationed at Limerick have resigned, owning to the dismissal of the leaders in the recent agitation for increased pay.'

The cricket came next.

AUSTRALIAN ELEVEN IN
ENGLAND
[By Submarine Cable]
Reuter's Telegrams
London, 28th August

The match between the Australian eleven
and an eleven of England was commenced
at the Oval today in the presence of a very
large attendance.

The Australians went in first, and were all
disposed of for a total of 63.

The home team in their first innings
obtained 101, all out.

When the telegrams arrived, *The Age* carried both day's play together, the first above the second in single column format. Play was described in the order it happened, factually and without any embellishment:

> London, 28th August
> The Australian crickets commenced their
> great match today, at the Kennington Oval
> (Surrey Club ground), against eleven of All
> England.
> The interest taken in the contest taken by the
> public generally was very great, and there
> was an enormous attendance at the ground,
> the Oval being thronged with spectators in
> every part.

Just as revealing are the two adjacent columns because they show how London-centric Australian life was, at least in the international sphere. Several news items concerned the campaign in Egypt but others covered the Duke of Albany's illness, the health of the Archbishop of Canterbury, wool sales and which ships had reached London.

The effect of England's defeat was clearly traumatic in England.

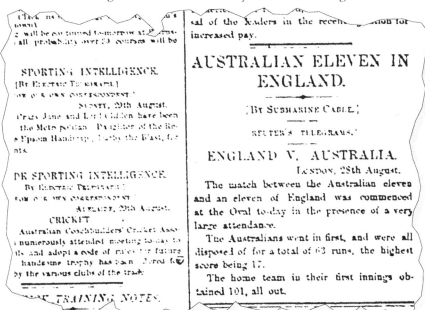

How the news reached Australia.

Cricket: A Weekly Record Of The Game wrote 'Australia will have just reason to be proud of the success its players have so worthily gained. It is not too much to say that to beat England has been the guiding star of an Australian cricketer's ambition. That ambition has been realised, much as Englishmen everywhere will regret the issue.' The Australians had done it, 'to be just, by sheer hard work, and all praise should unstintingly be given to the energy which in such a short term of years has placed Australian cricket on a level with the best of English production.'

The magazine also included a sort of funeral oration. 'Sacred to the memory of England's supremacy in the cricket-field, which expired on the 29th day of August, at the Oval.'

The Sportsman received angry correspondence in its letters column. One began: 'After the most disgraceful exhibition [...] is it not possible to select another team to play a final match with our visitors before they depart? [...] Nerve is what these Australians possess, and what our so-called England Eleven does not possess. Possibly the teeth of three of our eleven did not chatter when they walked to the wickets to face the demon bowler; but the remaining eight shivered and funked, and if these eight had played in the same style against fourth-form school bowlers they would have fared the same.' The writer picked his own team for the hypothetical return match and concluded that it, at least, would not give 'an awful fiasco of nervous play'.

The Australians went to Tunbridge Wells to play a United Eleven on 31 August and 1 and 2 September.

On the first day of the match the latest issue of *Cricket: A Weekly Record Of The Game* came out and in the column called 'Pavilion Gossip' could be read: 'In truth, the result has deadened the sky of English cricket. The Australians won by brilliant all-round play and no one, certainly not I, will have the slightest desire to minimise their victory.

'The important issues at stake made the play all round nervous and consequently untrue, and it was the influence of the title of the match, England against Australia, I believe, that produced the very evident general over-anxiety. [...] That five wickets should only have been able to add eleven runs, no matter what the bowling or the wicket, is a very painful reflection, one that will take us some time to get over.'

On Saturday the weeklies came out.

The Illustrated Sporting and Dramatic News wrote: 'No explanations or calculations of probabilities can alter the fact that an Australian team has beaten the pick of England cricket. We from time to time remarked on the thoroughness of Australian cricket, and this match proved it unmistakable. From the very first, the cricket was, to use an expressive term, sensational.

The fact that the best eleven we can place in the field was beaten, even if by only seven runs, is hardly a pleasant one to our notions of infallibility.'

The conclusion: 'In a limited sense may be regarded as a national disaster.'

The South London Gazette wrote 'When all things come to be considered, we find the real reason for the overthrow were first, the blameworthy nervousness of several of our batsmen and second, the unequalled bowling of Spofforth.'

The next issue of *Punch,* a magazine then so heavily into satire that each paragraph dripped with it, produced a poem (and this is what satire read like in 1882; if you don't know what the final paragraph means, I don't either):

THE LESSON OF THE LICKING

Well done "Cornstalks"! Whipt us,
    Fair and square!
Was it luck that tript us?
    Was it "scare"?
Kangaroo land's "Demon," or our own
Want of "devil," coolness, nerve, backbone?

Anyhow, stow, nagging!
    Whipt we are,
Boggling's bad as bragging:
    England's star
Seems, to some at least, here to have sunk
Through that worst of Captains, Captain Funk.

But the lesson's ready
    Dash and skill
Fail without cool, steady
    Nerve and will.
That's the best team that calmly pulls together,
Uphill or downhill, fine or dirty weather.

There they had us, HORNBY.
    Let the tip
Not be put, with scorn, by,
    They who'd whip
MURDOCH'S lot must ne'er be dashed or stuck,
Steady does it, Sirs, and Pluck is Luck!

A London journalist, Reginald Brooks, wrote an obituary in the *Sporting Times*:

'In affectionate remembrance of English cricket which died at the Oval, 29th August, 1882. Deeply lamented by a large circle of sorrowing friends and acquaintances. R.I.P.

N.B. The body will be cremated and the Ashes taken to Australia.'[1]

This appeared deep into the newspaper but struck a cord. Many read it and many remembered, especially the word Ashes. As it happened, a tour by an England team to Australia had already been set in motion before the match at the Oval. The Hon. Ivo Bligh, afterwards Lord Darnley, would captain it at the age of 23. A right-hand bat, he played for Cambridge University and Kent. The team included Barnes, Studd, Steel, Read and Barlow. Here was an immediate opportunity to redeem talk of The Ashes.

The Australians played Nottinghamshire, then I. Zingari at Scarborough. As that match began, *Cricket: A Weekly Record Of The Game* was inescapably caught up in the continuing fall out from the Oval. It wrote 'Players who only a few hours before had been deemed worthy of upholding the national reputation were transformed by the mere accident of failure into cricket villains of the deepest dye. To be unsuccessful is to be incompetent. Such is the verdict of public opinion, and the truth of this assertion has been fully tested by the batsmen who have been made the victims of popular resentment. [...] a victory by seven runs hardly furnishes a logical deduction that Australian cricket is so much superior to English as gives cause for such a universal wail of decadence. For the present it may be urged that the attitude of a certain class of writers to those who, after a thousand victories, have been once foiled, is hardly becoming. The utility of the apparently inexhaustible supply of anonymous abuse which has filled the columns of at least one paper during the week, is equally questionable.'

After I. Zingari, the Australians played Shaw's Eleven at Leeds then the North of England at Manchester. The first day of that was 14 September, the day Bligh's team sailed from Gravesend on the *Peshawar*.

The Australians played Shaw's Eleven again, at the Oval, an Eleven of Scotland in Glasgow and finished against an Eleven of England at Harrogate on 26 September. It meant that Bligh's team arrived in Australia and played several matches before the Australians got there.

They left Liverpool on the *Alaska* on 29 September for the United States. Their itinerary included two days in New York and a match there, and a match in Philadelphia. They were due to leave San Francisco on 21 October and reach Sydney on 16 November.

Mr and Mrs Clarke and their entourage were among the *Peshawar* passengers. Clarke and Bligh met, they liked each other and Clarke invited Bligh to bring the team to Rupertswood for Christmas and Bligh agreed – Clarke was President of the Melbourne Cricket Club, sponsoring the tour, but no doubt Bligh would have gone anyway. Rupertswood offered the sort of life to which Bligh was accustomed. The family had their own country house, Cobham Hall, a magnificent and historic building in Kent, and Rupertswood was in that world.

The *Peshawar* reached Ceylon (Sri Lanka) on 12 October, and the team played a match against Eighteen of Colombo who held on for a draw despite being 16 for 7 in their second innings. It left on Saturday 14 October and made good progress until the Sunday evening.

A journalist on board, described as 'A Special Correspondent', sent a full description to *The Adelaide Observer.*

A 'divine service' began at 8.00 and towards 9.00 people saw a vessel bearing down on them. 'She had then no light visible, and it was impossible to make out more than that she carried a good deal of sail.' She was 100 yards away and 'on the crest of a wave presented an appallingly grand appearance in the dim light'. The congregation at the service were only just dispersing when the alarm was given. 'In the uncertain light, and the sudden terror, many fell over the chairs and forms left from the service, and were struggling to rise when the crash came.'

The vessel ploughed into the *Peshawar* and 'the shadow of the terror gave place almost at once to a grave fear, and no one could guess what the consequences would be.' Mrs Clarke and Miss Snodgrass, her sister, came across the captain, and he told Miss Snodgrass to 'look after Mrs Clarke'.

'Mr W.W. Read, who was on the hurricane deck ... had to jump to the quarter-deck. Barnes

Ivo Bligh, the man who went to Australia to get The Ashes – and did. (Courtesy of Rupertswood)

113

was in his cabin, Bates asleep on the safe side of the deck, Barlow standing beside him. Morley had to run to the captain's bridge after they turned back from the starboard steps, where he would have been almost sure to have been injured, if not carried in to the water, and in one way or another all escaped injury.' In fact '…it was this unfortunate accident which caused the injury to Morley – a broken rib, undiscovered till some weeks later – and was probably chiefly responsible for his untimely death a year or two afterwards. By a curious fatality the Orient boat *Austral,* which was the alternative boat recommended to us for our journey, was sunk on arrival in Sydney Harbour, through carelessness in leaving ports open while coaling, so that we were unconsciously given the unusual choice between a ship that was run into and a ship that sunk – a cheerful alternative that might well have daunted the majority of us who were trying a big voyage for the first time. A horrid reminder of the fate that might well have been ours was the swarm of sharks surrounding the two ships on the morning after the collision; these monsters, according to common report, following the ships which carry many cargoes of coolies [unskilled labourers], as did the barque which was our assailant on this occasion.'[2]

Meanwhile… 'It is on board ship (during the terrifying collision) that Florence first comes to the notice of the dashing Ivo Bligh. He becomes deeply smitten by this spirited and attractive girl.'[3]

The *Peshawar* limped back to Colombo.

Allan Steel wrote to Bligh's parents: 'At Colombo, during our second visit, we played a cricket match against the Garrison, 18 of them. They were not up to much, though, as we got 180 and they only got 22 for 9 wickets. Ivo made nine and was then caught in the long field. As we had about four days to spend on shore whilst the damage received in the collision was being repaired, Charlie, George and myself took the train up to Kandy. Ivo wisely remained with Christian (an old friend of ours) at Colombo as the sea air was so much better for him than the muggy heat of the interior of Ceylon. […] The railway ride from Colombo to Kandy is supposed to be one of the most lovely in the world, it ascends about 2000 feet in twenty miles winding round the most precipitous precipices, the step of the carriages often overhanging.'

When the repairs were done the *Peshawar* ploughed on across the Indian Ocean towards King George's Sound, a natural harbour on Western Australia's south coast.

News of Clarke's Baronetcy came through on 29 October.

Steel was writing to Bligh's parents on 6 November because, as he explained, Bligh had 'met with a slight accident to his hand. His accident which though slight was rather painful at first occurred whilst we were engaged in a tug of war. He had the rope wound round his hand and a great strain suddenly coming from behind, the rope cut into the hand making a jagged sort of wound which I am very much afraid will prevent him playing cricket for at least three weeks.'

Steel went on: 'We have now, all being well, only four or five days to remain on board and I am sure we will all be glad to finish our voyage which has begun to seem almost interminable, as next Thursday we will have been eight weeks. The first match at Adelaide we are afraid will have to fall through as it was arranged for the 9th (next Thursday) and we do not expect to arrive there till that date.'

The *Peshawar* arrived at Glenelg, the disembarkation point for Adelaide, 10 days late on 10 November – as Steel said, the day of their first match, against Fifteen of South Australia.

'[…] the delay caused us to arrive at Adelaide on the night preceding the first day of the match as previously arranged. In the middle of the night our slumbers were disturbed by a cheery deputation from the Adelaide Cricket Club who pressed us with much hospitable insistence to prepare for a match next day against XIV of South Australia. So, after our long voyage, with all its attendant effects on cricketing eye and condition, we started our series of matches in this unprepared state.'[4]

Bligh's hand kept him out of the match but the tourists' visit created a fever of anticipation. *The Adelaide Observer* wrote:

'In these days of athleticism and of bone-and-muscle hero worship, it is not astonishing to find that a large portion of the public of South Australia have of late been exercised in mind regarding the approaching visit of the Hon. Ivo Bligh's team of cricketers to our shores. The abilities of the players have been canvassed and their performances analysed in order that some little idea may be gained of their merits. […] The late arrival of the mail steamer *Peshawar* was therefore much regretted […] it was not anticipated that the *Peshawar* would have been so delayed that she would not reach Glenelg till Friday morning.'

The *Peshawar* docked early and the players were taken to their 'respective' hotels – presumably different for amateurs and professionals – while the *Peshawar* sailed on to Melbourne. Bligh asked for the start of the match to be put back from midday to 2.00 and it was. Rain restricted play.

That evening the Governor of South Australia, Lt-Gen Sir William F.D. Jervois, patron of the South Australian Cricket Association, entertained the tourists at a vice-regal dinner. Jervois, a military man, had been at Woolwich and Chatham and may well have known Bligh, and there are suggestions that he married a cousin of Bligh's. He had been Governor since 1877.

S. S. Peshawur
6th November 1882

My dear Lord Darnley

As Ivo has met
with a slight accident to
his hand, he has deputed
me his correspondent to write
home for him. This accident
which though slight was
rather painful at first
occurred whilst we were
engaged in a tug of war,
He had the rope wound round
his hand & a great strain
suddenly coming on from
behind, the rope cut into the

The letter Allan Steel wrote to the Darnleys from the SS *Peshawur*. (Medway Archives and Local Studies Centre. Reproduced by kind permission of the Earl of Darnley and the Director of Community Services, Medway Council)

hand making a jagged sort
of wound which I am very
much afraid will prevent him
playing cricket for at least
three weeks; it is all the more
unfortunate as he was re-
covering his health so very
rapidly, that we were all
convinced he would with a
few days practise. be in his
old form once more.
We are now between King
George's Sound and Adelaide,
having left the former early
this morning. We had a

pleasant run from Colombo to King George's Sound, as the weather was very bracing especially after crossing the line. At Colombo, during our second visit, we played a cricket match against the Garrison, sixteen of them, they were not up to much though as we got 180 & they only got 22 for 9 wickets. Ivo made nine and was then caught in the long field. As we had about four days to spend on shore whilst the damage received

in the collision was being repaired
charlie; Georgie myself took the
train up to Kandy, I so wisely
remained with Christian (an old
friend of ours) at Colombo as the
sea air was so much better for
him than the muggy heat of
the interior of Ceylon. We had a
most enjoyable trip being sump-
tuously entertained by the Kandy
Club; the railway ride from Colombo
to Kandy is supposed to be one of
the most lovely in the world, it
ascends about 2000 feet in twenty-
miles winding round the most
precipitous precipices the side of
the carriages often overhanging

a fall of over 2000 feet. Below
was stretched out for miles the
most lovely tropical vegetation,
every species of plant which one
has so often heard of but never
seen were crowded in artless
confusion. After spending one day
& night at Kandy we returned
two at Colombo. Everybody on
board now has quite got over
the collision & it has almost
entirely faded from conversation.
We heard this morning at King
George's Sound that the result
of the inquiry has been to
throw all blame on the Captain
of the 'Glenroy' which has caused

great rejoicing on board the "Peshaum." We have now, all being well, only four or five days to remain on board & I am sure we will all be glad to finish our voyage. which has begun to seem almost interminable, as next Thursday we will have been eight weeks. Our first match at Adelaide we are afraid will have to fall through, as it was arranged for the ninth (next Thursday), & we do not expect to arrive there till that date, so in all pro-

bability we shall go on to
Melbourne, where we have to
play on Friday week.

Everybody is well, Morley having
quite recovered from his attack
of gout & with the exception of
Ivo's unlucky accident nothing
has ailed anyone.

I expect that next mail Ivo
will be able to write himself
as the wound is healing
quickly   Believe me

                    Yours very sincerely

    signed.   Allany Steel

                    Ivo

When the *Peshawar* reached Melbourne, the news of Clarke's Baronetcy – Australia's first – broke.

The Adelaide match was drawn.

'Immediately on its conclusion we started on the shorter voyage to Melbourne, some 36 hours if I remember right. This was our first experience of these coasting voyages, which, if the truth be told, came far too often in those days for the comfort and condition of the touring cricketer, undertaken as they were in smallish and not too well found vessels and on a rough coast.'[5]

The tourists beat Victoria.

'It must be noted that the weakness of the Victorian Eleven was greatly owing to so many of their best players having not yet returned from their English tour. We found the Melbourne ground excellent and very fast, but the light, especially for fielding, puzzling to English eyes. Probably the dark fir trees at the end of the ground partly accounted for this, but unquestionably an important factor was the extreme clearness of the Australian atmosphere as compared with the moister air of England.'[6]

The tourists went into the arduous and traditional 'walkabout' – matches at Sandhurst and Castlemaine.

'Our next long journey, Melbourne to Sydney, led us over the only railway between colonial capitals that was in use at that time. The Sydney ground we found very different from that of Melbourne; it was less surrounded by trees and consequently with a better light, but the turf, of a large-bladed flat-growing species of grass, was better to look at and field upon than it was for batting purposes. In our last big match we had to have a fresh wicket every innings, so badly did the turf stand the wear and tear of the game. Here, again, the absence of the Australian Eleven weakened our opponents sadly, and another easy victory came our way.'[7]

After a match at Maitland they played Eighteen of Newcastle at Newcastle on 8 and 9 December. Four days after this match – and no doubt eyeing the First Test, due on 30 December – Bligh was quoted as saying he hoped that when the tour was over he would have regained The Ashes.

The tourists went to Rupertswood, which could accommodate them easily. It had 50 rooms and stood at 'the end of a long, winding drive nestled among mature trees' past an exceptionally elaborate lodge and gates.

'A remarkable architectural expression of the more genteel, Victorian era. Its magnificent proportions and unique gardens lay testimony to the privilege and power that prevailed on these grounds. Built as a residence for Sir William Clarke, (first Australian born Baronet), it became a power seat in the great English tradition. Balls, hunt meets and week-end house parties were frequent. Anyone of note, in Victorian and Edwardian society, was

Rupertswood, where Bligh fell in love. (Courtesy of Rupertswood)

entertained by the Clarkes. Many historical figures visited Rupertswood, including Dame Nellie Melba, several Governors of Victoria and a rumoured visit by the Duke and Duchess of York, (later to become King George V and Queen Mary).'[8]

The tourists would be well entertained. Janet Clarke was a society hostess as well as a leading patron of good causes in Melbourne, and of course Miss Morphy was there, too. In fact 'an enormous house party was going on'.[9]

Rupertswood also had a cricket ground: by a great irony an oval.

On Christmas Eve, after what has been described as a 'congenial lunch', Clarke said 'Let's have a cricket match'. It could be organised in a few minutes because he had a pitch and he could round up a side of locals, mostly his own staff.

The pitch was on the side of the mansion – looking face on, to the left – and approximately 200 yards away. In fact at that time it wasn't a proper cricket ground but rather a paddock, without a pavilion: it was known as the cricket paddock. As the players made their way towards it they would have noticed a pronounced, and deceptive, slope. When they reached it they'd see the slope wasn't so bad.[10]

They played, and the tourists made the staff work hard ('the servants literally run off their feet retrieving the many fours and sixes')[11] and although, as it seems, nobody kept score the feeling was that the tourists had won.

Not that it mattered. The match had been a social affair, nothing more.

The chronology is maddeningly imprecise and the events themselves liable to several interpretations. This is hardly surprising because at the time what was happening was almost certainly light-hearted – someone has used the word jest – and, however clear it is in hindsight, nobody at Rupertswood can have had any notion of the weight the events would have to bear from 24 December down all the decades to here. They assumed enormous *subsequent* importance.

After the match Bligh made a speech, presumably thanking one and all in the usual way, and made mention of The Ashes.

It gave Clarke's wife an idea: she would provide some physical ashes. 'A tiny terracotta urn was produced from one of the ladies' dressing tables and given to Bligh as a personal gift and memento of his visit.'[12] On the lawn she – with three other ladies, one of them Morphy – burnt, or told a servant to burn, one or more of the bails and put them into a little pottery urn. It was the sort of urn anyone might have as an ornament or somewhere to keep small things like buttons. Nobody now knows if they were bails and one report, a hundred years afterwards, suggested Morphy's veil was burnt and those ashes put into the urn.

One of the staff, Pat Lyons, 'clearly remembered the afternoon many years later. It was his understanding that Lady Clarke, at dinner that evening, had presented Ivo Bligh with a pottery urn.' Lady Clarke said to all the diners that England and Australia have a real trophy to play for now. You can almost hear the laughter, polite, well-intentioned. They must have regarded it as a jest 'because that was all it was then'.[13]

Meanwhile... 'It is during this sojourn at Rupertswood that the romance between Bligh and Miss Morphy blossoms, but despite it being a closely guarded secret amongst the Rupertswood ladies it still manages to make the gossip columns.'[14]

The urn remained at Rupertswood.

The tourists went to Ballarat to play a local team of Eighteen on 26, 27 and 28 December.

'These matches against odds, it must be confessed, though they gave a pleasant opportunity to the team of seeing something of the country districts, from a cricket point of view were neither particularly helpful nor interesting; the cricket was too weak to be very exciting, and the grounds were none too well kept. However, it would indeed be ungracious not to add that everywhere the warmest and most hospitable of welcomes was extended to us, and every possible effort made to make our stay in each district as pleasant as possible.'[15]

They returned to Melbourne for the First Test which began on 30 December. There are reports that Clarke presented the urn to Bligh, while acknowledging 'the ladies of the household's efforts in its creation', before play. Since Clarke held official office – President of the Melbourne Cricket Club – such a presentation could bestow on the urn some sort of official status. Whether Clarke saw what this might really mean, whether he thought it was just a nice thing to do or whether he did it as a gesture to his wife is not clear.

It's a bit like arguing whether Shakespeare wrote the plays, and if he didn't who did? The precise, pedantic details of how we got them are fascinating but ultimately much less important than the fact that we have them.

The urn and The Ashes are the same. We have them.

There is another thing that is also unclear: the *real* status of the urn, and there is a clue about that. When Bligh married Morphy and returned to England to live in his mansion, he took the urn. 'Interestingly enough, no one really knew that the urn existed until Bligh's death in 1927.'[16] This suggests that up to then, when his widow presented it to the MCC at Lord's for public display, the urn was no more than a distant and amusing part of the family story, and of no interest to anyone else.

At Melbourne the Australians batted first, Murdoch made 48. Thereby hangs a tale. Steel would remember 'Murdoch and Bannerman seemed immovable. They had been in for about an hour, and every one of the regular English bowlers had been on and *off*. A suggestion was made to try C.F.H. Leslie. Now this gentleman, with all his great merits, was never, even in the estimation of his best friends, a great bowler. But on he went with pleasure [...] The first ball was a very fast one, rather wide, the second ditto, but the third one – "Ah, the third!" – was a head ball, designed after the manner of Spofforth's best; and it pitched on the middle of Murdoch's middle stump!

'The next comer was Horan, at that time the reputed best player of fast bowling in the Colonies. A very fast long-hop, wide on the off-side, was prettily cut straight into Barlow's hands at third man, and Mr Leslie had secured two wickets for no runs. He continued for another over or two, had Bannerman beautifully stumped by Mr Tylecote off a fast wide half-volley on the leg-side, and then retired in favour of one of the regular bowlers, after having, simply by wild erratic fast delivery, lowered three of the best Australians.'[17]

Bonnor, striking several balls into the crowd, finished the first day 60 not out. It rained overnight and Australia were quickly all out for 291. With conditions in his favour, Palmer (7 for 65) bowled England out for 177, so they followed on. Now Spofforth (3 for 65) and Palmer (3 for 61) cut deep into the batting but Giffen (4 for 38) wrecked the innings. England, all out for 169, left

Australia 56 to win and they got there for the loss of Massie.

The day after, Bligh wrote home:

> Melbourne
> Jan 3rd.

> My dearest father and mother,
> You will see on reading this why I address this letter to you both, as it is perhaps the most important letter I shall ever write to you. [...] To go straight to the point at once I want your permission to marry an Australian young lady Miss Florence Morphy. I will tell you the whole story. To begin with you doubtless remember how much I have told you of Mr and Mrs (now Sir W. & Lady) Clarke. Well, we have seen a great deal of them out here and their country house Rupertswood, Sunbury, has been quite a home to us. I have been there 4 times. I met this young lady both staying at the Clarke's (every time), she being one of Lady Clarke's greatest friends, and also in Melbourne and I am perfectly and most firmly convinced that she is the woman who would make my life a happy one.

> I do not mean to go into a description of her here but I will only say that as sure as I sit here she is a girl that all of you would love almost as soon as you saw her. A more truly loveable character I have never met in man or woman and whatever you think about the matter I must assure you most solemnly that this is no case of a young fellow being caught by a pretty face.

> [...] I have not told you yet that this young lady is very poor, her father who was a police magistrate having been dead many years and she and her mother have had hard work to support the orphan children of one of her sisters. [...] I honour and respect her all the more for it.

> [...] Could you send me a telegram when you get this letter just to say you have received it and do telegraph [...] to say that you give your permission.

> [...] Just been defeated by Australian XI. All the worst of luck – they had dry wicket Saturday – rain came Sunday, Monday morning and evening.[18]

The tourists went to Tasmania to play at Launceston and Hobart before returning to Melbourne for the Second Test. Something must have gone wrong with transmitting the news of the First Test defeat because, the day

Melbourne
Jan 3rd.

My dearest Father & Mother

You will see on reading this why I address the letter to you both, as it is perhaps the most important letter I shall ever write to you. Many thanks for your letters by the last mail which were written directly after you had read the accounts of the collision. I am so glad that you all did not realise the danger at first from the telegrams. Please thank all the others for their nice letters too. Now for the main subject of my letter. To go straight to the point at once I want your permission to marry an Australian young lady Miss Florence Morphy. I will tell you the whole story. To begin with you doubtless remember how ~~slightly~~ much I have told you of Mr & Mrs (now Sir W. & Lady) Clarke. Well we have seen a great deal of

The letter of love from Bligh. (Medway Archives and Local Studies Centre. Reproduced by kind permission of the Earl of Darnley and the Director of Community Services, Medway Council)

before the Launceston match, Bligh wrote home:

'I am much afraid from your telegram that the finish of our New Year's Day match must have been wrongly telegraphed. [...] It was a terrible bad piece of luck to begin our big match like that. They went in on a perfect hard wicket and got 250 for 7 wickets on the Saturday. It rained Saturday night, a little on Sunday and hard Monday morning and when I got to the ground I felt convinced that the match was practically over. Our lot played up well the first innings but 2nd innings when the wicket had improved a bit went to pieces rather and in the end we were beaten by 9 wickets. I personally had a bad time of it, as was only likely under the circumstances. I had only had 2 days practice on a fast ground and 2 innings both on slow grounds. I knew it was unlikely I should get runs, especially with my hand still weak and I did not. First innings rather unlucky pulled an off ball into the wicket 2nd innings with a long hop by Spof. Palmer's bowling was very good,

The wrong result, as Bligh tells his parents. (Medway Archives and Local Studies Centre. Reproduced by kind permission of the Earl of Darnley and the Director of Community Services, Medway Council)

his break back at times almost unplayable.

I think these first matches against inferior bowling have not been very good for us; people think they were in form when they really were not. But we are […] all in the best of spirits and generally jolly. I am getting stronger every day and can stand the cricket in the hot sun without inconvenience.

We are just commencing our Tasmanian trip with a wet Sunday at Launceston. It is a pretty little place and the river down which the steamer comes to get to the town is very picturesque. We play tomorrow and next day, go that night to Hobart, 8 hours rail.

[…] Morley has been laid up again with rheumatism in his knee, another stroke of bad luck. We feel his loss in the bowling very much. Leslie got 3 of the best wickets for 31 runs! Murdoch, Bannerman and Horan – on these good wickets a wild bowler like that seems the best chance of getting wickets.

[…] I am feeling as you may imagine in a rather perturbed state just now and I suppose shall continue to do so until the letter or telegram comes from you in answer to my letter. I do hope you have not thought that I have been rash or hasty in this or that I do not know my own mind. I am quite determined to do anything [rather] than give up Miss Morphy, and I think when that is the case although you might not be able to do much for me at any rate you would not with-hold your permission. […] If only I could see you and mother and talk it out with you I think you would not think me mistaken.

[…] I think most of the team will leave Australia about the beginning of April – George Vernon, C.B. Studd and I perhaps not for a fortnight later.'[19]

In the Second Test England batted first and solidly, led by Read with 75. They made 294 and then Billy Bates, round arm off-breaks, became the first Englishman to do a hat-trick in a Test Match. He finished with seven for 28, and now the Australians, all out 114, followed on – and met Bates again. He bowled them out for 153 (seven for 74) to give England the match by an innings and 27 runs. The Third Test at Sydney in four days would decide the success or failure of Bligh's self-stated mission.

After Melbourne Bligh had one of the bails made into a letter opener, which he presented to Lady Clarke (the family still has it). The fact that Bligh chose a bail for this is suggestive – no more, but no less – that he was repaying in kind (and courtesy) the bail which had been burnt and put in the urn.

Describing the first day at Sydney, *The Sydney Morning Herald* wrote 'Never in the annals of colonial cricket has there been such an important match ... no previous engagement of the kind has created such wide-spread interest throughout the Australian colonies. The issue of this great cricketing event ... will be anxiously awaited by thousands in England who would hail the news of a victory with as much enthusiasm as if British soldiers had won a great battle. The main object of Mr Blight and his companions in arms to the antipodes is to wipe out the disaster English cricket sustained at the hands of the Australians at the Oval and carry back, as Mr Bligh so happily puts it, "the revered ashes of English cricket".

'There could not have been less than 20,000 persons present, the pavilion being densely thronged by the cricketers of Sydney and the members of the Association ground, while the grandstand was so crowded as not to leave even standing room. The terrace in front of the stand was a favourite vantage ground, whence a good view of the game was afforded, while those less intent on the game of bat and ball chatted and promenaded on the velvet-like sward forming the lawn in front of the stand. The portions of the enclosure outside the reserves and stand were black with people, and the roofs of the outbuildings and even the top of the fence were covered with sightseers. The band of the Garrison Artillery, which played in the stand reserve, added some choice selections of music to the attractions of the day. The arrangements for the comfort and accommodation of the public were susceptible of much improvement, particularly in regard to the entrance to the ground and the grandstand, there were not a sufficient number of turnstiles for the number of people who went to the match, and ladies were subjected to much crushing at both the ground entrance and at the entrance to the stand. The luncheon arrangements under the stand were also sadly defective.'

Bligh stayed with a family at Paddington called Fletcher: the wife, Anne Fletcher – known as Annie – was the daughter of a Dublin couple who had migrated.

England batted first, Read and Edmund Tylecote both made 66, and they were all out for 247, leaving Australia enough time to make 8 without loss. Overnight rain, and showers during the second day, left Australia at 133 for one (Bannerman 68 not out). More overnight rain tilted the match towards the England bowlers, Australia all out for 218, but England collapsed on a difficult wicket to 123, leaving Australia needing 153 to win. They were 0 without loss at close on the third day. The weather improved on the fourth but Barlow created havoc with 7 for 40 and England had the match, and The Ashes, by 69 runs.

Interestingly, Bligh recalled that 'two wickets were allowed for the match,

ENGLAND first innings

R.G. Barlow	c Murdoch b Spofforth	28
C.T. Studd	c Blackham b Garrett	21
C.F.H. Leslie	b Spofforth	0
A.G. Steel	b Garrett	17
W.W. Read	c Massie b Bannerman	66
W. Barnes	b Spofforth	2
E.F.S. Tylecote	run out	66
W. Bates	c McDonnell b Spofforth	17
G.B. Studd	b Palmer	3
Hon. I.F.W. Bligh	b Palmer	13
F. Morley	not out	2
	Extras (b8, lb3, nb1)	12
	Total	247

1/41, 2/44, 3/67, 4/69, 5/75, 6/191, 7/223, 8/224, 9/244, 10/247

	O	M	R	W
Giffen	12	3	37	0
Palmer	38	21	38	2
Spofforth	51	19	73	4
Garrett	27	8	54	2
Bannerman	11	2	17	1
McDonnell	4	0	16	0

AUSTRALIA first innings

G. Giffen	st Tylecote b Bates	41
A.C. Bannerman	c Bates b Morley	94
W.L. Murdoch	lbw b Steel	19
P.S. McDonnell	b Steel	0
T.P. Horan	c Steel b Morley	19
H.H. Massie	c Bligh b Steel	1
G.J. Bonnor	c G.B. Studd b Morley	0
J.Mc. Blackham	b Barlow	27
T.W. Garrett	c Barlow b Morley	0
G.E. Palmer	c G.B. Studd b Barnes	7
F.R. Spofforth	not out	0
	Extras (b6, lb2, w1, nb1)	10
	Total	218

1/76, 2/140, 3/140, 4/176, 5/177, 6/178, 7/196, 8/196, 9/218, 10/218

	O	M	R	W
Morley	34	16	47	4
Barlow	47.1	31	52	1
Bates	45	20	55	1
Barnes	13	6	22	1
C.T. Studd	14	11	5	0
Steel	26	14	27	3

ENGLAND second innings

Leslie	b Spofforth	8
C.T. Studd	b Spofforth	25
Barlow	c Palmer b Horan	24
Steel	lbw b Spofforth	6
Read	b Horan	21
Barnes	lbw b Spofforth	3
Tylecote	c Bonnor b Spofforth	0
Bates	c Murdoch b Horan	4
Bligh	not out	17
G.B. Studd	c Garrett b Spofforth	8
Morley	b Spofforth	0
	Extras (b5, lb2)	7
	Total	123

1/13, 2/45, 3/55, 4/87, 5/92, 6/94, 7/97, 8/98, 9/115, 10/123

	O	M	R	W
Spofforth	41.1	23	44	7
Garrett	13	3	31	0
Palmer	9	3	19	0
Horan	17	10	22	3

AUSTRALIA second innings

Giffen	b Barlow	7
Bannerman	c Bligh b Barlow	5
Murdoch	c G.B. Studd b Morley	0
Horan	run out	8
McDonnell	c Bligh b Morley	0
Massie	c C.T. Studd b Barlow	11
Bonnor	b Barlow	8
Blackham	b Barlow	26
Spofforth	c Steel b Barlow	7
Palmer	not out	2
Garrett	b Barlow	0
	Extras (b6, lb2, w1)	9
	Total	83

1/11, 2/12, 3/18, 4/18, 5/30, 6/33, 7/56, 8/72, 9/80, 10/83

	O	M	R	W
Morley	35	19	34	2
Barlow	34.2	20	40	7

and we had now the advantage of first choice on two damaged specimens. The wicket of our choice furnished us with a difficult task in run-getting, and, with a total of 123, we set our opponents 153 to win. This, however, proved an impossible task, and Barlow and Morley bowled unchanged through an innings of 83. This match ended the career of Murdoch's great Eleven of 1882, and the ashes, so gallantly gained at the Oval, were once more supposed to be restored to English hands.'[20]

Tradition, if nothing else, insists that the urn was more formally presented to Bligh after the match. It is possible that the urn was taken from Rupertswood because Sydney was the deciding Test, and the Clarke family, as well as many other people, must have been well aware of the importance Bligh attached to his mission.

There would have been the perfect opportunity for a presentation, too. After the match 'the opposing elevens and the New South Wales Cricket Association met in the committee-room, when some complimentary speeches were made.

'Mr Murdoch proposed "The Health of the English team and their Captain, the Hon. Ivo Bligh." He did not begrudge them their victory, and, indeed, as they were to be beaten they were glad that the beating had been administered by the lion. It afforded him and the other members of the Australian team very great pleasure indeed to have the English team amongst them.

'The toast was received with three cheers.

'[Bligh] in responding expressed his thanks for the kind manner Mr Murdoch had proposed the toast, and assured him that the English team had enjoyed themselves very much indeed in the colony. [...] He called upon his team to drink to the health of "the Australian Eleven" coupled with the name of Mr Murdoch.

'The toast was enthusiastically received.'[21]

Before or following this dignified ceremony the urn could have been presented to Bligh, perhaps privately because if it had been done in public surely *The Sydney Morning Herald* reporter would have noticed.

Many, many histories say the urn *was* presented after the Test, but this may have begun as supposition – ordinarily that was the time it would have been presented, when the series had been settled – and hardened into 'fact' by weight of repetition, if nothing else.

One source[22] suggests that 'on his return to the Fletcher home from the after match celebrations', Annie Fletcher offered to make a velvet bag so that Bligh could store the urn in it. This implies either that Bligh had the urn with him – which in turn implies that it had been presented (well, re-presented) after the Test – or that Mrs Fletcher had heard about it, perhaps even from

Bligh in conversation.

Bligh accepted her offer and she made a 'beautiful brown velvet bag with the year 1883 embroidered on the front in gold thread'.

However, the final match of the tour was scheduled to be against Victoria at Melbourne, and there were several days free between the start of that and the end of the match before it for an improvised match against Australia at Sydney. Bligh might well have stayed at Rupertswood in between and would certainly have gone there anyway to see Miss Morphy. If he left the urn there after Janet Clarke gave it to him at Christmas, he knew he would be able to collect it before he sailed for home.

Significantly, *The Sydney Morning Herald* carried this in its match report:

'The result of the deciding encounter is extremely disappointing to the public, who nevertheless bore the reverse with composure. We have been justly proud of our cricketers and their deeds in the old country and our briefly enjoyed honours ... have been wrested from us by an adventurous band of cricketers who heroically set out from England to take back with them the laurels which our representatives so recently brought with them to Australia. Mr Bligh's most ardent hopes have been realised and he has now in his custody the "revered Ashes of English cricket", from which will be rehabilitated the supremacy of the English cricketers.'

On another page – what today we'd call the leader page – an unheaded item begins 'The Hon. Ivo Bligh's expressed intent to gather up the Ashes of English cricket strewn in Australia has so far been fulfilled. He has beaten the provincial eighteens and the colonial elevens, and in two out of three Test Matches has come off victorious. The victories have been as singular as unexpected.'

These repeated references to Bligh's phrase suggest that the idea of The Ashes had already taken some sort of root, at least among journalists as well as cricketers.

After Sydney the tourists went to Brisbane and Maryborough, 160 miles north of Brisbane. They were popular. 'During the tour, wherever the English team appears, large crowds come out to see them. They are treated most royally by dignitaries and the public alike. Rumours of a romance between Bligh and Florence captures the imagination of the public and spurs an unprecedented interest among fashionable young women in attending cricket games with a view of attaining eligible husbands.' [23]

The tourists returned to Sydney for the improvised match, a 'Fourth Test' hastily added to the schedule and not counting towards The Ashes. Before it, Bligh wrote to Mrs Fletcher to thank her for the velvet bag, and added that 'the ashes shall be consigned to it forthwith and always kept there in memory of the great match.'[24] Australia won by four wickets.

They played that final match against Victoria at Melbourne on 9, 10 and 12 March. The tour had been such a success for Melbourne Cricket Club that on 13 March, at a farewell dinner, the eight English amateurs were made Honorary Life Members. Morphy and her friends said to Bligh that the velvet bag wasn't 'grand enough' to hold the urn.

In thanks Bligh presented Sir William and Lady Clarke with a silver tray. The inscription said it was 'as a tribute of friendship & esteem by the English cricketers in Australia 1882–1883' and it carried the signatures of Bligh, Read, Steel, Charles and George Studd, Tylecote, Leslie and Vernon. The urn would stand on that at Rupertswood until Bligh returned to Australia to collect it and his bride, Morphy. He had proposed at Rupertswood but now had to go back to England.

This might imply, as I have suggested, that the urn had been there all the time. (The urn remained in her possession until he did come back, in February 1884.)

After Melbourne (which Victoria won by an innings and 73 runs), the team divided into three groups for the journey home. Reportedly the professionals set off almost immediately while the amateurs went to Rupertswood for a final visit. Mrs Clarke had pasted a poem – from the *Melbourne Punch*, 1 February – on to the urn:

> *When Ivo goes back with the urn, the urn;*
> *Studds, Steel, Read and Tylecote return, return;*
> *The welkin [sky] will ring loud,*
> *The great crowd will feel proud,*
> *Seeing Barlow and Bates with the urn, the urn;*
> *And the rest coming home with the urn.*

The amateurs left for England on 27 March but, for reasons anyone can understand, Bligh stayed. There was, or rather had been, a problem of social class. Bligh was nobility and Morphy wasn't. To get over this the Clarkes 'launch Florence into society with all the aplomb that is necessary. Indecently wealthy colonials are difficult to ignore, especially when [Clarke's father] had owned a land mass the size of Great Britain.'[25] On 23 April, more than a month after the Melbourne finale, he wrote to his father:

'Since writing my last letter I have made a great change in my plans. To my great astonishment the Lucases turned up after all by the last mail from India and I have settled to come back with them by the *Rosetta*. She is a nice ship and I have got a pretty good berth in her and it will be nice going with the L's. I shall get back a bit earlier too and will very probably be in time for the Varsity match or part of it. I think I shall probably go all the way round and not go to Brindisi. I am going with the Lucases and Miss Morphy to Sydney on Monday for four days and we shall come down here again by the *Rosetta*. [...] I heard from Vernon from Hobart where they stopped a few hours on the way to New Zealand that they have had a good voyage so far. The others in the *Paramatta* had it very rough between Adelaide and the Sound and they were most of them laid up again with seasickness.'[26]

A more leisurely age. (Medway Archives and Local Studies Centre. Reproduced by kind permission of the Earl of Darnley and the Director of Community Services, Medway Council)

Bligh and Morphy were married at Rupertswood on the 9th. Bligh wrote:

Alton
Mount Maledon
Feb 12

My dear Father,

I am writing you my first letter as a married man from a most charming place about 60 miles from Melbourne [...] lent us for our honeymoon. I arrived in Australia this last day week (Tuesday) and after 3 days of unexampled bustle and hurry the wedding took place on Saturday at Rupertswood. Florrie was looking so well when I came and in great spirits.

All the chief preparations had been made by Lady Clarke. [...] Florrie was delighted with all her presents from the family.

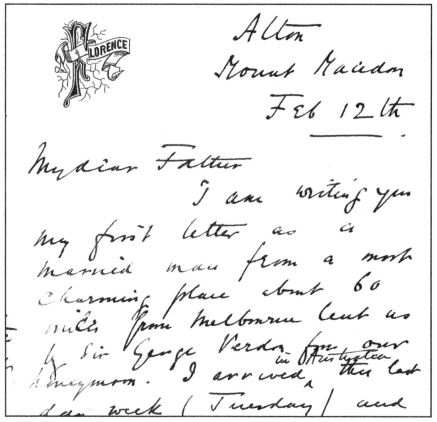

Married bliss... and a little hot news. (Medway Archives and Local Studies Centre. Reproduced by kind permission of the Earl of Darnley and the Director of Community Services, Medway Council)

It was a really lovely day but very hot, and the church rather stifling, which did not detract from the trepidation I felt. About 130 people were at the breakfast and the large ballroom was very prettily decorated for the occasion with various cricket designs. Florrie had eight bridesmaids and a very pretty lot they were. I gave them little gold brooches, gold bats with a ball in the middle, a design of Florrie's which turned out very well.

[…] I saw Murdoch the other day in Melbourne, he is in wonderful form now and has made some enormous scores lately. The Australian XI will undoubtedly be a very strong one [to England in 1884] especially if Spofforth goes, which he has as yet refused to do.

[…] Florrie sends you all her best love & is in capital spirits. I think there are not two happier people in this world than we are.[27]

Their first child was born in Melbourne before they returned to England and Cobham Hall, a pile so stately that English sovereigns, including Elizabeth I and Edward VIII, visited it. The hall, of red brick, is regarded as one of the most important in the country, combining Elizabethan, Jacobean and 18th-century styles.

That is where the urn stayed until 1927. By then, only six of the 22 players who played at the Oval in 1882 were still alive.

Notes

1. There was a fascinating insight into the background of the Ashes obituary on ABC Radio National's *The Sports Factor* in December 2002. An author, Jay Munns, explained that a great debate was going on in England at that time about cremation and Brooks' father belonged to a cremation society trying to have it made legal. Munns concludes that the obituary was in her phrase a 'double edged' sword in that by using 'cremation' and 'ashes' he was pushing the cremation debate.
www.ausport.gov.au/fulltext/2002/sportsf/s741889.asp

2. *History Of Kent Cricket,* Chapter XV, by the Earl of Darnley (Bligh).

3. *'The Lion and the Kangaroo:' The Ashes Story,* an essay by Marie Romeo of Rupertswood Mansion.

4. *History of Kent Cricket.*

5. Ibid.

6. Ibid.

7. Ibid.

8. www.rupertswood.com/docs/history.html

9. Marie Romeo op. cit.

10. Information about the pitch by Dominic Romeo of Rupertswood.

11. Ibid.

12. From a talk, *The Myth of the Ashes – how a concept became a reality* by MCC Archivist Glenys Williams, 2005.

13. www.rupertswood.com/docs/history.html

14. Marie Romeo op. cit.

15. Bligh op. cit.

16. www.rupertswood.com/docs/history.html

17. *The Badminton Library: Cricket,* Steel and Lyttelton.

18. Medway Archives and Local Studies. Reproduced by kind permission of the Earl of Darnley and the Director of Community Services, Medway Council.

19. Ibid.

20. *History of Kent Cricket,* Darnley.

21. *The Sydney Morning Herald.*

22. www.abcofcricket.com/A_Legend_Is_Born/ Velvet_and_Ash/velvet_and_ash.htm

23. Marie Romeo op. cit.

24. From the Glenys Williams talk. The letter is in the Museum at Lord's.

25. Marie Romeo op. cit.

26. Medway Archives and Local Studies. Reproduced by kind permission of the Earl of Darnley and the Director of Community Services, Medway Council.

27. Ibid.

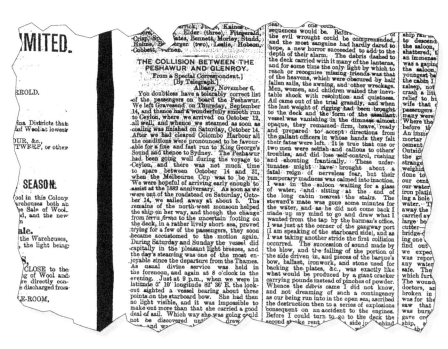

A mosaic of moments and memories: the *Peshawur* crash.

artly because the expenditure of the Clarence has created the at some day a safe and always ort will be in existence there. a course of years, however, have correctness of that impression l. It is not to be taken for the port of the Clarence is or of such a character as to war— as the terminus of a costly would be well for the Govern— er, before any further steps are the construction of a line from to the coast, that the question is not only what route should pt where is the port to be taken

n the whartage arrangements Quay and in the traffic of the , which are said to be under the of the Government, need a great deration if the public interest is cted. A new Government may s accession to power by prompt t it cannot establish claims ntidence of the public by taking which must either be retraced tious public inconvenience. Two set forth in the changes referred to. to provide additional shipping an at the ... Quay. The harbour

identified, tracked to their homes, remonstrated with privately, shifted to new scenes and better surroundings?

The Hon. Ivo Bligh's expressed intent to gather up the ashes of English cricket strewn in Australia has so far been fulfilled. He has beaten the provincial eighteens and the colonial elevens, and in two out of three test matches has come off victorious when pitted against the Australian Eleven. The victories have been as singular as unexpected. It was thought and maintained by competent critics at the start that the two representative teams were so evenly matched that victory would be practically decided by the preliminary toss. The first match, however, brought about a change of opinion. The Australians showed such superior form that an opinion went abroad to the effect that " the Englishmen are no match for them, we may count upon three victories, and the cricket championship of the world." The second match quashed all such predictions, rubbing out the Australian victory and leaving a clean page for the final contest. And now, that contest being ended, we acknowledge an all-round defeat, but naturally look about for the causes which have produced it. The first to appear is the losing of the toss. The Englishmen won that chance and went in to a magnificent score upon it; but made only an average score upon it; but the Australians began their uphill fight upon sodden turf in drizzling rain, and played at a disadvantage throughout the ...ings, yet still contrived to come within 29 of th... first score their opponents.

rse of the through the New E... the Clarence and Richmond. visit Tenterfield in fulfilment of stituents, and Grafton and so Richmond in response to special

The extension of the North Uralla to Armidale, a distan opened for public traffic on Th parations are being made to make tion worthy of the occasion. A are desirous of being present, a ment has had to make special the public in the trains. Speci run on the three days prior to which day no fewer than four Armidale. The specials on th Newcastle station at 6.15 a.m., at 7.50 p.m. On the morning o special trains will leave Newcas the other at 3 a.m. Visitors fr proceed by the trains on Thursda leave by the H. R. N. S. Compan which it has been arranged is p.m. this (Wednesday) evening Newcastle at about 2.30 a.m., visitors and the Ministerial speci requested to state that the com only be available by the trains ru which they have been issued.

The Hon. G. H. Reid, Minist tion, visited the Fort-street Mo The Minister was accompanied (Under-Secretary for Public I Parsons (Minister for Public tralia), and Captain Strong. Th ...t of the school,

The tour gets under way.

Mr. W. ... Crawfurd ...
Heatlee Bell, 9 st. 1 ...
Mr. J. H. Houldsworth's ...rana, 8 st. 12-15
(Lemaire)
ord Hasting's Beau Brummell, 9 st. 1 lb. (F.
Archer) ...
Mr.C. Blanton's The Prince, 9 st. 1 lb. (Rossiter)
Lord Calthorpe's Symphony, 8 st 12 lb. (Barker).
Mr. T. Cannon's Signophone, 9 st. 7 lb. (Owner).
Mr. L. de Rothschild's Chesterfield, 6 st. 10 lb.
(G. Fordham).
Mr. R. S. Evans's Waxaand, 8 st. 10 lb. (Goater).
Betting—2 to 1 each agst Signophone and Macheath,
100 to 30 each agst Beau Brummell and Adriana, and
8 to 1 agst The Prince.

On a course more suited to him Macheath
won very comfortably, and thus received the
prestige lost in the Champagne and Hopeful
Stakes. At the same time he does not look
the sort of colt to run well at Epsom, and
Signophone was hardly beaten on his merits,
as he was coughing before the race.

At Nottingham, Mr. Crawfurd, who has
been in the running vein since Goodwood, was
credited with the Handicap by the aid of
Edelweiss, a horse that has often disappointed the Bedford Lodge stable. Mr.
Crawfurd's horses are divided now between
Alec Taylor and Sherrard, and it is said
that the whole string will go to the hammer
during the Houghton week.

The Cesarewitch, to be run on October 10,
will only attract a small field. Geheimniss,
who was backed before the Leger, has since
been scratched, and another fancied animal
in Hackness has retired, her owner, Robert
Peck, refusing to allow her to run unless provided with a bet of 20,000 to 100. The merits
of this filly leaked out before the stable
commission was put in the market
and all the long shots were snapped up by
outsiders, who now have to regret their
eagerness in jumping at the good thing. The
filly is still in the Cambridgeshire, for which
she is about first favourite. For the Cesar-
witch Shrewsbury and City Arab, both three-
year-olds, are in about equal favour at 4 to 1,
while a lot of money has gone on Chippen-
dale, Corrie Roy, Pursebearer, Retreat, and
others at longer prices.

CRICKET.

THE HON. IVO BLIGH'S TEAM V.
FIFTEEN OF SOUTH AUSTRALIA.
November 10 and 11.

SECOND DAY.

The match was resumed Saturday morning.
The weather from first to last was delightful,
and in that respect contrasted most favourably with that which we have of late been
favoured with. As a consequence, also, the
pitch played much better, and was in every
respect a batsman's wicket. At the beginning of the game the attendance was not over
large; but as time drew on the crowd increased until there must have been over 7,000
spectators present. His Excellency the
Governor came down to the Oval after
play was begun, and he remained nearly the
whole of the afternoon watching the course of
the game. The following are the details of

THE PLAY
...ten minutes past 12 the Fifteen took the field,
...lowed by the not-out men, Barnes (10)
...Jones continued fr... the north
...got his last in h... lips for a
...first Barnes ... single
...Waldron ...

...of the chains. Another ch... being
...necessary, Barlow took Bates's place and
...ook the other end. Barlow sent down
...rs, and at length Giffen endeavoured to
cut h... but was caught by Bates at long-slip.
...—93. Pateman took his place, and in the last
...ball... Barlow's over cut him nicely to the pavilion
for 4, bringing 70 up. The next 10 appeared mainly
owing to Pateman's exertions, and then Noel gave
Steel a hot chance at point. The batsman showed
his gratitude by cutting Barlow for 2 and 4 in an
over. At 89 Pateman popped one from Barnes into
Noel's hands at slip, and the catch was accepted.
On Richards joining Noel there was a spell
of very slow play, the only relieving feature
being the fine fielding of C. T. Studd at
cover. At 93 Studd relieved Barlow, but the
separation came from the other end, Barnes
clean bowling Richards. 6—1—95. Slight, on
joining Noel, cut Barnes for a single, and got Studd
in the slips for 3, but at 99 Noel's long stay was
closed, he being bowled by Studd. 7—37—99. Noel
had been in two hours and a quarter, and only gave
one chance. Waldron snicked Studd for a single,
and brought up the 100. Steel was called on in
place of Barnes, and Slight played him to the off for
a single, and a little later he got Studd to the off for
4. Waldron in the meantime was keeping up a
wicket, several easy chances of scoring being
allowed to pass by him. 110 at length appeared; and then Waldron pulled Steel round
to leg for 4. The next ball was a possible
chance, but it resulted in a single. Slight
drove the last of the over finely to the off for a
double. In Studd's next Waldron made a splendid
straight drive for 4, and with 120 telegraphed
Morley was put on at the northern end. Waldron
got him to the on for 3, and as Studd was being
punished he gave way to Barlow. Both men kept
their places, and at 6 o'clock the score stood at 128
for 7 wickets. Score :—

THE ELEVEN.

R. G. Barlow, 1, c. King, b. Quilty 1
G. B. Studd, 2,1,1,1,1,4,4,1,1,1,2, c. Pateman, b.
Quilty 19
W. W. Read, 1,1,1,2, c. Gooden, b. Quilty .. 5
C. T. Studd, 2,1,1,1,1,1,1,1, b. Quilty 9
A. G. Steel, 2,3, b. Jones 5
W. Bates, b. Jones 0
W. Barnes, 2,4,2,1,2,4,3,1,1,2,1,1,4,1,4,1,1,3,1,1,1,1,
c. Giffen, b. Noel 42
E. F. S. Tylecote, 1,1,2,1,3,2,1,1,4,3,1,2,3,3,1,3,
2,1,3,1,3,4,2,1,1,4,1,4,1, c. Giffen, b. Quilty .. 59
C. F. H. Leslie, 1,1,2,1, b. Noel 5
F. Vernon, not out 3
Morley, b. Quilty 1
Sundries 6
—
Total 153

Bowling Analysis.
	Balls.	Runs.	Mdns.	Wkts.
Quilty	141	60	12	6
Hide	108	26	15	—
Jones	92	25	12	2
Noel	20	5	3	2
Bevan	60	20	8	—
Waldron	28	11	1	—

THE FIFTEEN.
J. Hide, 1,1,2, c. Leslie, b. Morley .. .. 3.
J. Noel, 8,4,1,1,1,8,1,1,2,4,1,1,1,1,2,4,2,1,2, b. C.
T. Studd 37
A. Jarvis, 1,3,1,1, b. Morley 6
W. Krill, 3, b. Morley 3
W. Giffen, 2,2,3,4,1,4,1,4,1,1,2,3,4,1, c. Bates,
b. Barlow 33
B. Pateman, 2,2,2,3, c. Steel, b. Barnes .. 9
T. Richards, 1, b. Barnes 1
W. Slight, 1,3,1,1,4,1,2,2,1, not out 16
A. E. Waldron, 1,1,1,1,4,1,4,1,3, not out .. 17
Sundries 2
—
Total for seven wickets 128

Bowling Analysis.
	Balls.	Runs.	Mdns.	Wkts.
Steel	68	38	6	—
Barnes	72	12	11	2
Morley	76	17	12	3
Bates	40	18	1	—
C. T. Studd		20		1
Barlow	13			
Ump...				

...4 and a co...
the bowling with mu...
signed the ball to Bruce... ...for the
change not being quite appr...alt, as his
bowling was evidently puzzling to both batsmen. Runs now came more freely, and
Tylecote scored several singles, and Studd 4
and 2 off Bruce's first three overs.
McShane relieved Edwards, and a few
singles were added. A couple of maidens
were then bowled, and Tylecote cut Bruce to
the chains. Next ball, however, the English
captain gave Kelly an easy chance at point,
but the ball was dropped. McShane bowled
four maidens in succession. A short adjournment then took place for refreshments.
Studd, who played a nice innings, fell a
victim to the first ball of McShane's next.
7—56—178. Leslie, the next man, did not score
for the first few overs. Tylecote in the meantime bringing up the score. Cooper again went
on in place of Bruce and Tylecote put him in
the slips for 3, Leslie opening his account by
hitting him next ball to the off for a similar
number. A single each brought 200 up amid
cheering, but in Cooper's next the captain
made a fatal mistake by stepping out too ball,
and Turner removed his bails. 8—37—200.
Vernon, who followed, started with a single
to square-leg. Leslie got the next to the
chains for 4. Vernon shortly afterwards repeated the performance, a few singles being
run during the interval. Logan took the ball
from McShane, and Leslie greeted the new
man by sending him through the chains at
leg for 4. Edwards relieved Cooper at the
Grand Stand end, and Vernon added a couple
of singles. Then Leslie drove Logan to the
chains for 4. Vernon after lifted Edwards to
leg for a similar number. Scott relieved Logan,
and Leslie drove Edwards for 4. Shortly
afterwards Leslie skied a ball, giving
Baker an extremely difficult chance,
which he did not succeed in taking.
As another change in the bowling was
deemed desirable McShane relieved Edwards.
Next ball Turner had a double chance
of stumping Vernon, or taking Leslie at
the wickets whilst running a bye, but both
opportunities were badly missed. A few
overs later Vernon was clean bowled by
Scott. 9—17—257. Morley, the last man,
commenced by putting Scott away for a
single. Leslie off Scott's next obtained 4
and 3, and put McShane away to the pavilion
fence for another 4. Bruce relieved Scott,
and the change produced the desired result,
for an over or two afterwards he clean
bowled Morley, and the innings closed at five
minutes to 5 for 273 runs. After an interval
of half an hour the Englishmen went into the
field, Swift and Scott taking the wickets.
Steel opened to the former and bowled a
maiden. Barnes took up the bowling at the
other end, and bowled a maiden to Scott.
Another maiden from Steel, and Scott, who
was relied upon for a big score, unfortunately
fell whilst returning after attempting a run,
and was run out. 1—0—0. Edwards filled the
vacancy, and Swift broke the ice by getting
a single off each bowler. He then cut Steel
for a couple, Edwards following by putting
Barnes away for three, but next ball he was
even out l.b.w. to a ball from Steel. 2—3—7.
Rosser, the next man, cut Barnes for 2, and
Swift secured a ...uple of singles. Bates re-
...ved Barne... ...nothing ... importance
...rs u...

Mission accomplished, as *The Sydney Morning Herald* reported.

Burning Embers

WITH HINDSIGHT everything is easy, logical, explicable and seemingly inevitable – although whether that is true for The Ashes is a matter of debate, not least because Bligh's insistence he was going to Australia in 1882–83 to get them might, afterwards, have fallen into the great silence. He had the urn at home on the library mantelpiece, almost nobody knew about it, the very phrase 'The Ashes' could easily have been dropped and England and Australia continue to play each other as they had been doing, for nothing more than the desire to play each other. It's what most countries do in most sports.

Instead The Ashes marked a unique, sentimental and romantic aspect of what cricket followers insist is a unique, sentimental and romantic sport, and the urn became an artefact of mythology – potent as any from ancient Greece – in a sport heavy with that in all directions. The fact that it stood on an ornate but otherwise entirely ordinary mantelpiece for half a century in a country house lost in Kent, and then stood at Lord's, and was intended to stand at Lord's, forever added myth to the myth.

The urn is precisely like the mermaid at Copenhagen. You can't believe how small they are, and in the next breath you're asking yourself how anything that small could project such a giant image. It's not in the eye of the beholder, it's in the mind of the beholder.

It is impossible to be rational about any of this and, if you broach the subject with those same cricket followers, they'll say 'exactly.' The rational would spoil the whole thing.

There is one inevitable aspect, however. The longer the series between the two countries has gone on, the greater the mythology because it has, progressively, more and more to feed on. That is why Kevin Pietersen's astonishing innings at the Oval in 2005 was much more than an astonishing innings: it took England from a position of great peril to impregnability, and that enabled The Ashes to be won for the first time for a generation, after many, many humiliations. The urn also brought a giant dimension with it every time the two countries played.

There were others. Because the Oval Test was invariably scheduled to be the last in any series in England, The Ashes often turned on it – not just 2005 but, famously, 1953 and 1926. We shall see.

There was a further dimension, built upon the extremely rational. The side holding The Ashes had only to draw a series to retain them and, as what the urn represented became obsessional, it sometimes spawned emasculated cricket. The end supposedly justified the means, and no captain wanted his name engraved on the great list from 1882–83 as one who lost them. In terms of posterity, a ragged, mediocre drawn series suited the defending captain much better than wonderful dramatics which ended in heroic loss. It wasn't always so. Again, we shall see.

So Bligh went home to tell his parents about the wonderful Florrie Morphy, returned to Melbourne and married her.

In 1884 the Australians toured England, again under Murdoch, to play three Tests. This was, of course, the first series when The Ashes existed and in that sense the first when, physically, they were at stake. England retained them 1–0.

The First Test, at Old Trafford, was drawn and England won the Second, at Lord's, by an innings. It was enough.

Immediately after that the Australians travelled to Sussex, and thereby hangs an amusing tale I can't resist about a man we have come to know well. Lord Hawke remembered 'by far the best lob bowler I ever played was the cobbler, Walter Humphreys. He was a really clever bowler, who put the ball both ways. His skill partially lay in the fact that he never pitched his ball high in the air. That was the undoing of Bonnor. The bearded giant laid a wager in the train to Brighton that he would hit "Punter" out of the ground at Hove, expressing himself very contemptuous of lobs. It was told to Humphreys that the big cornstalk had backed himself to hit him into the sea. As a matter of fact, Bonnor never got under one ball, being quite baffled by Humphreys keeping so low, and did not make even a boundary or score double figures in either innings.'

In the Third Test at the Oval in August the Australians made an astonishing 363 for 2 (Murdoch 145 not out) on the first day, in almost fantastic contrast to 1882, and went on to 551. England were in trouble in their first innings until Read, batting at 10, made 117 before Boyle bowled him. That opened the way to a draw. The series settled into the rhythm in which it has come to us, each series alternating between the two countries (with one exception: two sides went to Australia in, successively, 1886–87 and 1887–88).

Whether C.T. Studd knew, or cared, about this is unclear. He and his brother G.B. had toured with Bligh and during it, according to Studd's biographer,[1] 'two old ladies set themselves to pray that he would be brought back to God. The answer came suddenly. G.B., to whom he was especially attached, was thought to be dying. C.T. was constantly at his bedside, and whilst sitting there, watching as he hovered between life and death, these thoughts came welling up in his mind, "Now what is all the popularity of the world worth to George? What is all the fame and flattery worth? What is it worth to possess all the riches in the world, when a man comes to face Eternity?" And a voice seemed to answer, "Vanity of vanities, all is vanity". All those things had become as nothing to my brother. He only cared about the Bible and the Lord Jesus Christ, and God taught me the same lesson. In His love and goodness He restored my brother to health.' Studd was not only converted, he wished to convert everybody else, including the cricketers.

His career ended in 1884. He played several times against the tourists, and for MCC and Ground took 6 for 96 in the Australian first innings. Pardon wrote[2] 'At the commencement of the year we all should have laughed at the idea of a representative England Eleven without C.T. Studd, but the famous Cantab had done so badly against the Australians, and played their bowling in so timid a fashion, that his absence could not be regarded as a very serious loss.' He did not play in any of the Tests and prepared to devote the rest of his life to missionary work, starting in China.

England held The Ashes through six series from 1884.

Different men, different lives after the cold afternoon.

Edmund Peate was dismissed (in the even more painful meaning of the word) by the autocratic Hawke as a Yorkshire player in 1886, at the comparatively young age of 31. He continued in club cricket although he put on a lot of weight and died in March 1900, just after his 45th birthday. Hawke claimed that 'when I dismissed Peate, and years after, Peel, they stood by me and supported decisions which I have never regretted, however reluctant I was to take steps so drastic, but absolutely necessary for the morale of my team and the good of the game.' Well, maybe, your Lordship. It was his living you were taking away, though.

England lost The Ashes in 1891–92 when Grace captained England and Blackham captained Australia, regained them in 1893, held them in 1894–95 and 1896, and lost them in 1897–98.

That was March, and three months later George Ulyett became the first of the cold afternoon players to die, at Sheffield. He was only 46. He had been in poor health for some time and, by a terrible irony, caught pneumonia watching the Yorkshire v Kent match at Bradford.

Billy Barnes died the following March, also at 46. He'd always liked a drink, which brought him trouble during his career. When he retired he coached at Lord's before he took over running the Angel Inn in Mansfield Woodhouse, Nottinghamshire.

In 1899 the ethereal – and still mourned – Victor Trumper came to England for the first time, and W.G. Grace played his last Test innings at Trent Bridge. Richard Barlow, who'd opened with him on the first day at the Oval in 1882, stood umpire. Grace made 28 and 1, and bowled 22 overs in all. There *must* have been some banter between the two men.

The Commonwealth of Australia was formed in 1901, bringing six states together. About half the population of 3.8 million lived in cities and by now 75 percent had been born in Australia. The founders, understandably and perhaps inevitably, nursed futuristic ideals because they could create the future and did not feel shackled by what has been aptly described as the old world. One of the ideals centred round egalitarianism, another that the country should be one in harmony with itself and all its citizens. Other ideals involved basic human rights and democracy.[3]

The finish at the Oval in 1902, the crowd coming on.

By the Australians' tour in 1902, Trumper had become an immortal in the authentic and enduring sense. That series, for sustained unpredictability, is the only one which can stand comparison with 2005: Edgbaston was washed out after England dismissed Australia for 36, still their lowest total, Lord's washed out after England had lost their first two wickets for 0. Australia won easily at Sheffield, Trumper made 100 before lunch at Old Trafford, and Australia won by 3 runs. It brought them to the Oval where Gilbert Jessop of Gloucestershire, like Bonnor in everything except stature, scored a century in 75 minutes and England crept home by one wicket.

Trumper couldn't stop England regaining The Ashes in 1903–04 under Pelham Warner or retaining them in 1905. Interestingly[4] the phrase 'The Ashes' first appeared in *Wisden* in an article on the 1903–04 tour: 'Even in Australia an enthusiastic lady was good enough to send our captain an urn, labelled *"The ashes of Australian Cricket. Won by Captain Warner; assisted by captain Weather!"'* Warner wrote a book about the tour and called it 'How We Recovered The Ashes.'[5] The fate of the urn is unknown.

Harry Boyle died in November 1907 as the England team were travelling to Australia for a series they would lose 4–1. After 1882 his powers had waned, although he managed the 1890 side to England

That year Janet Clarke, who may have physically created The Ashes, helped organise a Woman's Work Exhibition. As with many women of wealth and position, she engaged in good works: the Charity Organisation Society, the Austral Salon, the Melbourne District Nursing Society, the Talbot Epileptic Colony committee, the Alliance Française, the Dante Society, the Women's Hospital Committee, the Hospital for Sick Children and the City Newsboys' Society.

Australia held The Ashes in 1909, beating England 2–1. The idea of The Ashes was sufficiently robust by now to be spawning imitations, or rather inspiring others to contribute. A Melbourne Cricket Club member presented the manager of the 1909 tour, Frank Laver, with an urn which had the ashes of stumps and bails from the Fourth Test, at Old Trafford.[6]

Murdoch died in 1911. His Test career essentially ended after 1884 but he played for, and captained, Sussex as well as London County. Although he died in Melbourne, his 'remains were embalmed, and brought to England for burial at Kensal Green' in west London. For all his disputes with Grace, they liked each other and became firm friends.[7]

England regained The Ashes in 1911–12 and a 'hollow gold sphere' – supposedly with the ashes of a bail – was presented to the captain, J.W.H.T. Douglas.[8] A triangular series (with South Africa) was organised in England in 1912. England met Australia in the First Test at Lord's and it ended in a draw.

A day later George Bonnor died at the age of 57. He remains a slightly sad figure because he was born a hitter and only a hitter, he couldn't accept that and tried to *bat*. It was like Hercules chaining himself. Bonnor was constantly getting out when he could have pulverised the attack as no other man on earth could have done.

The shadow of World War One began to creep across Europe, and then the darkness came.

Before the series resumed – at Sydney in December 1920 – many would be gone: Alfred Lyttelton in 1913 (aged 56), Allan Steel of the warm letter to Bligh's parents in 1914 (aged 56), Grace himself in 1915 (aged 67), Tom Horan in 1916 (aged 61), Richard Barlow in 1919 (aged 69). He'd kept on playing into his 60s.

As a country, Australia had made rapid strides since 1900, notably in agriculture, industry, government and social services, but the War extracted a terrible price: of the male population of three million, 400,000 volunteered to come to the aid of the Mother Country, 60,000 died and many thousands suffered injuries. However, the suffering did create the living Anzac legend which would become one of the country's most enduring values, representing unity and bravery.[9]

World War One bled a whole generation, opening the way to the Depression of the 1920s and the growing alarm of the 1930s when the dictators – Stalin, Hitler, Mussolini and Franco – eyed the world and intended to get hold of it. Sport represented escape and The Ashes a wonderful place of release.

Australia were immediately strong, winning 5–0 in 1920–21 and 3–0 in England in 1921.

Bunny Lucas died at his home at Great Waltham, Essex, in 1923, at the age of 66.

England went to Australia in 1924–25 and, although they lost 4–1, the Test they did win – the Fourth – was by an innings and 29 runs. It brought a measure of hope.

'Monkey' Hornby died in December 1925, at the age of 78. He'd been a real all-round sportsman, captaining England at Rugby and playing soccer for Nantwich as well, and then serving as President of Lancashire. His profession was schoolteacher. His wife's father founded *The Illustrated London News*. His grave at Acton, Cheshire, is carved in marble, with wicket, bat and ball.[10]

Australia came in 1926 but, just before the series began, Fred Spofforth died at Long Ditton, Surrey, at the age of 72. The first four Tests were drawn and that brought them to the Oval. England picked Wilfred Rhodes, one of the great all-rounders in the history of the game, who had played at

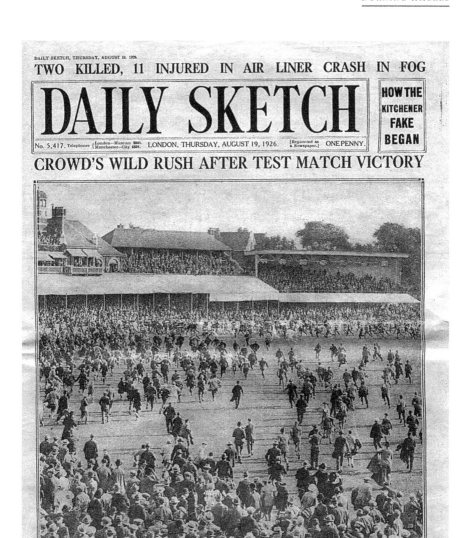

DAILY SKETCH, THURSDAY, AUGUST 19, 1926.

TWO KILLED, 11 INJURED IN AIR LINER CRASH IN FOG

DAILY SKETCH

HOW THE KITCHENER FAKE BEGAN

No. 5,417. Telephones {London—Museum 8841. Manchester—City 6591.} LONDON, THURSDAY, AUGUST 19, 1926. {Registered as a Newspaper.} ONE PENNY.

CROWD'S WILD RUSH AFTER TEST MATCH VICTORY

How the excited crowd at the Oval yesterday rushed across the ground to cheer the English eleven on their great victory over the Australians in the final Test Match. Unprecedented scenes of enthusiasm were witnessed, the crowd for a long time clamouring for speeches from favourite players.

Forty-four years after The Ashes Test the crowd come on at the Oval – England have got them back.

Nottingham in 1899 in the side captained by Grace; and so here was direct lineage to the cold afternoon. On a wet wicket Jack Hobbs made 100, his partner Herbert Sutcliffe 161, Rhodes took 4 for 44 and England won by 289 runs. The crowd swarmed on…

Warner wrote a book on the tour, *The Fight For The Ashes in 1926*, published by Harrap, London, who used an embossed image of the Darnley urn on the front cover. Harrap repeated this with three subsequent tour books.[11]

Ivo Bligh died in 1927 and his wish that the urn went to Lord's was carried out. George Giffen died that November, at the age of 68.

England went to Australia in 1928–29 and retained The Ashes. This was Bradman's debut and it is a sobering thought that of the men of 1882 only Bannerman, Read, Massie, Studd, Blackham, Garrett and Jones survived and could witness him take the whole game to another level. And Read was soon gone, at the age of 70.

These were hard years all over the western world, while in Australia the Depression cut deep into the ideal of egalitarianism as, inevitably, the rich survived more easily than the poor. Nor were Australian businesses spared.[12]

Bradman seized the 1930 series in England so that when Bannerman died, aged 79, during the Fifth Test at the Oval – another link in the lineage broken – Australia were poised to regain The Ashes. They did two days later. Bradman made 232 but was seen to be uncomfortable against the English fast bowler Harold Larwood, which made people think that might be the way to reduce his run-getting to human proportions. When Australia won, by an innings and 39 runs, the crowd came on and ran so fast to the pavilion that they beat some of the players there. These players cut a path through them and vanished up the pavilion steps. Later the captain, Bill Woodfull, said: 'We are very pleased indeed that we have achieved one of our great objects, the regaining of The Ashes. We have made hosts of friends in the old land.'

C.T. Studd died in the Belgian Congo in July 1931, his whole adult life devoted to the missionary work regardless of danger. His biography records it. 'At about 7 p.m. on Thursday he seemed to lapse into unconsciousness, and shortly after 10.30 p.m. passed to his reward. It was a fine going. He was smiling all through except when the actual pain seemed to grip him again. Even in his extreme weakness he was concerned about Elder, who had had an ingrowing toe-nail cut just a few days before, and was telling him to go and rest his foot. The last time he was with the natives at service was the five-hour one last Sunday, except for his usual morning prayers with his boys and a few others round his bedside on Monday morning. The last native he really pressed to get right with God was Chief Kotinaye. His last written word in a letter to the missionaries was "Hallelujah". The last word he spoke was "Hallelujah" too!'[13]

Jack Blackham died, at the age of 78, in December 1932 just as the infamous Bodyline series had begun in Australia – the logical conclusion of

TELEGRAMS,
LORD'S GROUND LONDON.
TELEPHONE Nº1
PADDINGTON 0144 (PAVILION.)
PADDINGTON 5884 (PAVILION.)
PADDINGTON 3131 (TENNIS COURT)
PADDINGTON 4675 (HOTEL.)

Lord's Cricket Ground,
London, N.W.8.

2nd July, 1928.

Dear Lady Darnley,

    The presentation of the Urn with the Ashes was formally mentioned to the M.C.C. Committee at their meeting to-day and they expressed great gratification.

    They much hope that you and Clifton will be able to present it in person and wonder if you could see your way to do so on Monday next during the Oxford v. Cambridge Match, when there will be a Committee Meeting at about 4.30 p.m.

    Possibly, however, you will not be coming to the 'Varsity Match, in which case they would be very glad if you could and would suggest another date.

With kind regards,
Yours sincerely,

Sec., M.C.C.

The Countess of Darnley,
    Puckle Hill,
      Cobham,
        KENT.

The Ashes go to Lord's, their home forever. (Reproduced courtesy of the MCC)

curtailing Bradman. England regained The Ashes. They did not hold them for long.

No Bodyline in England in 1934 and Bradman prospering again. They reached the Oval 1–1 and now the crowd gathered outside the pavilion in late August. Australia won by 562 runs: Bradman 244 and Bill Ponsford, who had an equal appetite for runs, 266. After this, Bill Woodfull, who captained the side, and Ponsford were 'presented with trophies intended to embody The Ashes concept'. Moreover, in the 'souvenir programme from 1934 we can see the first example of the Darnley urn's use in popular literature'.[14]

In July 1936 Gaumont made a film about The Ashes, to which Lady Darnley contributed a commentary. At the time, the match may have seemed distant but in one sense it wasn't. Three of the players – Massie, Garrett and Jones – were still alive.

Her notes for the commentary have survived but they do nothing to clear up the mystery.

'In November [crossed out] October 1882 the Hon. Ivo Bligh captained an English team going to Australia & a much read and famous paper, referred to him as "St Ivo on a pilgrimage to bring back the Ashes". They played

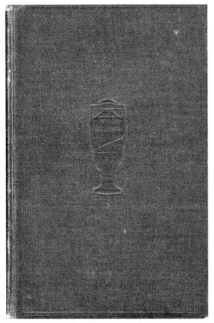
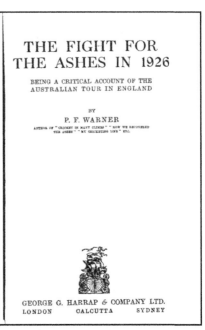

THE FIGHT FOR THE ASHES IN 1926

BEING A CRITICAL ACCOUNT OF THE
AUSTRALIAN TOUR IN ENGLAND

BY

P. F. WARNER

AUTHOR OF "CRICKET IN MANY CLIMES" "HOW WE RECOVERED
THE ASHES" "MY CRICKETING LIFE" ETC.

GEORGE G. HARRAP & COMPANY LTD.
LONDON   CALCUTTA   SYDNEY

Warner's book, and the urn is assuming its symbolic importance.

Murdoch's Australian eleven in 3 matches, winning 2 and losing one. When they had beaten Murdoch the 2nd time some Australian ladies headed by Janet Lady Clarke presented Ivo Bligh with a little terracotta urn about six inches high filled with the Ashes of a burnt bail – & on the outside of the urn was pasted the verses which *Punch* published at that time. [...] My husband treasured that little urn till his death. He had told me he wished it go to Lord's so I sent it there and there it is today.'

Australia held them in 1936–37 and England in 1938. The final Test at the Oval was timeless and, opening for England, Leonard Hutton made 364 – a new individual record for all Test cricket and, as it happened, exactly one more run than the 1882 match grand total.

Massie died two months later. His 55 seems puny in comparison to Hutton in every way except one, the context in which it was played. Massie won his match and, those 56 years later on the same midden, Hutton won his.

The shadow of World War Two began to creep across Europe.

Tom Garrett died in 1943, aged 85.

Australia held The Ashes during the war, of course, and continued to do that as the series resumed in 1946–47, then in England in 1948. The war changed Britain psychologically, politically and physically. Former Test player Jack Fingleton, now a journalist, wrote evocatively of the view from the ship bringing the tourists.

(1) This is "the true Story of the "Ashes" of English Cricket - the Game.

TELEGRAMS CAMAN KENT 14.
TELEPHONE SOLE STREET
STATION. SOLE STREET.

PUCKLE HILL
COBHAM
KENT.

21 July 1936

In 1882 after the Australians had defeated England for the first time, in a test-match, played in England, at the Oval 29 August of that year, when Massie's brilliant hitting laid the foundation for Australia's seven-run win, & Spofforth bowled like a Demon - it caused great consternation in England's Cricket circle.

On September 2nd in "The Sporting Times" appeared the following Memorial -

In affectionate Remembrance
of
English Cricket
which died at the Oval,
on 29th August, 1882.
Deeply lamented by a large circle of sorrowing friends, & acquaintances.

R. I. P.

N.B. The body will be cremated & the

153

② Ashes taken to Australia.

In ~~November~~ October 1882 PUCKLE HILL, COBHAM, KENT.

the Hon Ivo Bligh captained an English team going to Australia & much ~~famous~~ ~~of~~ ~~team~~ which ~~more~~ a~~n~~ ~~famous~~ even famous paper, referring to him as "St Ivo on a pilgrimage to bring back the "Ashes".

They played Murdoch's Australian eleven in ~~names~~ ~~of~~ ~~team~~ 3 Matches, winning two & losing one.

When they had beaten Murdoch the 2nd time, some Australian ladies headed by Janet Lady Clarke presented Ivo Bligh with a little Terracotta Urn, about six inches high, filled with the Ashes of a burnt Bail ~~and on the outside~~ ~~match~~ the Urn was pasted the verses which "Punch" published at that time as follows.

"When Ivo goes back with the urn, the urn, Studds, Steel, Read and Tylecote return return

3.

TELEGRAMS, COBHAM, KENT 14.
TELEPHONE, SOLE STREET, S.E.C.R.
STATION, SOLE STREET, S.E.C.R.

PUCKLE HILL,
COBHAM,
KENT.

The Welkins will ring aloud
The great crowd will feel proud
Seeing Barlow and Bates while
                        Then the hen
And the rest coming home with the Runs
Lady Clarke placed the Urn in
a red velvet bag embroidered with
Laurel leaves. When she presented it.
And my husband, I so Thigh Treasured
that little Urn, till his death for
he had told me he wished it to
St——; Marylebone Cricket Club at Lords — Sent it there
& there it is today.
The last time it was seen in
            I believe
Public was by the Luncheon
Table at "the Grosvenor House Hotel When
a luncheon was given to
Woodfull Captain of the Australian

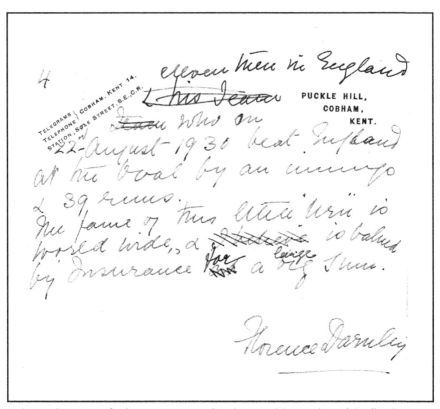

Lady Darnley's notes for her commentary. (Medway Archives and Local Studies Centre. Reproduced by kind permission of the Earl of Darnley and the Director of Community Services, Medway Council)

'All the way up from Tilbury we had seen the pitiful remnants of bombed-out buildings and homes. The London dock area had suffered enormously, but here was St Paul's defiant and magnificent while all around for acres were buildings razed to the ground. On the soil, much of it seeing its first London light for centuries, were growing in great profusion wild flowers and even trees. Wild flowers in the middle of London!'[15]

England would need a generation to get over this. Bradman's side bestrode the land like colossuses all the way to the Oval. There, England batted first on a rain-affected wicket and were all out for 52 in 2 hours 27 minutes (25 runs fewer than their second innings in 1882). Hutton made the top score, 30, just as Grace had made 32. Fast bowler Ray Lindwall took 6 for 20, which stood nicely against Spofforth's 7 for 44.

Australia replied with an opening partnership of 117, and then Bradman came down the steps and on to the field for the last time. It must have seemed a long journey. He was cheered all the way to the wicket and the England players gave him three cheers. He faced the Warwickshire leg-spinner Eric Hollies and played a defensive stroke to the first ball. The second, a googlie, beat and bowled him. He turned away, as Peate had done, and walked back into the shadows of the afternoon never to return.

If Peate had been alive, no doubt he'd have said in his Yorkshire accent 'At least I faced three balls.'

Australia retained them in 1950–51 and five months later Sammy Jones died in Auckland, New Zealand. As it seems, he bore Grace no ill-will for the run out. He was, after all, in his 90th year and it was, after all, 69 years ago.

And that was the last of them.

England had not held The Ashes since 1934 but were now poised to regain them at the Oval in 1953. They did when Denis Compton swept a ball to the boundary and Brian Johnson, commentating, cried out, voice strident with emotion: 'That's it! England have won The Ashes!' The crowd were already swarming on to the pitch...

Australia was evolving as a country. Millions of migrants were making a home there, bringing youthful energy, and across the 1950s the economy made strong progress. That found expression in major projects of national significance like the hydro-electric power Snowy Mountains Scheme. It found expression, too, in the spread of prosperity. Some 40 percent of Australians owned their own homes in 1947 but that rose to 70 percent by 1960.[16]

This prompted a former Australian Test player, Arthur Mailey, to write:

'Since the war more than a million migrants have taken up residence in Australia, and approximately half that number are foreigners. Of the non-British new arrivals I would suggest that one per cent know anything about cricket. [...] Whether cricket survives the shock of this invasion until the new settlers [...] absorb the game during their schooldays is a big question.'[17]

England retained The Ashes until 1958–59, and Australia held them through the 1960s. That included 1964 where Fred Trueman became the first man to take 300 Test wickets at the Oval, and 1968 when on a rain-affected wicket even worse than 1882 England's

S.P. Jones.

Derek Underwood took 7 for 50 and Australia were all out for 125. Underwood, a spinner, was swift enough to prevent batsmen using their feet to him and it may be that that August afternoon, on *that* wicket, he was the closest to Spofforth in pace, execution, control and mood. Of his 31.3 overs, 19 were maidens: of Spofforth's 28, 15.

Of course, comparing six-ball and four-ball overs is inherently misleading, but in the context of our story you can make the comparison because *every* individual ball bowled by these two bowlers brought twin problems for the batsman – how to survive it and then how to manufacture a run from it. (If you want to be pedantic and precise – why not? – Spofforth averaged 2.5 balls per run scored off him, Underwood 3.7. The discrepancy does not affect the central argument at all.)

England regained The Ashes in 1970–71, but they passed to and fro in the 1980s – although England dominated at the Oval in 1985 when Graham Gooch made 196 and David Gower 157 as they won by an innings and 94 runs. Mike Gatting retained them in 1986–87.

The urn was taken to Australia in 1988 as part of the country's Bicentennial celebrations.

After Gatting, the Australians held them for 16 years, an unprecedented run in peacetime and that, somehow, seemed to reflect the country itself and what it had become: 'one of the most cosmopolitan and dynamic societies in the world' speaking, apart from English, over 200 languages. Arthur Mailey had his answer, and Australia earned itself 'an international business reputation' with 'an innovative artistic community, diverse religious and cultural activities and variety in foods, restaurants, fashion and architecture'. In world terms, it had come a long way in a short time. We began our story with talk of the Mother Country, a small population almost exclusively British and Irish, and nightmare coach journeys into the bush. We end it somewhere else altogether.

Australia held them for so long it led to suggestions that, rather than be permanently at Lord's, the urn should be in whichever country held them but that met two objections. The first centred on the fragility of the urn which surely wouldn't stand up to repeated journeys into the indefinite future, however carefully packaged and handled. The MCC circumvented this by having a replica made in Waterford crystal and the winning captain is presented with that. The second centred on the legitimate view of the Darnleys. In 2002 Bligh's great-great-grandson pointed out that it belonged to the family and had been presented to Lord's in 1927 for safe-keeping. As a consequence, nobody else could decide to take it to Australia (or presumably anywhere else).

Interestingly, Australia won a six-match series 3–2 in 1997 but lost at the Oval, although Glenn McGrath took 7–76 in the England first innings. Was he, of all the Australian opening bowlers, the true successor to Spofforth? I've mentioned Underwood, a spinner. McGrath and Spofforth both opened, both controlled the area outside the off stump, both hoarded runs.

By 2001 Australian youth and vigour reached a climax when they won the series 4–1 and beat England at the Oval by an innings and 25 (Justin Langer 102, Mark Waugh 120, Steve Waugh 157 not out).

The urn *was* fragile. In 2003 X-rays revealed a serious crack in the stem and various other cracks, too. Glue used in previous repairs had begun to degenerate. It was entrusted to a leading conservation firm, Plowden & Smith Ltd.

In January 2004 Lord's announced:

'The recent restoration project has returned the urn to a stable but still delicate condition. The project included: an analysis of samples of the paint and adhesive used in the earlier repair; the subsequent removal – as far as possible – of the materials used in this repair work; and detailed restoration work in the damaged stem area.'[18]

The most famous artefact? Yes. Two countries playing each other at regular intervals for over a century is not unique to cricket, although it is rare in world sport. Many competitions have been contested for as long or longer – The Derby first run in 1780, the Open golf in 1860, Wimbledon tennis in 1877, the Modern Olympics in 1896, and so on – forcing us to conclude that those Victorians in severe clothing, top hats and bowler hats knew a thing or two about forging the matrixes of events which still intoxicate and fascinate us today. They are not, however, the same as just two countries forging their own dynasty of competition entirely between themselves. Any jockey may win The Derby, any golfer The Open, any tennis player Wimbledon but you have to be an English or Australian player to get yourself into The Ashes.

To find a true comparison you have to look at England and Scotland's Rugby teams playing each other for the Calcutta Cup from 1879. You might have been tempted to include the England v Scotland soccer series, which began in 1872, but that's defunct now and only a passionate memory. The Walker Cup, between American and British amateur golfers, was a comparative late-comer. It began in 1922. The Ryder Cup between American and British professional golfers was later still, 1927, the year the urn was moved to Lord's. By then The Ashes series was 45 years old.

Nor is gauging the importance of The Ashes an easy thing. Most of the world doesn't play cricket or understand it in the least (if they know anything about it at all) and baseball with its hollow World Series is in an even more remote position.

The story of the urn has a lovely charm of its own, and the urn itself endures as reality and myth at the same time. The fact that, like the statue of the Mermaid on the rock at Copenhagen, it is much smaller than you think somehow adds to the sense that this is something with several dimensions.

Reducing it to marketing terms, 'The Ashes' is a simple, evocative phrase which, as a brand name, could hardly be improved on because it's not like anything else, and it has soul. It's crisp in its brevity, which means it has fitted nicely in newspaper headlines for the last century and never cluttered news bulletins on television or radio.

None of this would have prevented it being a curious historical footnote but two strong factors went to work: there was no world cup of cricket and so it remained the paramount expression of the game, and it was contested by two countries with – one way and another – the resources to produce winning sides. Inevitably from time to time one country would dominate, occasionally for comparatively long periods, but that was constantly provisional. The other country would be back, and eventually always were. The series did not re-invent itself because it never needed to: generation succeeding generation took care of that.

Compare that with the Calcutta Cup and the inherent inequality because the wealth of talent Scotland can draw on, concentrated in the Borders, is small against England's nationwide structure. Between 1993 and 2006, England won every match except two. The Calcutta Cup, by its nature, could never be *the* expression of Rugby at its height.

Compare it, too, with the Oxford and Cambridge Boat Race, which began in 1829 and is an idiosyncratic – not to say downright eccentric – annual ritual and not to be compared with either the rowing world championships or the Olympics. It's not between countries, of course, but can stand in the overall context of merit.

Interestingly, The Ashes series has not been eclipsed by the World Cup – which only began in 1975, and is played to a limited overs format. Gradually, however, the series between other countries have assumed an importance of their own, notably England against the West Indies, first contested in 1928.

The appeal of playing *for* something – urn, trophy or whatever – is clearly demonstrated by its spread: the Frank Worrell Trophy (West Indies v Australia from 1960), the Wisden Trophy (England v West Indies from 1963), the Basil D'Oliveria Trophy (England v South Africa from 2004), the Trans-Tasman trophy (Australia v New Zealand from 1985) and the Sir Vivian Richards Trophy (South Africa v West Indies from 2000).

Interesting, too, that the Rugby League series between Great Britain and

The Oval 1882 set the stage for generations and here is the latest: Shane Warne making leg spin a deadly art form.

Australia has been played for The Ashes since 1908, a direct imitation of the cricket – and you know what the sincerest form of flattery is.

Even accommodating all this, The Ashes were alone until 1960 in the sense that nothing else in cricket *was* played for and then held until it was taken back by conquest, however long that took. The Ashes had an eternal and entirely unpredictable rhythm across the years. There were problems within that, though, because the country holding them needed only to draw a series to retain them and, at crucial moments in the 1960s and 1970s, that bred negativity to such a degree it began to provoke profound questions. Possession was not nine-tenths of the law, as the saying has it, possession was the law.

Kevin Pietersen who devastated Australia at the Oval, 2005.

A change in the psychology of cricket, perhaps fed by limited overs, which proved that its tempo could be increased, restored it to what it had been, and from 1989 the Australians virtually abandoned defence altogether for all-out aggression. They played some of the most devastating cricket ever seen, and it took England until 2005 to find a team to counter it.

Britain had been changing, too, from imperial power through the crippling, exhausting World War Two to recovery as a nation slightly lost within its past and future but now multiracial because, it, too had encouraged immigration. Perhaps it had always understood how to re-invent itself but, from the moment Margaret Thatcher shook the post-war consensus, an energy came back, and it was only a matter of time before the cricket team, as so much else, reflected that. The team which regained The Ashes one September afternoon in 2005 had plenty of energy and vigour of its own.

That they did it at the Oval returned the great story to where it began 123 years before. The latest episode (that's what it was) took its place quite naturally with 1926 and 1953. Cricket is a game which, to a sometimes obsessive degree, treasures its past and lives within it. I think it must be something to do with the statistics, which bring a great continuity. Spofforth's 14 wickets for 90 is still, as I write these words, the 13th best bowling analysis of all in a Test Match. The past is never far away.

It was very close when England went into the final day at 34 for 1, leading by 40 runs, in 2005 – the decisive stage when The Ashes would be regained or Australia would keep them. The Oval which Vaughan and Marcus Trescothick stepped on to would have seemed familiar to Massie and Bannerman: the gasometers, the flat-faced encircling buildings, the shape of the ground, the position of the pavilion, the wickets pitched in the same direction, a huge crowd prepared to surrender to their emotions.

The match moved to crisis: England at 127 for 5 at lunch – a lead of 133 – and plenty of time for this Australian side, loaded with heavy hitters, to get a total if they bowled England out quickly. This September afternoon, just like that September afternoon, a great gesture – of risk, of bravery – would settle it.

Kevin Pietersen did precisely what Massie had done. He seized the bowling attack and took it to pieces, blow by blow. He peppered the boundaries, these same boundaries Massie had peppered. His 158 was, in its value, just as Massie's 55 had been. Pietersen faced 187 balls and scored at 1.18 per run, Massie 60 balls at 1.0. Only in runs per minute were they significantly different: Massie made his 55 in 57, Pietersen his 158 in 285.

And when it was done that late August afternoon in 2005 the players appeared, as they had done in 1882, and the crowd cheered and cheered, as

Freddie Flintoff, yeoman with bat and ball.

they had done. It didn't matter that one crowd celebrated the victorious Australians and the other victorious Englishmen. Reading the newspaper accounts of both, apart from the names, it's hard to tell them apart. There's a timeless, unifying element at work here.

Timeless? On the other side of the world, at Rupertswood, there is a plaque on the side of the paddock, and the paddock is now a proper cricket pitch.[19] The plaque tells the tale of the origin – of what began there and grew – so that it embraced the Oval and Pietersen quite naturally.

It doesn't matter that the urn itself retains its mythical dimension nor that nobody knows what is actually in it. Some say a burnt stump, others a burnt bail, yet others a ball cover, not forgetting Morphy's veil. One claim hints that when Bligh had it in Kent, a servant inadvertently tipped it over and, presumably, the contents were lost. Ashes from a fireplace were substituted.

Modern technology, seemingly able to penetrate the most intractable of mysteries, could surely tell us what it contains particle by particle – but not knowing is deliciously better.

And there's a final paradox.

If the urn was empty, and had always been empty, that wouldn't change a thing.[20]

There remains, however, one supreme question: why did Peate do what we did? Shortly after the Oval Test, he was at Scarborough and somebody asked him. He replied that he thought he was a better bat than Studd – perhaps meaning in a better condition to bat on the day.

'Buns' Thornton overheard and pointed out that Studd had been running round in a blanket, Steel's teeth had been chattering and Barnes's teeth would have been chattering if he 'hadn't left them at home'.

Peate concluded he had to do it himself.

It was – and is – very simple. He was wrong.

Notes

1. *Studd* Grubb.
2. Pardon in *Bell's Life*.
3. www.dfat.gov.au/aib/history.html
4. Glenys Williams talk.
5. *The Fight For The Ashes 1926* P.F. Warner.
6. Glenys Williams talk.
7. www.cricinfo.com
8. Glenys Williams talk. The sphere is in the museum at Lord's.
9. www.dfat.gov.au/aib/history.html Anzac = Australian and New Zealand Army Corps which fought in World War One. The term became synonymous with all troops from Australia and New Zealand.
10. www.cheshiremagazine.com/Archives/monkey.html
11. *The Fight For The Ashes 1930* Warner; *The Fight For The Ashes 1932–33* and *The Fight For The Ashes 1934* J.B. Hobbs.
12. www.dfat.gov.au/aib/history.html
13. Grubb op. cit.
14. Glenys Williams op. cit.
15. *Brightly Fades The Don*, Fingleton.
16. www.dfat.gov.au/aib/history.html
17. *10 For 66 and all that* Arthur Mailey.
18. www.lords.org/latest-news/news-archive/completion-of-essential-repairs-to-ashes-urn,300,NS.html
19. Information courtesy of Dominic Romeo.
20. What might have changed everything, however, is this: suppose Mrs Clarke had had her inspired idea on the evening of 24 December 1882 and taken some cold embers from a fire to put in the urn. We might have been celebrating The Cinders all these years.

Appendix

The meticulous re-creation by John Kobylecky, and reproduced with his kind permission. If you're one of those people who instinctively recoils from anything mathematical, wait a moment. It is very straightforward.

The first column: the time when the over began.

The second column: the number of overs bowled.

The third column: who bowled the over.

The fourth column: the number of overs that the bowler has bowled in his current spell/how many maidens/how many runs he has conceded.

The fifth column: begins with the opening bat who took strike.

The sixth column: how many runs he has.

The seventh column: how many balls he has faced.

The eighth column: the other opener.

The ninth column: how many runs he has.

The tenth column: how many balls he has faced.

The eleventh column: the run total/number of extras.

Mr Kobylecky explains: 'The reason I do this is an important one of methodology. By their very nature, extras are not recorded in early scorebooks so any analysis has to track them down. Those figures inform the viewer where the suggested extras should be placed.'

The four-ball overs in the columns under each batsman are also straightforward.

0 = a ball the batsman did not score from.

1 or 2 or 3 or 4 = what the batsman did score.

b = bye.

w = wicket taken.

All this allows the match to unfold as it did at the time. Using AUSTRALIA DAY ONE as an example, Peate bowled to Bannerman at 12.10. Bannerman scored 3 from the fourth ball, retaining strike.

Ulyett bowled to Bannerman, who played a maiden.

Peate bowled to Massie, who scored a single from the third ball, passing strike to Bannerman, who did not score from the fourth ball.

Ulyett bowled to Massie, and they ran a bye from the first ball. Bannerman took a single from the second ball. Ulyett dismissed Massie with the third ball. Murdoch came in and did not score from the fourth ball.

And so on, throughout the table.

1	2	3	4	5	6	7	8	9	10	11			

AUSTRALIA
DAY ONE: Morning

First innings

Barnerman

Massie

Murdoch

Bonnor

Horan 00

Giffen 0

Blackham 000

Garrett 00

Boyle [Batsmen crossed]

Jones 0

Spofforth [Batsmen crossed]

LUNCHEON

DAY ONE: Afternoon

INNINGS CLOSED

ENGLAND

First innings

Dr Grace 00

Ulyett

Barlow

Peate

[Note: All odd numbered overs are bowled from the Gasworks (Gasometers) End]

1	2	3	4	5	6	7	8	9	10	11
15.53	014	Garrett	7-4-8	01	11	34	00		7	18/2
15.54½	015	Spofforth		w		35				18/2
			8-4-8	Lucas 000		3				18/2
15.58½	016	Garrett	8-4-13				0041	6	11	23/2
16.00	017	Spofforth	9-4-9				0 (4b) 01	7	15	28/6
16.02	018	Garrett	9-5-13	00		5	0 (lb)		17	29/7
16.03½	019	Spofforth	10-5-9				0000		21	29/7
16.05½	020	Garrett	10-5-14	1	1	6	000		24	30/7
16.07	021	Spofforth	11-6-9	0000		10				30/7
16.09	022	Garrett	11-5-15	000		13	1	8	25	31/7
16.10½	023	Spofforth	12-6-10	0		14	001	9	28	32/7
16.12½	024	Garrett	12-6-15				0000		32	32/7
16.14	025	Spofforth	13-6-14	4000	5	18				36/7
16.16	026	Garrett	13-6-17				2000	11	36	38/7
16.17½	027	Spofforth	14-6-17	01 1	7	21	1	12	37	41/7
16.19½	028	Spofforth	1-1-0	0000		25				41/7
16.21½	029	Boyle	1-0-2				2000	14	41	43/7
16.23	030	Spofforth	2-1-2	001	8	28	nb1	15	43	46/8
16.25½	031	Boyle	2-0-5	0		29	201	18	46	49/8
16.27	032	Spofforth	3-2-2				0000		50	49/8
16.29	033	Boyle	3-1-5	0000		33				49/8
16.30½	034	Spofforth	4-2-6				0022	22	54	53/8
16.32½	035	Boyle	4-2-5	0000		37				53/8
16.34	036	Spofforth	5-2-9	000		40	3	25	55	56/8
16.36	037	Boyle	5-3-5				0000		59	56/8
16.37½	038	Spofforth	6-3-9	0000		44				56/8
16.39½	039	Boyle	6-3-6	000		47	1	26	60	57/8
16.41	040	Spofforth					00w		63	57/8
			7-4-9				Lyttelton 0		1	57/8
16.45	041	Boyle	7-3-7	01	9	49	00		3	58/8
16.46½	042	Spofforth	8-5-9	0000		53				58/8
16.48½	043	Boyle	8-4-7				0000		7	58/8
16.50	044	Spofforth	9-6-9	0000		57				58/8
16.52	045	Boyle	9-5-7				0000		11	58/8
16.53½	046	Spofforth	10-7-9	0000		61				58/8
16.55½	047	Boyle	10-5-8	00		63	01	1	13	59/8
16.57	048	Spofforth	11-8-9				0000		17	59/8
16.59	049	Boyle		0w		65				59/8
			11-6-8	Studd 00		2				59/8
17.03	050	Spofforth		w		3	1	2	18	60/8
			12-8-11	Read 1	1	1	0		19	61/8
17.07½	051	Boyle	12-6-10	0020	3	5				63/8
17.09	052	Spofforth					w		20	63/8
			13-8-12				Barnes 001	1	3	64/8
17.13	053	Boyle	13-6-14				0004	5	7	68/8
17.14½	054	Spofforth	14-9-12	0 (lb)		7	00		9	69/9
				(Short break for an injury to Read)						
17.17½	055	Boyle	14-6-15	001	4	10	0		10	70/9
17.19	056	Spofforth	15-10-12	0000		14				70/9
				(Short break for an injury to Read)						
17.21½	057	Boyle					w		11	70/9
			15-6-17				Steel 002	2	3	72/9
17.25	058	Spofforth	16-10-14	001	5	17	1	3	4	74/9
17.27	059	Boyle	16-7-17				0000		8	74/9
17.28½	060	Spofforth	17-11-14	0000		21				74/9
17.30½	061	Boyle	17-7-18	0		22	001	4	11	75/9
17.32	062	Spofforth	18-12-14				0000		15	75/9

1	2	3	4	5	6	7	8	9	10	11
17.34	063	Boyle	18-7-21	0003	8	26				78/9
17.35½	064	Spofforth	19-12-18	0004	12	30				82/9
17.37½	065	Boyle	19-7-24	00		32	03	7	17	85/9
17.39	066	Spofforth	20-12-21	000		35	3	10	18	88/9
17.41	067	Garrett	1-0-4				0400	14	22	92/9
17.42½	068	Spofforth	21-12-25	0004	16	39				96/9
17.44½	069	Garrett					0w		24	96/9
			2-1-4				Hornby 00		2	96/9
17.47	070	Spofforth	22-12-29	3	19	40	001	1	5	100/9
17.49	071	Garrett	3-1-5	0		41	001	2	8	101/9
17.50½	072	Spofforth					w		9	101/9
							Peate 0w		2	101/9
17.53½										

INNINGS CLOSED

[Note: All odd numbered overs are bowled from the Gasworks (Gasometer) End]

AUSTRALIA - Second innings

DAY TWO: Morning

1	2	3	4	5	6	7	8	9	10	11
				Bannerman			Massie			
12.12	001	Barlow	1-0-4	2002	4	4				4/0
12.13½	002	Ulyett	1-0-3	00		6	03	3	2	7/0
12.15½	003	Barlow	2-0-8				0004	7	6	11/0
12.17	004	Ulyett	2-1-3	0000		10				11/0
12.19	005	Barlow	3-0-11				0003	10	10	14/0
12.20½	006	Ulyett	3-1-4				0001	11	14	15/0
12.22½	007	Barlow	4-1-11				0000		18	15/0
12.24	008	Ulyett	4-1-5	001	5	13	0		19	16/0
12.26	009	Barlow	5-2-11	0000		17				16/0
12.27½	010	Ulyett	5-1-10				0401	16	23	21/0
12.29½	011	Barlow	6-2-15				0040	20	27	25/0
12.31½	012	Peate	1-1-0	0000		21				25/0
12.33	013	Studd	1-0-4				4000	24	31	29/0
12.35	014	Peate	2-2-0	0000		25				29/0
12.36½	015	Studd	2-0-5	0		26	001	25	34	30/0
12.38½	016	Peate	3-2-4				4000	29	38	34/0
12.40	017	Studd	3-1-5	0000		30				34/0
12.42	018	Peate	4-2-9	0		31	401	34	41	39/0
12.43½	019	Studd	4-1-9				0004	38	45	43/0
12.45½	020	Peate	5-2-13	2020	9	35				47/0
12.47½	021	Barnes	1-0-3	002	11	38	1	39	46	50/0
12.50½	022	Peate	6-2-19				4020	45	50	56/0
12.52	023	Barnes	2-1-3	0000		42				56/0
12.54½	024	Steel	1-0-1	00		44	01	46	52	57/0
12.56	025	Barnes	3-1-4	0		45	001	47	55	58/0
12.58	026	Steel	2-0-5				0022	51	59	62/0
13.00	027	Barnes	4-2-4	0000		49				62/0
13.02	028	Steel					04w	55	62	66/0
			3-0-9				Bonnor 0		1	66/0
13.06½	029	Barnes	5-3-4	0000		53				66/0
13.08½	030	Steel	4-0-11				0200	2	5	68/0
13.10	031	Barnes	6-3-6	0020	13	57				70/0
13.12½	032	Ulyett	1-1-0				000w		9	70/0
							Murdoch			
13.16½	033	Barnes	7-4-6	000w		61				70/0
				Horan						
13.21	034	Peate	1-0-4				0400	4	4	74/0
13.22½	035	Barnes	8-4-8	1	1	1	(2b) 01	5	7	78/2

1	2	3	4	5	6	7	8	9	10	11
13.24½	036	Peate	2-1-4				0000		11	78/2
13.26	037	Barnes	9-4-9	0001	2	5				79/2
13.28	038	Peate		w		6				79/2
				Giffen w		1				79/2
				Blackham						
			3-1-8	40	4	2				83/2
13.37	039	Barnes	10-5-9				0000		15	83/2
13.39	040	Peate	4-1-10	1 0	5	4	01	6	17	85/2
13.40½	041	Barnes	11-5-10	000		7	1	7	18	86/2
13.42½	042	Peate	5-1-14				2024b	11	22	94/6
13.44½	043	Barnes	12-5-15	01 1	7	10	3	14	23	99/6
13.47				Rain stopped play – LUNCHEON TAKEN						
DAY TWO: Afternoon										
14.45	044	Peate	6-2-14	000w		14				99/6
				Jones						
14.49	045	Barlow	1-1-0				0000		27	99/6
14.51	046	Peate	7-3-14	0000		4				99/6
14.52½	047	Barlow	2-1-1	000		7	1	15	28	100/6
14.54½	048	Peate	8-4-14				0000		32	100/6
14.56	049	Barlow	3-1-7	0240	6	11				106/6
14.58	050	Peate	9-4-15	000		14	1	16	33	107/6
14.59½	051	Barlow	4-2-7				0000		37	107/6
15.01½	052	Peate	10-5-15	0000		18				107/6
15.03	053	Barlow	5-2-9				0002	18	41	109/6
15.05	054	Peate	11-6-15	0000		22				109/6
15.06½	055	Barlow	6-3-9				0000		45	109/6
15.08½	056	Peate	12-7-15	0000		26				109/6
15.10	057	Barlow	7-3-12	00		28	03	21	48	112/6
15.12	058	Peate	13-7-16	0		29	001	22	51	113/6
15.13½	059	Steel					01	23	53	114/6
				Jones run-out after completion of the run						
			1-0-1	Spofforth 00		2				114/6
15.17½	060	Peate	14-7-19	00w		5	3	26	54	117/6
				Garrett						
15.20½	061	Steel	2-0-2	0		1	001	27	57	118/6
15.22	062	Peate	15-7-21				2000	29	61	120/6
15.23½	063	Steel		2	2	2				122/6
				Murdoch run-out attempting to complete a third run						
			3-0-4				Boyle 0w		2	122/6
15.26½				INNINGS CLOSED						
		[Note: All even numbered overs are bowled from the Gasworks (Gasometer) End]								
ENGLAND		-	Second innings							
				Dr.Grace			Hornby			
15.45	001	Spofforth	1-1-0	0000		4				0/0
15.47	002	Garrett	1-0-2	1	1	5	001	1	3	2/0
15.48½	003	Spofforth	2-1-2	001	2	8	1	2	4	4/0
15.50½	004	Garrett	2-1-2				0000		8	4/0
15.52	005	Spofforth	3-1-3	01	3	10	00		10	5/0
15.54	006	Garrett	3-1-4	001	4	13	1	3	11	7/0
15.55½	007	Spofforth	4-1-9				4002	9	15	13/0
15.57½	008	Garrett	4-1-5	001	5	16	0		16	14/0
15.59	009	Spofforth		1	6	17	w		17	15/0
							Barlow w		1	15/0
			5-1-10				Ulyett 0		1	15/0
16.06½	010	Garrett	5-1-8	0003	9	21				18/0
16.08	011	Spofforth	6-1-12	0020	11	25				20/0

16.10	012	Garrett	6-2-8				0000		5	20/0
16.11½	013	Spofforth	7-1-19	403	18	28	nb0		7	28/1
16.14	014	Garrett	7-2-10	1	19	29	001	1	10	30/1
16.15½	015	Spofforth	8-2-19				0000		14	30/1
16.17½	016	Spofforth	1-0-2	0200	21	33				32/1
16.19½	017	Boyle	1-0-1	00		35	01	2	16	33/1
				[Short break for an injury to Boyle]						
16.26½	018	Spofforth	2-0-3	00		37	01	3	18	34/1
16.28½	019	Boyle	2-0-6	04	25	39	01	4	20	39/1
16.30½	020	Spofforth	3-0-10	2	27	40	401	9	23	46/1
16.33	021	Boyle	3-0-7	00		42	01	10	25	47/1
16.35	022	Spofforth	4-0-14	021	30	45	1	11	26	51/1
16.37	023	Boyle	4-1-7	0000		49				51/1
16.39	024	Spofforth					0w		28	51/1
			5-1-14				Lucas 00		2	51/1
16.43	025	Boyle		20w	32	52				53/1
			5-1-9	Lyttelton 0		1				53/1
16.47	026	Spofforth	6-1-18	003	3	4	1	1	3	57/1
16.49½	027	Boyle	6-2-9	0000		8				57/1
16.51	028	Spofforth	7-2-18				0000		7	57/1
16.53	029	Boyle	7-2-11	0002	5	12				59/1
16.55	030	Spofforth	8-3-18				0000		11	59/1
16.57	031	Boyle	8-2-12	001	6	15	0		12	60/1
16.59	032	Spofforth	9-3-23	041	11	18	0		13	65/1
17.01½	033	Boyle	9-3-12	0000		22				65/1
17.03	034	Spofforth	10-4-23				0000		17	65/1
17.05	035	Boyle	10-4-12	0000		26				65/1
17.06½	036	Spofforth	11-5-23				0000		21	65/1
17.08½	037	Boyle	11-5-12	0000		30				65/1
17.10	038	Spofforth	12-6-23				0000		25	65/1
17.12	039	Boyle	12-6-12	0000		34				65/1
17.13½	040	Spofforth	13-7-23				0000		29	65/1
17.15½	041	Boyle	13-7-12	0000		38				65/1
17.17	042	Spofforth	14-8-23				0000		33	65/1
17.19	043	Boyle	14-8-12	0000		42				65/1
17.20½	044	Spofforth	15-9-23				0000		37	65/1
17.22	045	Boyle	15-8-13	01	12	44	00		39	66/1
17.23½	046	Spofforth	16-10-23	0000		48				66/1
17.25½	047	Boyle	16-9-13				0000		43	66/1
17.27	048	Spofforth	17-11-23	0000		52				66/1
17.29	049	Boyle	17-10-13				0000		47	66/1
17.30½	050	Spofforth		0w		54				66/1
			18-12-23	Steel 00		2				66/1
17.34	051	Boyle	18-10-17				4000	5	51	70/1
17.35½	052	Spofforth		w		3				70/1
				Read 0w		2				70/1
			19-12-25	Barnes 2	2	1				72/1
17.40½	053	Boyle	19-11-17				0000		55	72/1
17.42	054	Spofforth	20-13-25	00 3b		4	w		56	75/4
							Studd			
17.45	055	Boyle		w		5				75/4
			20-11-19	Peate 20w	2	3				77/4
17.48				INNINGS CLOSED						

[Note: All odd numbered overs are bowled from the Gasworks (Gasometer) End]

Bibliography

Altham, H.S. and E.W. Swanton, *A History of Cricket,* George Allen & Unwin, London, 1938.

Alverstone, the Rt Hon. and C.W. Alcock, *Surrey Cricket: Its History And Associations,* Longmans, Green and Co., London, 1902.

Barker, Ralph and Irving Rosenwater, *Test Cricket England v Australia,* B.T. Batsford Ltd, London, 1989.

Beldham, G.W. and C.B. Fry, *Great Batsmen: Their Methods At A Glance,* Macmillan and Co. Ltd, London, 1907.

Booth, Keith, *The Father Of Modern Sport,* The Parrs Wood Press, Manchester 2002.

Caffyn, William, *Seventy-One Not Out,* William Blackwood and Sons, London, 1900.

Cotter, Gerry, *The Ashes Captains,* The Crowood Press, Marlborough, Wiltshire, 1989.

Darnley, the Rt Hon. The Earl of, – Chapter 5 of *The History Of Kent Cricket,* Eyre and Spottiswood, London, 1907.

Egan, Jack, *The Story Of Cricket In Australia,* The Macmillan Company of Australia in association with the Australian Broadcasting Corporation, 1987.

Ferguson, Niall, *Empire: How Britain Made The World,* Penguin Books, London, 2004.

Fingleton, Jack, *Brightly Fades The Don,* Collins, London, 1950.

Frith, David, *England Versus Australia. A Pictorial History Of The Test Matches Since 1877,* Lutterworth Press, Guildford, Surrey, and Richard Smart Publishing, 1977.

——— *The Trailblazers,* Boundary Books, Cheshire, 1999.

Giffen, George, *With Bat & Ball,* Ward Lock and Co., London, 1897.

Grace, W.G., *Cricket,* J.W. Arrowsmith, Bristol, 1891.

————— *'WG': Cricket Reminiscences,* James Bowden, London, 1899.

Grubb, Norman P., *C.T. Studd Cricketer and Pioneer,* The Religious Tract Society, London, 1933.

Hawke, Lord, *Recollections and Reminiscences,* Williams & Norgate, London, 1924.

Johnson, Paul, *The Offshore Islanders,* Pelican Books, London, 1975.

Lilley, A.A., *Twenty-Four Years Of Cricket,* Mills & Boon, London, 1914.

Mailey, Arthur, *10 for 66 and all that,* Phoenix Sports, London, 1958.

McCleary, G.F., *Cricket with the Kangaroo,* Hollis & Carter, London, 1950.

Moyes, A.G. ('Johnnie'), *Australian Cricket: A History,* Angus and Robertson, Sydney, 1959.

Mulvaney, John and Rex Harcourt, *Cricket Walkabout,* Macmillan Ltd London, 1988.

Pardon, Charles F., *Australians in England 1882, 1884 Bell's Life*, London, 1884.

Pullin, A.W., *Alfred Shaw, Cricketer* Cassell and Co. Ltd, London, 1901.

Standing, Percy Cross, *Anglo-Australian Cricket 1862–1926,* Faber and Gwyer, London, undated.

Steel, A.G. and the Rt Hon. R.H. Lyttelton, *Cricket,* (in the Badminton series) Longmans, Green and Co., London, 1909

Thomson, A.A., *Odd Men In,* Museum Press Ltd, London, 1958.

Warner, P.F., *How We Recovered The Ashes,* Chapman and Hall, London, 1904.

Webber, Roy, *The Australians in England,* Hodder and Stoughton, London, 1953.

Wynne-Thomas, Peter, *The Complete History Of Cricket Tours At Home And Abroad,* Hamlyn, London, 1989.

Index

Printed in Great Britain
by Amazon

51161830R00102